Restoring the Tallgrass Prairie

A Bur Oak Original

RESTORING THE

Tallgrass Prairie

An Illustrated Manual for Iowa

and the Upper Midwest

By Shirley Shirley

University of Iowa Press ⎁ Iowa City

University of Iowa Press, Iowa City 52242
Printed in the United States of America

Design by Karen Copp

Printed on acid-free paper

Library of Congress Cataloging-in-Publication Data
Shirley, Shirley.
　　Restoring the tallgrass prairie: an illustrated manual for
Iowa and the upper Midwest / by Shirley Shirley.
　　　　p.　　cm.—(A Bur oak original)
　　Includes bibliographical references (p.　　) and index.
　　ISBN 0-87745-468-X, ISBN 0-87745-469-8 (paper)
　　1. Prairie plants—Iowa.　2. Prairie plants—Middle
West.　3. Prairie plants—Iowa—Identification.　4. Prairie
plants—Middle West—Identification.　5. Restoration
ecology—Iowa.　6. Restoration ecology—Middle West.
I. Title.　II. Title: Restoring the tallgrass prairie.　III. Series.
SB434.3.S48　1994
635.9′5—dc20　　　　　　　　　　　　　　94-7374
　　　　　　　　　　　　　　　　　　　　　　CIP

01　00　99　98　97　96　95　94　C　5　4　3　2　1
01　00　99　98　97　96　　　　　P　5　4　3　2

*This book is dedicated to all those who had a part
in my discovery of the tallgrass prairie and to my grandchildren,
Jennifer and Jessica Cano, Rachel Cassata, and Sara Morledge
Hampton, and to any future grandchildren and generations.
May their lives be fuller because of this information, and may their
love of nature continue to grow.*

Contents

Preface

IOWA WAS AT one time in the midst of the tallgrass prairie, but today few Iowans know what a prairie looks like. They are not aware of which species of plants are native and which are alien or cultivated. That is because less than 1 percent of the prairie remains, mostly in obscure places along rivers, steep banks, railroads, and cemeteries. As the sites have diminished, so have all the species that depended upon the prairie for existence. Friends ask, "Was that a prairie that I played in when I was little?" and "How do I know if the seeds I am collecting are native?" Little knowledge has been passed down on how to recognize plants of our native heritage.

We are often not aware of our losses and their value until they are gone. Elderly people describe the flowers that used to grow thick in our area, attracting butterflies and birds, but these flowers are no longer found. Crested irises, lady slippers, snow trilliums, wild lilies, showy orchis, and cardinal flowers were commonplace only fifty years ago but now are virtually impossible to find. Native plants such as these are especially susceptible to herbicides and changes in the environment. The chemical contact weakens the flowers that do survive, so the seedpods may be mutated and unable to produce a normal offspring. Many have been lost through cultivation and construction.

Prairie restoration is more than saving our native wildflowers and grasses. It is a matter of saving all forms of life associated with the prairie biome. It represents the foundation and stability of our very life. Native plants are appearing in small garden borders and large restorations. Small areas are important in creating new interest in the prairie world. However, the greater the diversity of plants we restore, the greater the return of all forms of life associated with the prairie. The academic world is showing increased interest in the prairie, and scientific studies are being done to understand the complexity of our native plants. I have written and illustrated this book with the hope that Iowans and others living in what was once the tallgrass prairie will be able to identify a prairie remnant and propagate native species.

My recent discovery of the tallgrass prairie has been enlightening and enjoyable. I have always enjoyed woodland wildflowers and nature in general and could not believe the tallgrass prairie had eluded me for half a century. It all began with the seeds. I volunteered to help Doug Sheeley, Hardin County roadside manager, collect native prairie seeds and later helped catalog eighty-six prairie remnants in this county. My interest grew, and there was no turning back. Studying the writings of Willa Cather, David Costello, Aldo Leopold, Rachel Carson, John Madson, and Robert Waller, I gained a deeper insight into the history of the native tallgrass prairie and the need to preserve it.

Iowa is located in the center of the tallgrass prairie, which extended to all the states touching Iowa's border, on into Ohio, and all the way from Texas north through the Dakotas and into Canada. Many of the plants, therefore, extend into the tallgrass prairie beyond Iowa where conditions are similar.

The prairie restoration methods I propose are not the only or the best ways, as this information is in constant change. Compare the information that I have learned with your own research and experience to better undertake restoration of the tallgrass prairie.

Prairie restoration is relatively new, and knowledge is changing as we learn. Roger Tory Peterson states, "This is a time of enormous change in people's thinking. People have begun to see that life itself is important—not just ourselves, but all life. We have a new awareness of the sanctity and fragility of nature. The older I get the more I feel the interconnectedness of things all over the world. The healing of the land has begun. We are learning from our mistakes of the past, but we have so much more to learn. This involves not only methods but a way of life. Humans can become more responsible members of the natural communities by recognizing they are only one part of a complex system. When that is accomplished, we will enjoy our place in the natural ecosystem. The legacy is ours. We are the caretakers." I hope this book will help others find the joy of the majestic prairie that once covered our state of Iowa and much of the Midwest. The strength and complexity of our heritage are found in the prairie roots and seeds.

Wildflowers of the Tallgrass Prairie by Sylvan T. Runkel and Dean M. Roosa; *The Audubon Society Field Guide to North American Wildflowers, Eastern Region*; *Peterson Field Guides, Wildflowers Northeastern/Northcentral North America* by Roger Tory Peterson and Margaret McKenny; and *Grasses* by Lauren Brown were used for plant identification. An advance checklist from the forthcoming *The Vascular Plants of Iowa: An Annotated Checklist and Natural History* by Lawrence J. Eilers and Dean M. Roosa (hereafter referred to as Eilers) was followed for the nomenclature. Locations of plants in Iowa were obtained from Eilers and from Paul A. Christiansen's *Distribution Maps of Iowa Prairie Plants*. Seedlings were sketched from plants grown by the author. The majority of species-flowering plants, fruits, and seeds were sketched in Hardin County, Iowa. Variations in pH are results of soil testing with an Instamatic pH meter on sixteen prairie sites within a hundred-mile radius of Eldora, Iowa. The information on harvesting was obtained by personal experience and observation.

Acknowledgments

MY KNOWLEDGE OF the tallgrass prairie began with Douglas Sheeley, Hardin County roadside manager, who taught me how to identify the native species and where to find them on over eighty remnant sites in Hardin County. This learning experience with collection of seeds continued as I cataloged the sites.

Throughout the whole process my husband, Bob Shirley, and my children, Greg Shirley, Janet Cano, Carolyn Cassata, and Diane Morledge Hampton, who now live out of state, gave me constant encouragement, guidance, and support.

My prairie walks with Sylvan T. Runkel, Joel and Joyce Hanes, Al Kollasch, Pauline Drobney, Alan Wade, Paul Christiansen, and Carl Kurtz were also invaluable in identifying and learning more about the prairie. John Fleckenstein and Ron Harms added the dimension of identifying butterflies on their prairie foray. Alan Wade and Howard Bright shared information with me from their prairie seed catalog businesses. Mervin Wallace sent information on methods used in roadside management in Missouri, and Lee Burris and Al Kollasch added insight to the section on soil management and selection. The coffee that Bernie and Sy Runkel gave me to discuss the prairie with knowledgeable people was also appreciated. Thanks to Connie Knospe, the Eldora librarian, who obtained many books for my use through interlibrary loan, and Ann Rathburn Morton, who loves books and life. Thanks also to the many who watched with encouragement as my roadside prairie took shape and grew in front of our home.

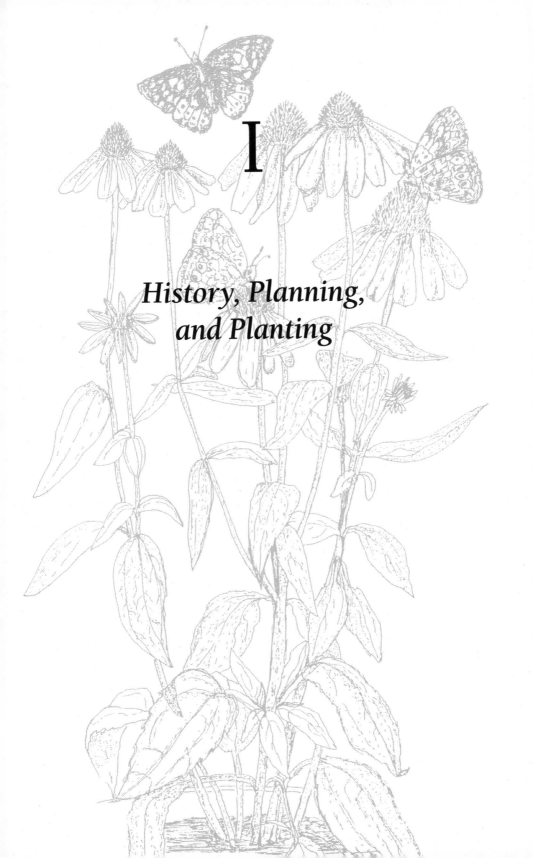

I

History, Planning, and Planting

Leaders in the History of the Tallgrass Prairie

THE TALLGRASS PRAIRIE covered 250 million acres of the Midwest for over 8,000 years. This prairie had been dominated by over 30 species of grasses and over 250 forbs, which had been kept alive by the natural prairie fires. Willa Cather describes the prairie of copper drenched in sunlight in so much motion as if it were running to the sea.

By the 1900s this prairie was on the brink of destruction after only half a century of intervention by the steel moldboard plow. There was less than 1 percent of native prairie remaining in Iowa. At this time a vision for the movement to save the prairie first came from the studies of Bohumil Shimek, a University of Iowa botanist. In 1917 he became one of the founders of the *Iowa Conservation Magazine*, whose purpose was to help create state parks. He proposed an extensive prairie protection plan, but it was not implemented. The prairie continued to receive little attention until Dr. Ada Hayden's vision and life were devoted to saving the prairie. Without her efforts, the prairie could have easily slipped away. She was the first woman and the fourth person to receive a doctorate in botany from Iowa State University. Her documentation of more than 100 tracts of native prairie with 32 that she felt were suitable for preserves was completed in 1945 and published in 1946. By 1965 the Iowa State Preserves System was created.

Since then more than 63 areas have been dedicated as state preserves. The 240-acre prairie near Lime Springs in Howard County was dedicated to Dr. Hayden on May 7, 1968. Shimek and Hayden were forward-thinking conservationists, ahead of their time. Their studies and reports continue to be of value.

State and county conservation boards, roadside management programs, private groups such as the Nature Conservancy and the Iowa Natural Heritage Foundation, and university scholars have played a large role in prairie preservation. Through their efforts to inventory sites and to provide education, research, and management, many prairies are being protected. The Loess Hills area in western Iowa is receiving significant attention for its unique natural heritage. It is of the utmost importance that we continue to care for these pristine areas.

In nearby Wisconsin the need to reverse the trend of the vanishing prairie was recognized. J. T. Curtis and Grant Cottam had the vision of restoration as the means to increase the diminishing native plants. Curtis, who was inspired by Aldo Leopold in the 1930s, studied techniques for prairie restoration at the University of Wisconsin's prairie at Madison. Henry C. Green and Neil Diboll followed, continuing to set standards for restoration.

As early as 1917 Texas recognized the wildflower as a roadside asset to control erosion. In 1929 it was used for roadside beautification purposes. Use of native plants to control weeds along the roadside was first attempted in 1970 during the energy crisis. Lady Bird Johnson advocated the 73,000 miles of highway in Texas as potentially the biggest garden in the world. The state now estimates the savings of this program at $8 million a year. Integrated roadside vegetation management continued to grow across the United States as the benefits were seen. In Iowa the Living Roadway Trust Fund was set up by the 1988 session of the Iowa Legislature, and 3 percent of Resource Enhancement and Protection (REAP) funds were channeled in this direction in 1989. Bill Haywood was a pioneer in this program, and Al Ehley has played a significant role. In 1992 the Integrated Roadside Vegetation Management (IRVM) program became incorporated under the name Association for Integrated Roadside Management (AFIRM).

Lady Bird Johnson also founded the sixty-acre National Wildflower Research Center in Austin in 1982, which continues to provide information on wildflowers for each state, listing local species and seed sources. She felt that cultivated plants were taking away from our unique regional distinctiveness, stating, "I like diversification. I like the varied look of the United States. I'm just trying to keep a habitat, some room, a place to live so we won't be a homogenized country." Her desire was to maintain a local character. Wildflowers give a peace and continuity to life, a refreshment to the spirit. The center has studied over 300 species, and scientific research for demonstration and test plots includes a pollinator garden to attract birds, butterflies, and insects. The center continues to provide increased knowledge of propagating and managing native wildflowers and grasses.

Wes Jackson founded the Land Institute in Kansas to study native plants as agricultural crops. The Illinois bundle flower and eastern grama grass are two that are being studied. The Leopold Center for Sustainable Agriculture at Iowa State University in Ames is also developing profitable farming systems that conserve natural resources.

Establishment of the Walnut Creek National Wildlife Refuge at Prairie City, Iowa, was approved on September 5, 1990. The U.S. Fish and Wildlife Service, Department of the Interior, has given a $10 million grant to restore the prairie. Planting began in the spring of 1992 with 4 acres of forbs near the office and 73 acres of big bluestem. In the fall 168 species of seeds were collected and purchased to plant 400 acres the spring of 1993. Only seeds collected within 38 Iowa counties were used in order to preserve the gene pool of the area's native prairies. Thus far, 4,922 acres have been purchased, and authorization has been granted to purchase an additional 8,654 acres for the restoration. Pauline Drobney, refuge biologist, states it will take twenty years to finish planting. Environmental teaching is already under way, with hundreds of teachers and students participating in activities on the site.

Many have played a role in increasing the interest in and knowledge of the tallgrass prairie. We are looking for direction to find the secrets that the prairie once held in order to sustain our quality of life. A wealth of knowledge is waiting to be found in our "prairyerth."

Planning Your Site

Learning to Recognize and Identify Native Plants

In order to plant an authentic native prairie, you must first study native plants in their natural setting. To the average person the small remnants of prairie that are left may look like just another domestic pasture.

To locate a natural prairie, get to know other people who have been interested in native plants. Directories of state preserves can be obtained from departments of natural resources in most prairie states, and private organizations such as the Nature Conservancy have directories of prairies they are conserving. Nature walks organized to prairie sites and membership in prairie organizations are the best way to learn about prairie propagation. In Iowa, prairie walks and nature hikes are published weekly in the *Des Moines Sunday Register*'s Big Peach Section (it is good to see the paper including noncompetitive events in the sports section). Knowledgeable leaders identify and teach about prairie plants on these walks. Take the time to visit a variety of sites. You will find no two alike. A list of organizations interested in restoration is provided at the end of this book.

Members of the Iowa Prairie Network, a statewide organization divided into six districts, share their prairie experiences. The purpose of the net-

7

work is "to learn about, teach about, enjoy, and protect Iowa's prairie heritage." One of my best prairie experiences was a September walk on the eighty-acre prairie of Joel and Joyce Hanes near the Floyd County Fossil Park at Rockford, Iowa. They are active officers in the Iowa Prairie Network. Their dedication and the extent of their efforts were evident as we viewed the 170 species they have cataloged since purchasing and managing their native prairie in 1988. Four types of gentians and ladies' tresses, only a few of the diminishing species, were included. As an added plus they have discovered on their property an area of sea fossils that date back 375 million years. They were deposited when the Middle Devonian period brought inland seas washing over the area from Muscatine to Mason City. And as if this wasn't enough for one day's experience, Joyce then led us to an Aldo Leopold bench overlooking a breathtaking view of the Iowa landscape that included several small towns. During the day concerned people offered information on methods and management of prairie remnants that were being lost to woody encroachments.

The prairies in the Midwest vary from tallgrass in the black soil where grasses grow higher than your head, to sand prairies where growth is more sparse, to bedrock loess prairies existing on steep hillsides where grazing is difficult and farming impossible, to very wet fens and boggy areas. Railroad rights-of-way and cemeteries are also excellent places to find surviving native plants.

Quickly I discovered that each prairie takes on a personality of its own. This is true even in a small geographical area because of the lay of the land and the soil content. Notice where the forbs and grasses are growing. Are they on a north slope, a south slope, or flat land? Is it a high prairie on top of a hill or a low prairie in a valley? What is the moisture level, available sunshine, and consistency of the soil? Is the vegetation formed in a mosaic pattern of clumps and bunches? What plants are found growing together?

For example, in July hoary vervain may be in masses at the top of a pasture, while pale coneflowers, flowering spurge, purple prairie clover, and porcupine grass are giving way on one slope and ox-eye and prairie coreopsis are beginning a blaze of color around the bend. Down along the wet bottoms slough grass is growing tall where blue flag and Michigan lily have just ceased blooming. The beauty of this private twenty-five-acre prairie exists because it has never been plowed and is lightly grazed. Two bulls are there this year and cause little disturbance to the plants or to me while I sketch (permission had been given to me by the owners to study the plants). Light grazing can have an effect similar to burning. The little spring flowers had their colonies in May, and the fall plants will also be giving a new array of color. Each month and nearly each week the prairie takes on a new appearance. This natural look is hard to obtain in a restoration because it takes years of natural adaptation and succession to become established.

The patterns of plant succession will alter as the habitat changes, until a dynamic equilibrium with the environment becomes stable and self-maintaining. In the prairie this is limited by the average soil-moisture availability. Only if the land composition changes can one prairie segment develop into another. On barren ground annual weeds, including aliens such as ragweed, appear. Next short-lived perennials such as black-eyed Susan and alien quack grass fill in. When conditions are favorable, the slow-growing, hardy plants become established, while the short-lived plants are crowded out. The long-lasting perennials such as lead plant, compass plant, bluestem, and Indian grass indicate the later stages of succession. Greater diversity of native species is an indication of a better prairie, the goal of all restorationists. The prairie can be limited to secondary succession from disturbance due to plowing, overgrazing, other animal activities, and chemicals and will revert to some of the earlier stages. Many of these changes become predictable as you learn to look for plants indicating a well-established prairie. The plants that are most numerous will be the ones that will be the easiest to propagate in an environment similar to their native habitat. Patience is important and rewarded when you propagate some of the long-lived perennials.

With an awareness of native plants, you can create a permanent succession of an ever-changing panorama of color with native wildflowers and ornamental grasses. These delicate yet incredibly durable perennials will give you years of enjoyment. Time spent in site analysis and preparation as well as proper seed selection is well worth the effort to get off to a good start in your restoration.

Choosing Your Site

The discovery of the beauty of the native species can be experienced on a small scale in a border or in a larger planting of a native prairie meadow. Regardless of size, special considerations can be incorporated to also attract wildlife. Perhaps you have had your eye on a key area in your community such as a highway, gateway corridor, county fairground, public building, park, golf course, or maybe an area that has been abandoned. An ongoing beautification project can be divided up into team areas, and seeing each other's work develop can bring an exchange of ideas and results. These more ambitious projects can be approached with the help of local permits, landscape designers, city and park commissioners, qualified native seed sources, master gardeners, and a group of volunteers. Wildflowers are beginning to appear in public landscapes where everyone can enjoy their beauty and learn of our heritage. When located near high schools and universities, prairies afford easy access to outdoor classrooms. Commercial land can also profit from the benefits of a native restoration. Cost of upkeep is significantly less. The land we have altered can be revitalized with native plants. Planned landscaping and restorations are critical to the survival of the tallgrass prairie.

Divide your project into visual areas, taking into consideration the needs of your family, wildlife, and community. Then figure the cost of your plan in both finances and time. Use graph paper and let each square represent one foot or scale it to your convenience. Sketch in the existing buildings, trees, and all that is significant on the property, remembering that prairie plants require sunlight. Include short-range as well as long-range plans, rating the projects by number in priority. Save room in your plan for later developments, including a pond. Benches added to parks and backyards can provide a relaxing opportunity to view birds, butterflies, and other creatures attracted by the plants. As seen in English country gardens, paths add another visual effect. Prairies require less maintenance of mowing, watering, and fertilizing, thus cutting the energy cost as well as the use of herbicides and fertilizer. Compare the total cost of planting and upkeep between your bluegrass sodding and prairie plantings. The difference should be significant. Most prairies become quite drought tolerant and chemical free once established. This saves the caretaker a lot of time and expense in upkeep once the prairie is established.

Be aware of the time involved to maintain the prairie when planning the amount of space. Start small. Mixes can be obtained for areas as small as 1,000 square feet (31.63 by 31.63 feet, the size of a nice double garage). When creating a new planting it is best to use only local native plants and seeds to avoid contamination of the native gene pools. Do not expect instant beauty that eliminates all maintenance. People get discouraged with wildflower projects when they do not understand proper selection of native species and establishment practices. Many of the native plants live from fifty to one hundred years, so like trees they take time to grow. For the first two or three years maintenance will be quite time consuming, but once established the prairie plants with their tenacity and longevity will give you many rewards with less labor and expensive maintenance.

Your landscaping prairie will want to be flowing and lucid. Curved lines are more attractive than straight where borders exist. Observe how the natural prairie grows in clumps, with an irregular form. This natural design can be incorporated even in small borders. In addition to planting flowers in irregular clumps, also vary the heights of the flowers in the border. In keeping with nature, plant the garden in vertical layers. Place flowers that grow less than 18 inches in front and over 2 feet in back, with an overlapping in the middle with the irregular clumps. Be aware of color, blooming period, and foliage. Some plants die back, while others are very decorative for the remainder of the season.

Native meadows appear as weeds to many, and city ordinances must be observed. One gardener's weed is another gardener's flower, salad, wine, medicine, fiber, dye, or poison. You can think of your meadow as conscientious neglect. We have been asked by farmers, when gathering wildflower seeds, "What are you going to do with those things?" Some species of weeds that are present in the early succession of a prairie planting have value as a food for wildlife. As the prairie plants mature, the undesirable weeds will lessen and be totally eliminated. If you wish to turn parts of your sunny lawn into prairie, the sod or weeds can be killed with a layer of black plastic placed on it or cut away with a sod cutter, and then the soil prepared for planting. A larger lawn can be partially cut back with strips of prairie borders running through it.

On a larger scale, seeds can be planted for a prairie meadow or in the landscaping of individual gardens separated by paths or lawn. The multiple areas can vary from short grass mixes to tall grass mixes and will relate to one another with the farthest being visually attractive from the distance as well as close up. Well-planned landscapes will have different mixtures of seeds depending on the soil and the visual effects desired. Some of the more aggressive forbs and grasses, such as prairie coreopsis, wild bergamot, goldenrods, sunflowers, some coneflowers, asters, cord grass, and switchgrass, can be attractive in back edges, patches, or large drifts.

Including Wildlife Habitats

With the decline of the prairie, many insect and animal species have lost their habitats. Diminishing species become indicators of the extent to which our environment is being robbed of its natural beauty, diversity, and resources.

Strips of prairie adjacent to other habitats can be very useful. They are needed next to ponds for waterfowl and songbirds and serve as a filter to trap agricultural runoff of pollutants before they enter surface- and ground-water supplies. Widths of 100-foot borders can also be used along wetlands, hedgerows, fencerows, woodlands, and conservation strips to maintain the soil and usefulness to wildlife. Grassy strips make good corridors to move between habitats.

Even a small patch of prairie can attract a wide variety of wildlife. The National Wildlife Federation has a Backyard Wildlife Habitat Program. It encourages elimination of most turf grasses, conservation of water, reliance on natural pest control, fewer commercial fertilizers, composting, mulching, and the use of native plants. Information is provided and habitat numbers are assigned to those who register their wildlife habitat.

A wildlife habitat or refuge must provide the basic needs of shelter, food, water, and protected areas for reproduction. Individual species of native plants can attract the type of wildlife that you desire. Bees, birds, butterflies, bats, and other animals are drawn to flowers' fruits and scents. Small ponds are helpful in providing water, which is sometimes overlooked in a wildlife garden. Butterflies need puddles with wet sand or mud on which to perch and drink, because they cannot drink from open water. If you are fortunate enough to have a pond, you may also benefit from the attraction of waterfowl.

Refrain from using chemicals such as herbicides, pesticides, or fungicides when you want to attract wildlife. Chemicals that are used on your lawn can be a critical factor in preventing successful wildlife gardening.

Butterflies are second in importance only to bees as plant pollinators. Plant diversity is dependent on the pollinators present. The butterfly is provided with something even more convenient than the long bill of the hummingbird. Its proboscis is a flexible tube that coils up just below its jaws and like a spring uncoils to be inserted into flowers with long tubes. A tiny bulb just above the proboscis may be inflated or compressed with muscles, working like a syringe to bring the fluid into its body.

As captivating as butterflies are, their decline has gone almost unnoticed and unprotested. Butterfly collecting used to be considered innocent but is now on the list of antienvironmental occupations. We need to take into consideration the plants in our prairie that attract butterflies. The appendix lists species of butterflies and the plants they are attracted to. You will notice as the season passes that new butterfly species arrive as the new flower species bloom. Therefore, to attract certain species of butterflies, plant the types of forbs and grasses that they like to feed on. Butterflies choose nectar plants for food and host plants to lay their eggs where newly hatched caterpillars will feed.

Hummingbirds are drawn to many of the same plants as butterflies. When you plant a variety of both nectar and food plants, more species will come to your prairie. Caution is given in the discussion of burning prairie meadows to burn in sections at different intervals to prevent destroying the eggs or chrysalides of the butterflies and other beneficial insects.

Butterflies feed in the daytime and like an area in the sun sheltered from the wind. Adding windbreaks such as fences, hollow stumps, and thick brush under some of the trees and placing flat stones at various sunny locations in the garden for basking will encourage them to use the area. They live by sunlight from the time they emerge from the chrysalis to dry their wings and take flight, and they rely on their eyesight with preference for flowers with yellow, blue, purple, and red blossoms. They are drawn by a single splash of color. Butterflies can see ultraviolet light which is visible on petals and thus leads them to the nectar even on overcast days. Single blossoms with short flower tubes, such as phlox, asters, and black-eyed Susan, provide some of the nectar sources for butterflies. They prefer the simple native flowers over the fancy cultivated varieties.

Moths, bees, dragonflies, and damselflies are also important aspects of the prairie. The honeybee, brought to this country by early colonists, is credited with the pollination of numerous plants and provides honey as a result of its work. Moths are active at night, so they depend on their sense of smell to locate flowers. Moths prefer flowers that emit a strong scent and open at night with white, pale yellow, or pink petals. Some flowers have patterns that also guide the bees to the nectar by ultraviolet nectar guides. Dragonflies feed on flies, gnats, and mosquitoes. Their large eyes can see moving objects 18 feet away, and they grasp their prey with their legs or jaws and eat it while flying. It has been said that humans could not live in some areas if dragonflies were not present to reduce the number of mosquitoes. A damselfly is any of a species of slow-flying dragonfly with long wings that fold over its back when at rest.

Birds feed on insects and the native grass seeds in your prairie. Birds require considerable space in which to live and reproduce. As the prairie becomes extinct we lose species of birds, sometimes bringing others who adapt to nonnative habitats. Dickcissels and grasshopper sparrows are two species that are dependent on grasslands. Birds have different eating habits, but many will visit wildflowers to feed on insects, spiders, and seeds. They feed on flower as well as grass seed. Valuable food sources range from the small plants such as violets to the composites and goldenrods. Wildflowers and grasses also provide nesting materials, nesting sites, and protective ground cover. Ponds in the meadow and birdbaths in the backyard habitat provide water. Birdbaths should be changed every three days to keep the birds happy and to keep mosquitoes from breeding in the stagnant water. Addition of native shrubs and trees on the perimeter of your prairie will add to your bird population. Corridors provided for burning the prairie will be needed to prevent the encroachment of trees. Care must also be taken when mowing and burning the prairie to protect nesting birds as well as insects.

Deer and small mammals will also be attracted to your prairie, where locations permit. The ultimate prairie restoration includes buffalo, prairie-chickens, and other animals found on the native prairie.

Analyzing Your Site

Now you have observed natural prairies and chosen the location, size, and purpose of your prairie. You have an idea of the appearance that you want to create and the wildlife that you want to attract. Note which areas are in the sun and which are in the shade. Keep in mind prairie plants' requirements of sunlight, moisture, and soil content. The prairie flourished because of natural fires and control of tree invasion, making sunlight available. The early pioneers, when they first saw the prairie, thought it was not fertile because of the lack of trees. They soon discovered the richness of the soil. Taller plants and hill slope can also be important factors that influence the amount of sun reaching the native plants, which need from five to eight hours of sunshine per day.

Before selecting your seed and plant species, you must determine what kind of soil you have. The correct species selection can be made only when correct analysis of the soil is done. The Midwest prairie grew on all types of soils from mucks and clays in fens and potholes, to rich loams on broad plains, to dry sands on steep hill slopes. Consequently, there are wildflowers adapted to all types of soils, and they need only to be selected correctly. However, it is important to remember that humans have made many alterations to the soils where prairie once grew. The richer soils in mesic and wet sites are now often growing perennial alien grasses, crops, and trees as well as aggressive weed species. Soils at some sites have been chemically disturbed through the use of pesticides, fertilizers, and dumping of wastes. At other sites soils have been severely eroded and/or compacted. In order for your prairie to thrive you must manage the particular soil at your site. This is not difficult provided you know a little bit about your soil.

The prairie uses the soil as a site for root growth, as an anchor, as a water reservoir, as a supplier of nutrients, and as a venting system that exchanges carbon dioxide produced in the soil for oxygen from the atmosphere. These elements are all required for growth of the plant to take place through the nourishment of the roots. Generally, the ideal soil consists of about 50 percent pore volume and 50 percent solid volume. "Loose" and "friable" are two common terms applied to a soil that has the ideal amounts of pores and solids. The pores are where the gases are exchanged, the water is held, and the roots grow. It is important to note that plant roots do not ever grow through solid soil or through excessively dry or excessively wet soil; rather, they only grow in pores of moist soil. Beneficial organisms, microbes, and earthworms are at the base of the chain that gives life and structure to the soil. In a healthy soil they are part of nature's way of protecting and feeding plants.

In the ideal soil about half the pore volume will consist of "macropores" (large pores), and the other half will consist of "micropores" (small pores). The large pores will generally be full of air, but during storms they will temporarily fill and freely drain excess rainwater, thus preventing water ponding on the surface and drowning the prairie. The small pores should always be full of water, giving the soil a moist feel. Most prairie plants will grow best if the rate of water drainage is one-quarter inch per hour or faster. This can be measured by digging a small hole in the soil, filling it with water, and timing how rapidly the water level drops. Drainage can be improved by adding compost. Sand and clay alone can become very compact.

Ecologists often classify prairies according to five soil moisture conditions: dry, dry mesic, mesic, wet mesic, and wet. Dry prairies grow on sandy or gravelly soils which are often calcareous (very alkaline). They are usually on hilltops or steep slopes, resulting in more rainwater and snowmelt running off and infiltrating the soil; hence their name. Dry mesic prairies grow on deep mineral soils and are found on moderate and gentle slopes. Mesic prairies grow on well-drained humus-rich soils and are found on flat landscapes. Mesic conditions refer to locations where there is no runoff or runon of rainwater or snowmelt so that the amount of water infiltrating the soil equals the amount of precipitation landing on the soil. Wet mesic and wet prairies grow on soils located on the low, flat lands along river floodplains and in the potholes present throughout the Midwest. Both the floodplains and the potholes commonly have water runon that results in their being flooded each spring.

The solid portion of the soil is composed of minerals and organic matter. The minerals are grouped according to texture. Texture simply refers to particle size: sand (0.05 to 2 mm in diameter), silt (0.002 to 0.05 mm in diameter), and clay (smaller than 0.002 mm). When a soil contains a mixture of sand, silt, and clay, its textural class is loam. In other words, soil can be referred to as being "sand," "clay," "loam," or even intermediates of these such as "sandy loam."

Sand feels gritty and will not stick together by itself. It generally is light colored and dries rapidly. It warms quickly in the spring, drains freely, and generally neither supplies nor holds many nutrients. Harold Rock reports success broadcasting seed on undisturbed sandy soil where there are many open spaces and little competition from other plants. This technique was very successful for Indian grass, big bluestem, little bluestem, and certain forbs that readily grow in sandy soils. Fall-planted areas produced flowering plants within three to four years.

Silt feels like bread flour. When moistened it also behaves like bread flour in that it adheres to your hand better than to itself. Silty soils tend to hold large amounts of water while still permitting the ready exchange of soil gases with atmospheric oxygen. Like sand, though, silt generally neither supplies nor holds many nutrients.

Clay when moist sticks to itself, feels smooth, and can readily be made into a ball or any other shape. In fact, the type of clay in soils is often very similar to the clay used in sculpturing and ceramics. Thus, moist clay soils tend to be very moldable and when dry tend to consist of very hard clods. If these clods are struck by a hard object, they often shatter into dust. Clay soils are usually rich in nutrients and stay moist longer than silty or sandy soils. However, clay soils generally do not permit adequate amounts of oxygen to reach the roots unless they are first amended with either sand or, preferably, organic matter. Transplants work better in clay than seeds, and seeds will benefit from clean straw and watering regularly for the first two months of establishment. Losses can be high on raw clay soils, and it is best to amend them with organic matter before planting.

Soil types in which species grow best are listed under individual species. The humus (organic matter) in soil is generally as important as the mineral particles, even though organic matter contents are normally quite low.

Typical contents of organic matter in prairie soils range between 1 and 10 percent. Organic matter is so important because it provides the soil all the positive features already discussed about sand, silt, and clay as well as being an energy source for worms, ants, bacteria, and so forth. The presence of these organisms is essential to a healthy prairie because they control the amounts and rates at which nutrients will be supplied to roots. In other words, an adequate supply of organic matter in soil will result in a sustained prairie because the organic matter is a natural source of fertility and porosity as well as being the fuel that drives the nutrient cycle which naturally maintained the prairie over millennia.

Soils with high contents of organic matter are generally black or dark brown in color and often have a spongy feel. It is important to note that not all organic matter is equally beneficial. Fresh organic matter in the form of leaf litter, manures, or composts provides considerably more nutrients than woody materials. Another valuable source of organic matter comes from green manure crops such as buckwheat, clovers, or vetches. These are called green manures because of their high nitrogen content, which is added to the soil by literally plowing them into the soil while they are still green (actively growing).

Another important aspect of organic matter is that it, along with clay, acts as a glue which binds the silt and sand together into aggregates. These aggregates are known as soil structure or peds. Normally what you see when you pick up soil is the soil structure and not the individual sand, silt, clay, and organic matter particles. Good soil structure is crucial to healthy plants because structure is what ensures good porosity and, thus, good root growth, water movement, and air movement. Crumb or granular structure is ideal at the soil surface.

The last important aspect of soil that you need to know something about in order to best establish your prairie is soil pH and its relationship to soil fertility. In itself pH is simply the measure of the amount of hydrogen ions in any substance. Its importance in soils stems from what it tells us about acidity, neutrality, and alkalinity, which directly affect nutrient availability. Acid soils are those with pH values below about 6. Alkaline soils are those with pH values above about 7.5. Neutral soils have pH values between about 6 and 7.5. The majority of wildflowers will do best at a soil pH of 6.5, and many have a wide tolerance for pH. Many wildflowers can survive in soils having pH as low as 3 or as high as 8; however, they will grow much better if the soil pH is between 6 and 8. Plants generally grow best when the pH is in this neutral range because it is in this range that most nutrients such as phosphorus, calcium, potassium, and magnesium are most available. Under more acidic conditions, iron, aluminum, and trace elements often become toxic. Also, nitrogen release from organic matter is often inhibited when soil pH drops below 5.5. Likewise, under alkaline conditions, nutrient availability decreases, thus limiting plant growth.

The following list gives the common range present at different sites:

Limestone ledges and outcrops	pH 7–8
Undisturbed wildflower patches	pH 6–8
Recently limed cultivated fields	pH 6–7
Sand hills	pH 5–8
Uplands and meadows lacking limestone	pH 5–6
Hardwood forests	pH 4–5
Peat bogs	pH 3–5

Soil pH is extremely variable, and even experienced soil scientists are often wrong when asked to predict pH based simply on the appearance of the soil. You would not want to lime any soil automatically, thinking this would improve it; its contents may already be highly alkaline. Large amounts of plant food become increasingly "locked up" when the soil pH is over 7. Consequently, I strongly recommend that you test your soil prior to planting or amending. Any of a number of quick, inexpensive, and simple-to-use soil test kits or pH meters with probes are available for measuring soil pH. Simply buy one from a reputable dealer and follow the directions given. Alternatively, the Extension Service will analyze your soil pH and make recommendations. They do this for a very low price, and the information they provide can be of great help in deciding whether you need to adjust the soil or choose plants that will adapt to the soil. The best way to reduce pH is to use compost, regularly introducing decaying humus. This not only reduces pH gradually but helps hold plant foods and moisture. Peat is another useful soil conditioner of an acidic nature. Remember that each type of prairie flourishes only within a certain range of soil pH.

In summary, matching your prairie to the soil is very important. Plants grown out of their natural habitat can acquire disease or be more prone to insects. You can readily evaluate these factors except for pH simply by sight and feel. It is beautiful to see how free-spirited the wildflowers really are. They choose the soils and environments that are most suitable. This characteristic will be apparent as you work with the native plants in your setting.

3

Obtaining and Selecting Plants and Seeds

Removing Plants in the Wild

With native plants diminishing in number, it is ecologically detrimental to dig up wild plants. All plants should be left in their preferred environment in the wild. Some have deep taproots that cannot be disturbed for transplanting once they are established. (However, if you discover that an area is going to become a construction site, then do try to save the plants from being destroyed. Carefully remove them with a large amount of soil around their roots. Transport them in moistened burlap bags. Find an environment as similar to the natural habitat as possible. Of course, obtain permission from the landowners before removing the plants.)

Recently I stopped at a steep hillside native prairie along a major highway to see why the butterfly weed that I had sketched was no longer in bloom. To my sadness I found large holes in the ground where the plants had been, with the plant tops and flowers cut off and lying on the ground. This is an example of a plant with a long taproot that is easily broken and can be moved only when dormant or very small. Because of its brilliant color it is seen from the roadway, and people try to transplant it while it is in bloom. Its beauty is its demise. As early as the 1930s this plant was reportedly becoming scarce in some areas where it formerly grew in abundance and was even considered aggressive. Now it has nearly disappeared.

Some wildflowers may be picked without depleting the population if they are abundant. When done early in the season, this sometimes promotes the plant to bloom again. Do not disturb the roots of the plant when picking wildflowers. Picking flowers can inhibit them from forming seeds. This can be used to your advantage if you have a plant that you do not want to multiply by seed and become aggressive. Flowers should not be picked on public land.

Other groups, such as orchids and gentians, should never be picked. Leave any bloom growing on a species that is not abundant. Endangered species, of course, should not be disturbed. Rare species need to be protected. When they are found they need to be handled by knowledgeable people. Notify county and state conservationists before discussing your find with others. Iowa's federally threatened prairie plants include the western prairie fringed orchid, Mead's milkweed, and prairie bush clover.

Finally, do not eat or use any plant that you cannot positively identify as harmless. If you have even the slightest doubt, leave it alone.

Harvesting Your Own Seeds

The importance of seed management must not be overlooked. Since our goal in collecting seeds is preservation of our native plants, we must be aware of protecting and leaving enough seeds in the prairie sites so as not to hinder their growth potential. Collecting native seeds for propagation close to the restoration site is beneficial. Gathering seeds from native remnants by hand is time consuming but important in the survival of the prairie. On a beautiful fall day it is enjoyable and rewarding, an experience you will long remember.

Sites for seed collection are often found along railroads, rivers, cemeteries, and roadsides. To gather your own seeds, first receive permission from the landowners, whether public or private. This includes parks and roadsides, which are owned by city, county, state, or federal governments. All these sites are under management and care and not free to our taking. You will need gloves, clipping shears, a bucket with a handle, paper bags, and marking pencils or pens.

Most seeds are ready about a month after the plants finish blooming. Many will have pods that change from a flexible green capsule to a firm golden or brown capsule, and most seeds turn dark when mature. Do not get in a hurry and harvest them before they are mature and dry. However, you will need to watch the plants that throw seeds from their pods. These are mainly small spring and summer varieties, such as the violet, phlox, and puccoon. Tie a thin muslin bag around the seed head so the seeds are not lost. Once the colorful bloom is gone, small plants are difficult to find. In the summer the taller plants quickly shoot up and hide them. For example, it is disappointing to go back and not be able to find a wood lily when the red petals are gone and the plant is surrounded by tall sawtooth sunflowers. I once went back to find a Michigan lily that I had sketched in bloom, only to find it surrounded by cord or slough grass that had grown from about three to five feet in only ten days. Shooting star and white camass are also rapidly lost in the overstory in June. This fast growth takes place especially in the wet areas. When the small plant is blooming, mark it with a strip of soft, colorful fabric, or stake a flag by it to find the plant when the seed heads have formed. Some of the summer flowers such as flowering spurge also throw their seeds. Fall plants tend to hold their seeds for a longer period, some throughout the winter in a sturdy pod. These help you in the spring to identify the new plants as they emerge if you are familiar with last year's remaining dried seed pods. The grasses and many forbs clustered to a stem will remove easily when ripe and will strip off with your gloved hand. Other seed heads can be clipped off into a bucket. One species is harvested at a time and then placed in a paper bag and labeled for date, species name, and location collected. A few days of drying in the paper bag will make the seeds easier to remove from the seed head.

Do not deplete the seed source of an existing area. Collect from 10 to 75 percent of the seed heads depending on whether they are in short supply or a common species that is locally abundant. Leave a conservative amount on the site for continued growth. Also, if you are collecting late in the season and a lot of seeds have already fallen, you will be able to collect a higher percentage of existing seeds. It is critical to understand that annuals and biennials are dependent on the seed supply that falls in their area to reproduce, as their root systems die in one to two years. Be aware of these species, because if all the seeds are taken they will die out from their natural habitat. It is important to leave seeds where they have proven that proper conditions exist for their growth. This is an issue that we must share with the media, as some prairies are being swept clean of the seeds that are produced, endangering the continued stability of the site.

On a larger scale, the forage harvester is the typical combine used by farmers in the past and may be used to harvest native forbs and grass seeds. Carl Kurtz of St. Anthony, Iowa, uses an old Allis Chalmers combine to harvest native seeds. He uses this machine because it is lightweight. He has over thirty-five species of forbs with less than 25 percent of grasses in the area that he combines. When this method of harvest is chosen, species that ripen and hold their seeds in the fall must be selected. The time that they can be combined is limited to about a two-week period in the first half of October. Self-propelled combines can be used, but some do better than others in combining the fluffy seeds. The combine is set to cut 8 to 10 inches off the ground. Airflow must be limited almost completely so the seeds are not lost, and leaves and stems need to be dry to go through the combine. The mixture of chaff and seeds is in a ratio of about 5 to 10 percent seeds from this method. When planted in this form, it needs to be mixed well for even distribution.

Cleaning and Storing Seeds

Hand-picked seeds will need threshing. Many seeds can be removed by placing the seed heads in a paper bag and shaking it. Others will need beating or crushing. For a small amount of seeds you may rub the fruit, capsule, and pod between two bricks. Leave a few stems in so that the seeds are not crushed. Another method is to use a rolling pin. Purchase a hammer mill to do the threshing on a mechanical basis. Keep the hammer mill full to avoid cracking the seeds. Small plot threshers can be adapted with special rubber-coated concave bars to reduce damage to fragile seeds. Clearance between the cylinder and the concave bars should be 1 1/2 inches beyond the diameter of the seed. Awns can be debearded by the hammer mill.

After threshing, remove the stems and leaves. This may be done with a tea strainer or by hand screening. Construct a screen with window screen or hardware cloth in different sizes and attach it to a wooden frame that is an easy size to handle. Particles larger and smaller than the seeds need at least two sieves, which may be purchased from Seedboro. Screens used for farm sprayers are also effective. Another source is the soil sample sieves that soil conservationists use to separate soil particles for particle-size analysis.

There are several methods of finer separation. You may use air screens, air separators, specific gravity separators, belt separators, or hand separators. Air screens have round holes, oblong holes, or screens. The top screen removes the large particles, and the second screen allows the trash to pass but retains the seeds. Screens with a mesh of 1/32 inch, 1/16 inch, 1/8 inch, 1/4 inch, and 1/2 inch are good to have. Adjustment is needed for the rate of feed, airflow, and oscillation of the screen's pitch. Keep the top screen nearly full. Air separators operate with aspirators or pneumatic principles of terminal velocity. The South Dakota Seed Blower is an example. Air forced from a vacuum cleaner with the hose connected at the back of the tank is another method. If you want to do your separating by hand, put the crushed material on a newspaper and tilt while blowing or put a sheet on the ground outside and let the wind blow away the chaff as you drop the crushed material. To determine if seeds are viable, use the flotation method. Leave the seeds in water for fifteen minutes; the viable seeds will sink.

Seeds are best stored in an airtight container at a cool temperature. If space allows, a refrigerator is ideal. Seeds should be stored at a temperature between 40 and 60 degrees F. Seeds remain viable from one to ten years, but it is best to try and plant them within one year of collection. For longevity of storage, moisture content should be between 5 and 14 percent. Pods and legumes have a higher moisture content. In open storage, seed moisture increases with cooling. Rapid drying or temperatures above 100 degrees F will damage seeds. A simple way to measure the moisture content is the bite test. If the seed feels rubbery, the moisture content is too high. Clean Ziploc bags should be used for storage to prevent fungus growth. A desiccant such as silica gel may be added to the seeds to control moisture content. If the seeds contain insects, which are most often found in legumes, cut a three-inch piece of no-pest strip and enclose it in the bag; store the bag in a cool place for ten days to two weeks.

Recognizing the Difference
between Native and Alien Seeds in Selection

When purchasing seeds, buy from a reliable source where the seeds are grown locally. Gardeners and conservationists seek out nurseries that propagate their own plants and seeds. Do not purchase seeds from those who obtain them from the wild. Seeds need to be labeled clearly as to species and the amount of each when purchasing a mix. Mixes can contain all sorts of combinations of natives, aliens, and cultivars grown in different sections of the country. A native plant is one that grew in our country without human introduction. Exotic, alien, and introduced are terms used for plants that were originally grown outside this country. Some were brought to this country intentionally by the pioneers, while others were brought inadvertently. Many continue to thrive. Naturalized refers to plants that were introduced by humans and have escaped cultivation long enough to have survived normal climatic changes in an area. Some of these have become aggressive and are considered noxious. Others grow in a controlled manner and have become an asset.

Natural selection refers to adaptation of plants to a region where they can survive the climate and day length. For example, native switchgrass grown in the northern United States will not grow in the South. It is best to use seeds gathered within one hundred miles of the site. The distance will vary according to topography, sunlight, and moisture. This area will be wider from east to west and narrower from north to south. The advantage of collecting your own seeds is that you know you have a local ecotype.

The terminology "wildflower" on a package can be misleading. Some of the beautifully packaged mixes of regional formulations of wildflowers contain no native seeds. Others have inexpensive fillers. Mixes may contain a combination of annuals and perennials that gives a lot of bloom the first year but is not adapted to form a permanent stand. Some broad mixes are formulated for a wide variety of conditions. Those seeds that do not adapt do not grow and are wasted. Nature abhors a vacuum, and weeds grow into these open spaces. Purchase only native seeds of local ecotype selected for your site analysis.

The majority of seeds planted will be native perennials for a well-established planting. Native annuals adapt and reseed themselves quite well, but there are few native annual wildflowers in the tallgrass prairie. Several years of patient establishment are needed when working with a native prairie, but it is well worth the effort. Although a bad year might diminish the bloom, the native prairie forms dense networks of roots that preserve them from extreme heat, cold, and drought of the harsh prairie climate.

Avoid these alien species by reading the labels of the seeds you purchase: yarrow, winter cress, rattlesnake grass, bluebell, bachelor's button, ox-eye daisy, shasta daisy, chicory, crown vetch, cosmos, Queen Anne's lace, dame's rocket, day lily, common St. John's wort, sweet pea, tiger lily, bird's-foot trefoil, loosestrife, butter and eggs, white sweet clover, yellow sweet clover, rough-fruited cinquefoil, bouncing Bet, soapwort, common groundsel, common tansy, common dandelion, Mexican sunflower, yellow goat's-beard, salsify, oyster plant, crimson clover, red clover, white clover, butter daisy, and hairy vetch. The following plants often used in borders are also aliens: pot marigold, bachelor's button, cosmos, sweet William, maiden pinks, African daisy, California poppy, globe amaranth, baby's breath, strawflower, candy tuft, blue flax, statice, sweet alyssum, forget-me-not, baby blue eyes, Shirley or field poppy, and annual phlox. The mere presence of these plants displaces native plants that have to compete for the limited soil and space.

Ask to what extent the seeds are cleaned. Prices vary greatly because of the amount of cleaning done. Some companies debeard the fluffy plants and some remove hulls when possible, giving more viable seeds per ounce, a better buy at a higher price. Forbs are more expensive than grass, and knowing the percentage of each in the mix will help when comparing prices of different mixes from different companies.

The amount of seeds purchased should be based on pure live seed (PLS) for native grass seed. Total pounds of PLS is obtained by multiplying the number of bulk pounds by the purity and germination percentages determined when the seeds are tested. This gives an accurate estimate of the amount of viable seeds expected to germinate. It is possible that only 75 percent of the seeds would be PLS, making a difference on how much you need.

Standardized germination testing has not been developed for all wildflowers. The tetrazolium (TZ) test stains the live material in seeds and tells only what percentage of the seed has live tissue. It doesn't tell how many will germinate or lie dormant.

Alan Wade of Prairie Moon Nursery, Winona, Minnesota; Neil Diboll of Prairie Nursey, Westfield, Wisconsin; and Howard and Donna Bright of Harpers Ferry, Iowa, are very dedicated to prairie restoration, to serving you, and to improving our environment. This is evident in the teaching information included in their catalogs to assist you in successfully establishing your prairie. They have individual seed packets as well as mixes for your soil requirements, wildlife attraction of birds and butterflies, tall or short prairie, and flowers and grasses good for drying. They also have prairie plants available. Research is constantly taking place to develop a mix that will combine seeds in an amount that will give the best succession of bloom for your soil. If you are not within an appropriate distance from their nurseries to receive plants or seeds for your ecotype, investigate the practices of a nursery or seed source near you. A list of many suppliers is in the appendix.

Formulating Your Own Seed Mix

Putting together your own mix is a challenge but rewarding. You may gather your own seeds, buy individual packets, or add your selection of forb or grass seeds to a properly selected commercial mix.

First measure your area and convert it to square feet so that you know how much seed to order. There are 43,560 square feet in an acre, so divide your number by this. If you will be planting 5,000 square feet, for example, you will be planting .115 or close to one-eighth of an acre.

One acre requires 8 to 20 pounds of seeds. Based on 10 pounds of seed per acre, you would need 4 ounces per 1,000 square feet (see table 4) or 20 ounces per 5,000 square feet using average-size seeds. The greater

Table 1. Seeding Rate per Acre

Forbs		Grasses		Total
%	Lb.	%	Lb.	Lb.
13	2	87	13.0	15.0
33	4	67	8.0	12.0
50	6	50	6.0	12.0
62	8	38	5.0	13.0
69	10	31	4.5	14.5
75	12	25	4.0	16.0

Table 2. Seeding Rate per 1/8 Acre (5,000 square feet)

Forbs		Grasses		Total
%	Oz.	%	Oz.	Oz.
13	4	87	26	30
33	8	67	16	24
50	12	50	12	24
62	16	38	10	26
69	20	31	9	29
75	24	25	8	32

Table 3. Seeding Rate per 1,000 Square Feet

Forbs		Grasses		Total
%	Oz.	%	Oz.	Oz.
17	1.0	83	5.00	6.00
30	1.5	70	3.50	5.00
50	2.5	50	2.50	5.00
60	3.0	40	2.00	5.00
70	3.5	30	1.50	5.00
76	4.0	24	1.25	5.25
84	6.0	14	1.00	7.00

Table 4. Amount of Seed Needed According to Area

Seeds in a Pound	Pounds per Acre (43,560 square feet)	Ounces per 1,000 Square Feet
9,000,000[a]	0.5	0.2
3,200,000	1.0	0.4
1,800,000	2.0	0.8
850,000	3.0	1.2
600,000	4.0	1.6
500,000	5.0	2.0
473,000	6.0	2.4
370,000	7.0	2.8
320,000	8.0	3.2
250,000	9.0	3.6
200,000[b]	10.0	4.0
138,000	12.0	4.8
122,000	15.0	6.0
102,400	20.0	8.0
73,000	25.0	10.0
7,000[c]	30.0	12.0

[a] Order fewer small seeds.
[b] Average size.
[c] Order more large seeds.

Table 5. Estimated Seed Order for 1,000 Square Feet

Species Chosen	Seeds per Oz.	Price	Amount Seeds Purchased
Lead plant	17,000	$2.00 1/8 oz.	2,125
Butterfly weed	6,400	2.00 1/8 oz.	800
Sky-blue aster	82,000	2.00 1/16 oz.	5,125
Milk vetch	16,000	2.00 1/16 oz.	1,000
Prairie coreopsis	12,500	2.00 1/16 oz.	781
Pale coneflower	5,000	4.00 1/4 oz.	1,250
Prairie smoke	34,000	2.00 1/16 oz.	2,125
Rattlesnake master	8,000	2.00 1/2 oz.	4,000
Round-headed bush clover	10,000	2.00 1/4 oz.	2,500
Prairie blazing star	8,000	4.00 1/2 oz.	4,000
Purple prairie clover	18,320	4.00 1/4 oz.	4,580
Stiff goldenrod	46,000	2.00 1/2 oz.	23,000
Total	263,220	30.00 2 3/4 oz.	51,286

amounts will be needed for hand sowing as opposed to drilling. Also soil with moisture can sustain more growth and will be able to accommodate the larger amount. Another factor is size of seed, as calculated in table 4. Seeding rates as high as 18 to 30 pounds to the acre have even been used when native seeds need to out-compete weed seeds waiting to germinate. Wildlife habitats can be sown with smaller amounts of seeds, counting on some of the present seeds beneficial for food and cover.

From the figures in tables 1 through 3, calculate the total weight of seeds needed for the size of your site. Then determine what percentage you want in grass and in wildflowers if you are mixing the two. For a dense stand of forbs you should have from 60 to 75 percent forbs, while at least 50 percent grasses should be planted in a wildlife meadow for food and cover.

Tables 1 through 3, based on a full acre, 5,000 square feet, and 1,000 square feet, will help you determine the amount each of grass and forb seeds that you will need in a total mix. The table weights are figured on hand broadcasting. Use 2 pounds per acre less if drilling, or cut the amount of grass seeds in half. A cover crop of oats may also be seeded at a rate of 20 pounds per acre, 40 ounces for 5,000 square feet, or 8 ounces for 1,000 square feet.

You are ready to formulate your order. Go to your catalog and choose your mix or formulate your own. Write down all the species you wish to order. The number of forb species that you would be looking for in a mix would be at least 12 for 1,000 square feet and 16 for 5,000 square feet. For an acre you may want to use up to 30 species of forbs. A wide variety of species will help your area to sort and develop communities of plants that are adaptable to your location, and the greater the diversity, the greater your prairie's long-term stability.

The easiest plants to establish are in the Asteraceae (sunflower) and Fabaceae (pea) families. Rely on these and add others for interest that are adaptable to your site's conditions. If a species is known to be aggressive and easily reseeds itself, use smaller amounts. For example, Prairie Moon Nursery used to put 5 ounces of gray-headed coneflower in their mix, but now they have found that 1 ounce gives a better mix.

The amount of each species ordered will be determined by the amount of seeds available, size of the seeds, and cost. One ounce of average-size seeds contains 12,500 seeds; one pound, 200,000. I recommend that you plant 30 to 60 forb seeds per square foot. Therefore, if the seeds are large, the number of seeds per ounce will be less, and you will order more by weight. Total the weight of your order and adapt the amount for different species to come up with the total amount of weight and seeds per square foot that you need. Each species in the study has an estimate of the number per ounce and per pound. This varies depending on the quality of the seed. To help you formulate your own mix, estimate the amount needed by the number of seeds in a pound (table 4).

Table 5 shows how you would figure your own mix for a 1,000-square-foot planting. First, choose plants for your soil type (these are for sandy loam, mesic to dry moisture, full sun, and neutral pH 6–7.5). Plants were also chosen for season, height, and color variety (April to September, mostly moderate height, and a variety of color). About twelve species are recommended (twelve were chosen). I then consulted the catalog for cost and size of packages available. Then, looking at the seed size, I chose enough to equal 2 3/4 ounces. From the twelve species the total number of seeds ordered is 263,220. I found the mean number of seeds per ounce (263,220 ÷ 12 = 21,935). I converted this to pounds for use in table 4 (21,935 × 16 = 350,960). This indicates that the seeds are slightly smaller than average and that the order of 2 3/4 ounces is adequate. Since 51,286 seeds were actually ordered, this gives me 51 seeds per square foot as recommended. According to table 3, I am close to the ratio of 60 percent forbs and 40 percent grasses for the total planting. Therefore, to complete the order I need 2 ounces of grass seeds, and I will order 1 ounce of little bluestem (PLS) at $2.00 and 1 ounce of side-oats grama (PLS) at $2.00. The total cost of the 2 ounces of grass seeds is $4.00, and the 2 3/4 ounces of forbs is $30.00. The total order for the 5 ounces of seeds for the 1,000 square feet is $34.00.

Selecting Seeds for Roadside Management

The purpose of roadside plantings is to provide safety, drainage, an area for snow removal, access, and information to the traveling public. In dealing with the roadside terrain, however, additional considerations will need to be dealt with. The different functions of each zone of the rights-of-way must be addressed when planning the site. To begin with, the environment must be considered. The area may be hot and prone to drought, the fill is generally poor and compact, the ditches slope, air quality is poor due to exhaust emissions, runoff may be polluted, and undesirable perennial vegetation may already be present. There will be several areas that reflect how plants will sort themselves into micro-habitat conditions. Plants with higher moisture requirements will do well in the swales and borrow ditches. Lower-growing species and those most tolerant will grow on the immediate shoulder if frequent mowing is done. This area can also be planned to reduce mowing, reflecting a great cost reduction. Taller grasses and woody species will be found along guardrails, walls of drainage structures, and fence lines. They can be utilized for erosion control and good drainage. These factors call for more study and research on how plant structure can be utilized in managing the roadside in a cost-effective way, as well as in beautification projects. Once established, the native grasses have vast root systems and can choke out brush with a two- to three-year burn plan.

Native wildflowers can become well adapted for areas on roadsides between the ditch and the adjoining property line where the least disturbance occurs. There are also a number of short species that can grow in the median and in-slope areas. Planting native grasses with a cool-season mix brings faster green-up and more rapid growth. According to Peter Schramm, prairie biologist at Knoxville College, Galesburg, Illinois, big bluestem and Indian grass as the basic mix with a liberal amount of little bluestem thrown in is recommended. Indian grass is an ideal roadside grass. A combination of 60 percent Indian grass, 25 percent big bluestem, 10 percent little bluestem, and 5 percent switchgrass is recommended. Another approach would be mixing 40 percent Indian grass, 40 percent big bluestem, 15 percent little bluestem, and 5 percent switchgrass, or the switchgrass could be omitted. Where a lower height of grasses is advantageous, little bluestem and side-oats grama are used. Dominant forb species include coneflowers, silphiums, rattlesnake master, blazing star, white sage, stiff goldenrod, and purple and white prairie clover. Mosaic plantings with more forbs can be done in rest areas, cloverleafs, and areas where showy flowers will attract attention. Native species are proving themselves along with burn management to be very effective in roadside areas.

For droughty soils the relative amounts of little bluestem and side-oats grama should be increased in the mix, lessening the amounts of big bluestem, Indian grass, and switchgrass. In low-lying areas or for heavy soils, switchgrass should be increased and little bluestem and side-oats grama decreased.

Before native seed plantings are started, the common offenders must be eradicated. Tall fescue should be killed with glyphosate (Roundup) before planting and spot-eliminated the first two to three years. A native planting is not recommended where fescue, sericea lespedeza, or bird's-foot trefoil exists in large amounts as the seeds can stay viable in the soil for several years. If fescue, sericea, or bird's-foot trefoil is growing around the outside of the planting, it is mowed to a distance of 40 feet in Missouri for the first two to three years to prevent seeds from blowing into the planting and getting established. Crown vetch was thought to be the answer to soil erosion along the roadside and was widely planted. It has proven to be very aggressive, and water has washed the soil through the root base. There is no reliable method of eradicating it from an area, aside from sterilizing the soil. You can sterilize the soil with black plastic cover for two months in the spring. Roundup will kill the plants, but the seeds will continue to come up for a number of years. Because of their fast-trailing lateral growth, it is very difficult to kill the plants that come up in a wildflower planting without killing forbs and grasses. The seeds can wash downhill also, so do not plant native seeds below crown vetch.

Gathering and farming local native seeds are being done to meet the need for seeds to be replanted. Doug Sheeley, Hardin County roadside manager in Iowa, who has cataloged the native prairie remnants in the county, obtained permission to harvest them and planted the seeds on a plot of donated land at Caulkins Campus near Iowa Falls. The seeds will later be harvested for roadside maintenance within Hardin County, keeping the local ecotype pure. Sheeley is an active participant in the organization supporting the integrated approach to roadside vegetation management.

The Iowa Ecotype Project is dealing with the problem of native seed availability by asking volunteers to collect three specified varieties of species each year. The seeds collected are sorted into three zones running from north to south in Iowa. These seeds are channeled through the Association for Integrated Roadside Management (AFIRM) office at the University of Northern Iowa and sent to the USDA Plant Materials Center (PMC) at Elsberry, Missouri, where they are developed for use by commercial growers. The species collected from 1990 to 1993 were side-oats grama, round-headed bush clover, Canada wild rye, purple prairie clover, wild indigo, prairie dropseed, ox-eye, June grass, pale coneflower, Indian grass, little bluestem, and prairie blazing star. This project will meet the needs of local ecotypes at a reasonable price to increase the seeds available for roadside management. According to Bob Dayton, agronomist for the Soil Conservation Service, "This project puts Iowa ahead of the other states in preserving the native seed and making it available on a commercial basis."

Starting Seeds Indoors

PLANTS ARE USEFUL in a border and to fill in bare spots in a larger restoration. It is also helpful to be able to identify the seedlings when you want to do some weeding.

Follow methods in the species section to break dormancy for successful germination. Seeds can be stratified during the winter for the recommended period and planted in February or March. Some will germinate within a week, while others can take over three months. Germination will vary with species, temperature, moisture, and the age of the seed. Be patient and keep watering your flat. The best surprises are those seeds that take maybe four months to germinate. Many will take from seven to twenty-one days. Some that are slower to develop will be kept in the flats longer and benefit from the use of a cold frame. A sturdy root system is needed before they can be transplanted into the permanent location. Seeds that quickly lose their viability or become dormant when dried will benefit from planting in flats in the summer or fall and placed in a cold frame for the winter for a natural stratification. In February they can be brought into the greenhouse for germination.

You will need 3-inch-deep flats, growing media, peat pots or containers 2 1/2 to 3 inches across, and garbage bags or covers for your flats to keep the moisture in. Plastic trays that allow watering from the bottom are beneficial. I like the 10-by-20-inch tray with seventy-two cells and clear plastic lid to start and keep separated small amounts of different species. If you choose to use plastic containers that you have accumulated, be sure to punch holes in the bottom to allow for drainage. Wash used containers in soap and water and rinse them in a bleach solution of a quarter cup of chlorine to a quart of water. Peat pellets may be used for easy-to-grow plants or those that resent transplanting. Pellets expand to seven times their size when placed in water to form about a 2-inch column encased in a plastic net. Peat pots are a fine choice. Just fill them with the growing medium and plant. They allow water to evaporate from all exposed surfaces and will dry out faster than plants in plastic containers. You will also need markers and a permanent marking pen to clearly label and date the seed planting.

There are a variety of germinating materials. Sphagnum moss is very acidic and useful for plants that tend to damping-off. It is difficult to moisten evenly, however, so it is best to get a mixture containing both sphagnum moss and vermiculite or perlite. Vermiculite has a neutral pH and contains magnesium and potassium, elements necessary for good root growth. Perlite is a volcanic ash and provides good aeration. It tends to rise to the surface. Seed-starting mixes can be purchased at most garden centers. Instructions are given on the mix for adding water before the mix is put in the tray to get the correct moisture content. Benomyl fungicide may also be used to prevent damping-off. Before sowing the seeds, drench the sowing medium with half a tablespoon per gallon of water solution and allow the medium to drain for two hours before planting. Garden soil is not recommended for starting seeds. It may contain weed seeds, fungi, and insects and does not allow for good drainage and aeration.

Place the medium in the flats and water from below. Pat the medium down before planting. Sow twice as many seeds as you hope to grow. Some will need an even larger ratio if they are difficult to germinate. Seeds should be covered two times their thickness, unless they are light sensitive. These seeds, which are usually very fine, are not covered at all with planting medium. To retain moisture, a clear lid or clear plastic bag is attached to the flat. Dark bags may be used on other seeds. Remove the bag when sprouting occurs. Clear lids that remain on the flat need to be adjusted for proper moisture content and temperature. Let the flats air if the growing medium has absorbed too much moisture. Keep the flats at a temperature of 65 to 70 degrees F. Sunny windows are unlikely to provide enough light for your seedlings. If you're not lucky enough to have a glassed-in porch or greenhouse, fluorescent lights may be used as instructed. Plants benefit from eight to twelve hours of light a day. Keep artificial lighting at least 3 to 6 inches above the plants.

The first growth that you will see are the cotyledons, also known as seed leaves, as they store food. Dicotyledons have two seed leaves that emerge in the seedling before the true leaves appear. Monocotyledons appear as a blade of grass.

Next the true leaves appear. When four true leaves appear, you may transplant to peat pots or sectioned flats. Handle the seedlings by the leaves to prevent breaking the stem. A clean ice cream stick is useful in removing the seedlings from the flat. Stem seedlings can be planted up to their true leaves. Rosette seedlings should sit on the surface of the soil. If stems have fine hairs, they can trap water and lead to leaf mold, so plant them in slightly mounded soil for drainage. Do not place in full sun for several days, until the seedlings have recovered from the transplanting shock. Single-stemmed plants benefit from pinching back by removing the tip of the plant. Check the roots once a week to make sure they have not become root-bound. If they are coming out of the bottom of the pot, transplant.

In May and June large-enough plants can be placed outdoors. Soil temperature should be 60 degrees F and past the danger of frost. Plants should be 1 to 1 1/2 inches tall and kept at a temperature of 50 to 55 degrees F for one to two weeks. This will produce stockier, heavier-stemmed plants. A cool porch or cold frame is ideal. Place on a south-facing exposure. The frame may be made with glass, fiberglass, or plastic, double layered with ventilation in between. Paint the inside walls white to reflect the sun or insulate with 1-inch Styrofoam. If the lid is not raised when it is hot, the plants may die, quite a disaster after all the care you have given them. The temperature should be raised only 10 to 15 degrees F in the daytime and 5 degrees F at night. The final week before transplanting outdoors, keep the frame open. After planting outside, keep the plants watered for several days. Fertilizer is not recommended for native plants.

One common mistake with peat pots is to plant the rim of the pot above ground level. The peat pot then acts as a wick and draws water away from the plant's roots, releasing it into the air. Break off the rim if you are unable to bury the pot.

Do not be concerned if you do not have a greenhouse or indoor facilities to start your seedlings. Seeds can be successfully germinated in the garden. For control and cultivation you can start them in rows or squares where they can be identified, weeded, and transplanted later. Outdoor planting is used entirely by Prairie Moon Nursery in Winona, Minnesota. The general planting can be started after the danger of frost is past and up to early July. One-year-old lead plant, purple prairie clover, white prairie clover, and butterfly weed need winter mulching to prevent frost heaving, which can be fatal to these plants.

5

Preparing the Site for Planting

PREPARING THE SOIL is the most important step in the success of your prairie. The time to get rid of as many weeds as possible is before planting, rather than after they have grown on a newly seeded site. Study prairies and other restorations and start small so that you can properly manage your planting.

The 1991 Code of Iowa "Primary Noxious Weeds" lists quack grass, perennial sow thistle, Canada thistle, bull thistle, field bindweed, horse nettle, leafy spurge, hoary cress (perennial pepper-grass), Russian knapweed, tall thistle, musk thistle, and buckthorn. "Secondary Noxious Weeds" are wild mustard, velvetleaf (butterprint), cocklebur, wild carrot, shattercane, buckhorn plantain, red (sheep) sorrel, curly dock, smooth dock, poison hemlock, multiflora rose, wild sunflower, teasel, purple loosestrife, and puncture vine. Landowners are ordered to control them from maturing by cutting or other means. These are the major weeds and aggressive plants that must be controlled in Iowa.

Some of the weeds most prevalently encountered in the prairie plantings in Iowa the first year are pigweed, amaranth, velvet leaf, foxtail, buttonweed, and smartweed. You may also encounter the annual weeds shepherd's purse, common purslane, crabgrass, and common groundsel. Annual weeds and grasses are not much of a problem in the long term and can act as a cover crop in the first year. They tend not to recur after about the second year. The perennial weeds broad leaf plantain, mouse-ear chickweed, alien clovers, bromegrass, horsetail, quack grass, field bindweed, hedge bindweed, and dandelion will cause more of a problem. Perennial weeds may spread vegetatively by producing stolons or rhizomes or by spreading root systems.

Common disturbance indicator species are quack grass, smooth brome grass, Canada thistle, field bindweed, hedge bindweed, yellow nutsedge, leafy spurge, sweet clover, Kentucky bluegrass, timothy, and reed canary grass. These are difficult plants to deal with when the prairie is establishing and should be eradicated before planting. Analyze your weed problem. It can be a big disappointment if these weeds are allowed to compete with your expensive native seeds. The loss can result in more maintenance effort and the need to buy additional seed. Use one of the following methods to eradicate weeds before planting:

1. Till the soil frequently for a full year before planting so that the weed seeds are allowed to germinate; then remove the plant before it goes to seed. Planting oats at a rate of 96 pounds (3 bushels) per acre between September 1 and October 1 or winter wheat at a rate of 90 pounds (1.5 bushels) per acre from September 1 to October 30 will stabilize the soil and provide humus when turned under in the spring. In preparing a new site that does not have a cover crop, till no deeper than 1 to 2 inches to prevent stirring up weed seeds. An exception to this is when the weeds are very thick. The first tilling will then need to go perhaps 6 to 8 inches deep to loosen the weeds. Then rake the roots out with a harrow. This is best done when the soil breaks up easily and can be done several times from different directions.

2. Till in the fall, and disk and harrow the site as early as the ground can be worked in the spring. Fall tilling is especially helpful when perennial vegetation such as pasture sod, hay fields, and lawns is being eliminated. Planting a winter cover crop such as annual grain rye or oats is recommended a couple of weeks before your area's average date of first frost. After spring disking wait two or three weeks for weeds to emerge and harrow again. Repeat two or three times during April and May and into June. Just work the surface soil so that weed seeds from deeper soils are not brought to the surface.

3. Turn the soil and place a jute-back carpet or black plastic on the area for a year before planting, allowing no weed growth. Be sure to anchor the

edges of the material well to keep it in place. This will kill the weed seeds present.

4. Chemical treatment with Roundup may be applied two or more weeks after the site is disked and harrowed in the spring. Spray on actively growing weeds at the 2- to 5-inch stage, using 1 to 1.5 percent solution for annuals and a 2 percent solution for perennials. Repeat two or three times if weeds are heavy. One application in the spring may be sufficient if the soil has been tilled previously, or apply in the fall after crop removal. One week after the last application, drill the seed to avoid disturbing the soil base.

Roundup is a nonselective but environmentally sound herbicide. This is the choice of herbicides because it breaks down quickly after contact with the soil so it doesn't linger to interfere with seeding. It is best applied in the fall and once again before planting to clean a new area, and then followed with spot application during the growing season. Unlike soil sterilants, Roundup is ideal for preparing sites because you can plant seven days after spraying. A low pressure is used when spraying to produce large droplets that will not drift. It is not volatile, therefore it has no fumes or odors. On shallow soil little disturbance is then needed to prepare the seedbed. It will not leach into the soil to harm the roots of desirable nearby plants, and soil microbes break down into naturally occurring substances like water, nitrogen, and carbon dioxide. It must be sprayed or touched with a wand on actively growing, green vegetation; it will then move into the root system to kill the underground parts. *It will kill any green plant with which it comes in contact.* Browning of the treated plants usually occurs in about seven days, and in another week the roots and total plant are destroyed. Therefore, allow two weeks for the herbicide to degrade before cultivating. Always read and follow all label directions, seek competent application advice, and wear protective gear.

5. Spring burning, when possible, is good if your ground is infested with thistles. If Atrazine has been used in your field within the past two years, it will be necessary to plant a smother crop of corn or sorghum to hold the soil for a year and control unwanted weeds while the Atrazine breaks down. Some prairie grasses can tolerate some levels of Atrazine, but prairie flowers cannot tolerate any.

6. Tilling must be continued throughout the growing season or you can cease cultivation after a month and sow a green manure crop such as buckwheat or sorghum. Green manure crops must be mowed or tilled under before they set seed. An annual grain such as rye will prevent erosion over the winter, when spring planting is planned, or a mulch could be applied.

7. No-till has the advantage of not stirring up weeds and rocks, creating a loose seedbed. This is effective only in an area of minimal weed seed content. Seeds may be broadcast on undisturbed sandy soil where there are many open spaces and little competition. They were also successful with small-seeded species on closed sod of the moist-mesic habitats in the fall of the year with gentians and other species.

8. The quickest way to remove the sod in lawns is to remove the top three inches of grass and soil using a sod cutter. The ground will be lower but possibly weed-free. If soil is added be aware of the seed content. Sod cutters can be rented. If you prefer to remove the sod by cultivation, it will need to be done two to three times approximately one week apart. If quack grass or Johnson grass are present, till for a full year. When herbicides are used to kill actively growing grass, cultivate after everything has turned brown. This will take about two weeks after application.

In the end the bed needs to be weed-free and firm for planting in the spring. Roll using a cultipacker or cast-iron field roller or by adding weight to the metal flap that drags behind the tiller blades before planting to get a good firm seedbed.

When correct seeds are selected for your soil, amendments will not have to be made unless you have extreme conditions of inadequate soil as already explained. Extreme clay or sandy soils lacking loam that have not been able to sustain any vegetation indicate that the soil needs correcting before the investment of native seeds. Rock in a fill may also prevent success.

Fertilizer is not applied before planting because the weedy species respond quickly, choking out the native perennials. Native plants respond best without fertilizer.

Planting

YOUR DECISION TO plant in fall or spring is based on the factors of weed competition, moisture, and stratification for germination. Seeds planted in May and June, with the first two weeks in June being preferred, avoid competition with the early, rapid weed growth. Forb seeds that prefer cool soil, as listed, will lie dormant until fall or the next spring. Warm-season prairie grasses and forbs will not germinate in cool soil, and best results occur in early June. When rainfall is adequate, plantings may be made as late as July 15, but moisture for three to four weeks following planting is essential.

Nurse or cover crops may be planted with the native grasses and forbs, with planting between May 1 and July 10 at the rate of 20 pounds (5 gallons) of oats, 5 pounds of annual rye (or an increase of 7 to 8 pounds on slopes), 10 pounds of annual flax, or 18 pounds (2.75 gallons) of winter wheat per acre. These crops will reduce weed growth where weeds often try to come up before the prairie plants are established. They generally do not reseed themselves. Do not use agricultural grain rye as chemicals in its roots suppress the germination of other plants, and do not use bromegrass. Be sure your seeds are weed-free.

Late fall planting around November 1 has the advantage of natural stratification and gives a wider variety of species an equal start. When fall planting, add winter wheat to the native mix at a rate of 18 pounds (2.75 gallons) between October 15 and November 15. October is too late for oats. As already stated, some seeds in fall planting can be lost to birds or other animal predators. Earlier fall planting may cause early sprouting and winter kill, as native grasses may germinate in ten days if the weather is unseasonably warm. They can also be seeded without tillage into an oat stand. The oats will winter kill but give protection from heavy spring rains.

Frost seeding between late October and late March, when there is no snow cover, can be done. Freezing and thawing will mix the seeds with the soil. This method can also be used for reseeding bare spots on an established field.

Grass-Forb Competition

Forbs have difficulty competing with a heavy stand of grass. A matrix such as Canada wild rye, oats, or timothy can be added to the forb mix to provide a temporary fuel matrix, erosion control, and weed replacement. If forbs are planted alone or in a ratio of three to one with native grasses, they can become established with the matrix. Carl Kurtz advocates planting 20 pounds of mixed flowers and grasses per acre using at least two times the weight of forbs as grass seed. Try to use as much variety (diversity) of local seed types as possible. The greater the diversity, the greater your prairie's long-term stability. If you plant only forbs, when they are established you can plant the native grasses using the No-till Rangeland grass drill or overseeding in the fall after a burn.

A mosaic planting is another method that allows forbs to compete with grasses. Small plantings with a wide variety of species can closely simulate natural prairie remnants when edges are blended with the mixes. Different sections are planted at the same time with different seed mixtures. Little bluestem and side-oats grama are less competitive, and when only 1 pound of grass seed per acre is added to the forbs they can be planted along the viewing area. For the background a mix with taller grasses can be increased to 4 to 8 pounds, still including many forbs in the mix. In a third area, a dense planting of 10 to 14 pounds of tall grasses per acre can be applied with some of the more competitive forbs. The patterns of the different plants can be very attractive. Besides the height of the plants, mixes can be formulated to be planted on different soils.

Grass-forb competition can also be influenced by differential seed conditioning. This is done by cold-damp stratification of the forbs, excluding legumes, while leaving the grasses dry. When they are mixed together and planted, the forbs will germinate as soon as moisture is adequate, while the grasses will be delayed from one to three weeks (see Schramm, *Prairie Restoration*).

Planting Techniques

Planting techniques will be chosen by the location and type of planting that you are doing and will range from hand broadcasting, drill seeding, endgate seeding, hydroseeding, Easy-flow fertilizer spreading, to cultipacking.

For hand broadcasting mix four parts clean, fine, damp sand with one part seed for better distribution. Even distribution is more difficult by hand. Be careful not to sow too heavily or you will run out. The seeding rate should be thirty to sixty seeds per square foot. It is best to sow lightly from one direction and then repeat, sowing from a different direction on the second pass. Seeds need to be sowed 1/4 to 1/2 inch deep. Proper depth is important because if seedlings are to survive they must emerge quickly and begin to produce their own food. If they are too deep, they will lack light or exhaust their food supply before emergence. When planted alone, forb mixes should be 1/4 inch deep and grasses 1/2 inch deep. Very fine seeds can be kept out of the mix and sown on top of the soil after it is packed. The other seeds can be worked into the soil with a rake, harrow, or straight disk. Firm soil is important so that the seed has contact with the soil and moisture. Packing is needed with spring plantings if walking on the area compacts the soil more than 1/2 inch after sowing and raking. Use a roller or cultipacker, drag old bed springs, or even drive a car on the area to pack down the soil. If the area is small you can pack the soil by walking on it.

Garden fertilizer spreaders also may be used for a small area. Hand-held cyclone seeders become clogged with a variety of native seed mixes and should be used only for cover crops of oats or rye.

When planting more than half an acre with clean seeds, a drill or hydro-seeder should be used. Well-known drills are the Truax and Nesbit. The Nesbit has a picker wheel in the large box for the fluffy seeds (bluestems, Indian grass, blue grama, etc.) and a brush wheel for the fine seeds (switchgrass, lovegrass, legumes, etc.). Jim Truax of Minneapolis says that his broadcast seeder design is user-friendly and gives controlled seeding rate and distribution of wildflower and grass seeds. With the Truax drill, set depth bands to 1 inch to achieve 1/2-inch-deep planting and set them at 1/2 inch to plant 1/4 inch deep. Use horticultural-grade vermiculite rather than sand for stratification when you plant with the Truax to avoid damage to the drill. The John Deere rangeland drill, as modified by the Miller Seed Company of Lincoln, Nebraska, has been reported as being as successful as the Nisbet grass drill. This drill uses a gravity feed for the fluffy seeds and a fluted feed for the fine seeds. The John Deere Power Seeder is also equipped to handle chaffy seeds.

Seeds are dropped at established rates when furrows are cut into the ground. More even coverage can be obtained by removing the double-disk opening and disconnecting the tube which can be removed or left hanging. A chain or rubber tire can be dragged behind to work the seeds into the soil and help pack it. The seeds are planted in rows, but going over the same area from a perpendicular angle will give a more natural look. Peter Schramm, in his discussion of mosaic planting design to duplicate nature, discusses the art of using the Nesbit drill as taught by Wilson in 1970. He refers to the drill being the brush, the seed mix the paint, and the operator the artist. Fewer seeds are needed than in hand broadcasting because the germination rate is higher. The Truax design uses a baffle system to broadcast the seeds so they are distributed over the entire area. A roller then presses the seeds into the soil. Other features facilitate planting fluffy or irregular-size seeds, and it adapts to the rigors of rough sites with increased efficiency and versatility.

The Rangeland Grass Drill with Zero-Till attachment can be used on no-till or disturbed land prepared with a rotary or flail mower. It will cut through the heaviest trash or frozen ground and still achieve good soil-to-seed contact. It has limitations on very wet or sloped land. Some experts recommend that Roundup be used before no-till seeding.

Endgate seeders used with clean seeds mount on the back of a wagon. They are commonly used to sow oats and legumes. Good results can be obtained seeding an area 5 to 6 feet wide. Prairie seed grass in an endgate seeder continually bridges and requires constant attention, however.

Hydroseeders may be used on sloped or wet areas. Sloped hydroseeding from the bottom forces the seeds into the ground for better soil contact. Sloped sites need mulching. On wet ground remove an impeller or two on the hydroseeder to prevent clogging.

Easy-flow-type fertilizer spreaders may be used to distribute seeds when they are mixed with heavy trash. These spreaders plant an area about 6 feet wide and can be rented from a fertilizer dealer. Follow with a spiked-tooth harrow to work the seeds into the soil. Plant on a windless day and go over two times if necessary. Have someone in the spreader push the seeds down to keep an even flow.

Cultipackers can provide uniform seeding rates and depths. Appropriately sizing one to a tractor may be difficult. A roller bar on the cultipacker packs the seeds into the soil for good contact. Cast-iron field rollers also give a good firm seedbed, which is important for seeds to acquire moisture for germination. It also gives some protection against water erosion when the soil is unprotected or a cover crop is needed.

Maintenance

Postseeding Management

Water the soil for three weeks after planting for good germination. Water one-half-inch deep during seed establishment if rain does not provide this within a week. If you can water thoroughly right after planting, by all means do so. Irrigation beyond three weeks may stimulate weed growth. Sandy soil may need watering more frequently.

Nature's Green and Soil Alive! contain a natural blend of soil enzymes and activators that work together to improve the quality of your soil without fertilizers. They stimulate the existing beneficial microorganisms in the soil, helping to break down organic matter and improving the moisture retention and texture of the soil. They attach to your garden hose and can be applied directly to your wildflower area after seeding.

Mow when weeds grow above the seedlings at a height of 10 to 12 inches, shading by 50 to 70 percent. Mowing above the seedlings will need to be done perhaps twenty-one to thirty days after the seeding date. Organic farmers do this to avoid using herbicides. Native perennials are growing roots the first year, and the aboveground growth is small. On the first mowing cut back to 2 to 4 inches with either a sickle or rotary shredder. Keep the plot mowed to about 6 to 8 inches until late September. The height you set the mower will be determined by the height of the prairie plants. The blade must clear the height of the desired seedling. Set it 2 to 8 inches above them, maintaining the understory of native plants and removing the over-story of weeds. The preferred method is the flail mower. A rotary mower is better than a sickle-bar mower, as it produces smaller cuttings, reducing the chance of smothering the grass or forb seedlings. The cuttings will settle in to form a fine mulch. Do not allow any weeds to set seeds. Foxtail and other weeds can completely smother out the native seedlings. Continue this process as needed during the first year. A lawnmower at its highest setting can be used on smaller areas when large equipment is not available. Do not leave clippings bunched up in piles. In a total stand of wildflowers, foxtail and other grasses can be treated with Ornamec Grass Herbicide. It does not control broad-leaf weeds or sedges and will not harm wildflowers, but it will kill native grasses.

Do not use herbicides for broad-leaf weeds unless no forb species have been planted. Pure grass stands may be sprayed with broad-leaf weed killers such as 2,4-D at a rate of 2/3 pint to 1 quart per acre without damage to grasses. Broad-leaf weed killers do not kill foxtail or other cool-season grasses, so mowing may still be required. Atrazine can also be used on warm-season grass stands to kill cool-season grasses; however, it is believed that some warm-season grasses may be adversely affected. This postseeding weed control is the most important part of a successful establishment, es-pecially in a dry year according to Carl Kurtz. Since 2,4-D kills the worms and the birds that feed on them, organic farmers prefer not to use it. As stated before, do not use 2,4-D or Atrazine with wildflowers. If bromegrass or quack grass develop heavily, prairie grasses will have little advantage and seeding may have to be redone.

In management of restorations and reconstructions that have not been allowed natural burning, one must use Roundup with caution. Though Roundup has been strongly advocated as the herbicide of preference for spot application, some recommend not using Roundup because of the pos-sible destruction of the understory by wind drift. It is possible to lose some of the native plants along with the undesirables, and thus organic means should be strongly considered.

A light covering of weed-free straw is beneficial. Mulch with oats, wheat, or grain free of perennial grasses. Do not use baled hay. As mentioned ear-lier, this is especially important with purple prairie clover, lead plant, and butterfly weed to prevent frost heaving.

Inexperienced restorationists almost always are convinced they have a failure the first year. The top growth amounts to a narrow, straight leaf with the grasses until late summer. At the end of the first year prairie annuals such as black-eyed Susans will be dominant. The planting will look messy because the prairie seedlings above ground are still small. They may have only 6-inch wispy tops. Annual weeds may still be present. But continue patiently, remember that roots are being established, and prepare for spring burning if there is enough thatch buildup. Usually this is not needed until the third year.

Second Year

Hand weeding or spot application of an herbicide is your best defense in the second year. Weeds not only take away the water and nutrients from the seedlings but they shade and smother some of the young plants. Weeds present now are mainly biennial. In the second year, curly dock can be a problem. The roots take hold so that it requires a spade to dig them out. But if they are not removed, the prairie will crowd them out in a few years. Hand weed or apply spot application of Roundup to individual plants such as Canada thistle, sweet clover, or sour dock. Mix one part Roundup with two parts water (a stronger solution) and apply by hand with a brush applicator. These applicators can sometimes be purchased through grain elevators and feed stores. Thistles should be cut or spot sprayed before they go to seed. Taproots of dandelions, wild parsnips, and burdock should be cut below the ground or spot sprayed also.

Mowing after the first year should only be done if necessary and limited to once or twice a year no lower than 8 inches. It may be required to control foxtail in midsummer where grasses have not become well established. Mow very early in the spring and then avoid mowing until July 15 to protect ground-nesting birds and butterflies. Mowing is used when burning is not possible. Most management should be limited to pulling problem weeds or chemically treating individual plants such as Canada thistle or sour dock. Individual Canada thistle plants cannot compete with vigorous prairie stands and in most cases are smothered in three or four years.

Grazing can have similar effects as mowing. However, if overdone it is hard on the prairie. An old pioneer's advice, "Take half and leave half," will keep your planting of native pastures healthy and vigorous for many lifetimes. Done in conservative measures, grazing keeps the prairie growing, but it is no substitute for burning. Studies are being made on the effect early migratory and nomadic movements of grazing animals had on the prairie.

Fertilizing continues to be unnecessary.

The short-lived perennials Canada wild rye, gray-headed coneflower, ox-eye, wild bergamot, and showy tick-trefoil will become established and may bloom. The large-flowering yellow species will make a pleasing display and may last for three to four years or longer while the longer-lived plants are being established. Annual weeds should be nearly gone. Black-eyed Susan is still reseeding itself but appearing more on the edge of the stand.

Third to Fifth Years

Burning will be beneficial beginning about the third year, depending on when enough growth has accumulated to provide fuel. Others advocate burning every year if annual weeds such as foxtail and old witchgrass are present. The one exception is on steep slopes, where erosion may have exposed the new root systems. Then burning can be done every three to four years, rotating the sections that are burned each year. A prairie with grasses added to the forbs allows a greater matrix for burning. Native plants with their deep rooting systems are adapted to recover from the burns. The benefits of burning are more vigorous plants and the recycling of important nutrients. Competition from the overstory is lessened, letting the sun reach the soil. Microbial activity increases in the blackened soil as the soil temperatures are increased. Organic matter is then broken down, releasing nutrients for plant growth. Nitrogen, phosphorus, and potassium become available. Fire is a natural process in the ecosystem and helps to reduce woody plants and other invaders. Burning stimulates prairie plants to produce aboveground vegetation and induces more seeds to germinate. It also reduces time and cost to the landowner when compared to conventional methods such as mowing or spraying. Failure to burn may result in a prairie of nearly all grass and few forbs in a matter of five years, and the grass itself will become less productive.

Be aware of your local codes on burning and notify the fire department, gas pipeline companies, and your neighbors that you will be burning. Establish a firebreak by mowing a perimeter of the field at least 8 feet wide three times a year to protect areas outside the field. Special safety precautions and equipment are needed when burning. Further guides to proper burning techniques should be obtained. Volunteers are always needed at a burn site, and this is a good way to learn the proper methods. Burn schools are also held by various prairie and conservation groups.

Once a prairie is established, butterfly chrysalides and eggs and other wildlife will be destroyed during burning. Butterfly species have different seasons for propagating, and this timing should be studied when this is a concern. Burrowing mammals are more tolerant of annual burning than ground-nesting mammals. Burning helps correct the unnatural microvertebrates in an unhealthy field. Burning different sections each year on a rotating basis will afford refuge for those animals and insects that would be harmed. Pheasants enjoy wintering in the tallgrass area, but fortunately they tend to nest in alfalfa fields. However, usually only one-third to one-half of the prairie is burned at a time to protect the wildlife that has been established at least five years. Setting up a rotation plan for burning will ensure that wildlife will not disappear from the area.

Timing the burn is important. It should be done when the native prairie is turning green in the spring and native grasses are 1 to 3 inches tall. Spring burning in March or April can help control perennial weeds, small trees, and cool-season grasses and stimulate the native grass at the same time. It helps to establish seeding of warm- and cool-season grasses by stimulating growth and opening up weedy areas to allow existing seedlings to dominate these areas. The period of optimum burning is about ten days, so plans should be made to burn at the beginning of this period to allow for delays due to inclement weather. Wind speed and direction, frontal passages, field moisture, relative humidity, and temperature in addition to the amount of vegetation in the field affect how the fire will burn. Optimum conditions are a steady wind of 5 to 15 mph and humidity between 30 and 60 percent, with a temperature range of 60 to 70 degrees F. Prescribed precautions must be met in case the fire gets out of hand. Learn from those experienced in using a backfire and headfire to control the burn. Fires are easier to control when they are used as a management tool. Accidental fires in areas that have been allowed to accumulate vegetation can cause costly destruction. Natural barriers such as roads, driveways, streams, lakes, and mowed borders around the prairie help establish fire lanes. By June burning can damage spring forbs such as the prairie violet and blue-eyed grass. Fall burns, after the prairie has gone dormant, do not suppress the prairie but lack the advantage of sudden ground-warming that a spring burn produces. Ash from fall burns is washed away by winter precipitation.

Established woody plants, however, are not always controlled with spring burning. Occasional fall burning, alternated with spring burning, will bring a more complete eradication. The injury to undesirable woody plants causes them to weaken over winter from fungi and disease. Sumac, aspen, and other tree encroachments are aided by spring burning, resulting in their increase. Mowing can also increase woody plants three to one. To eliminate the woody growth chop or chainsaw it at ground level in late spring or early summer, followed by mowing and burning in the fall. Another alternative is to cut smaller trees and girdle larger trees. A mixture of 1/4 Crossbow and 3/4 diesel fuel painted on woody growth may also be effective in killing it. Annual burns will then eventually eliminate the new growth of the woody plants. Fall burning has the disadvantage of removing winter cover for wildlife. It also has less value in stimulating the growth of prairie species to compete with the nonprairie species and should therefore be limited.

In an area where burning is not possible, mowing in late fall or preferably early spring is another option if cuttings are removed to avoid a buildup of thatch. This should only be considered for urban property and home landscaping. Mowing should not be considered unless very heavy foxtail stands persist, indicating that seeding has failed and may need to be done again. Weeds should be minimal and can be pulled individually.

Do not fertilize unless the plants show signs of deficiency, such as light foliage. Nitrogen can cause soft vegetation growth to increase and delay flowering. This will shorten the life of a perennial and will encourage weeds. If fertilizer is needed, use a ratio of 1 part nitrogen, 3 parts phosphorus, and 2 parts potassium, or use 60 pounds of phosphorus and 40 pounds of potassium per acre.

On an existing prairie it is sometimes necessary to replant or overseed areas that do not have adequate forbs and grasses. This can be done to a native prairie remnant as well as to a prairie that has been planted but where more species are desired. Choose spot planting, partial overseeding, or complete reseeding. When a small stand of native plants is present, seeds mixed in sand can be hand sown on the surface in the spring to increase the stand. Some of the most successful showy prairies have had forbs started from seed indoors in the spring and spot planted into the prairie in the fall or early spring. This method gives you more control of the results that you want to achieve. Grasses and forbs grown in pots that you started during the soil preparation time or purchased can be planted 12 to 15 inches apart. Adding transplants or a plug of plants can be beneficial when the root mass has not yet filled in. Then water and mulch the area.

When spot planting is done, prepare at least a square foot for each plant. Allow sufficient space for root growth and other plant competition.

In areas that are weak, till curved strips of about 3 to 8 feet, making the new planting blend in naturally with the existing area. Sufficient sections need to be cleared so that plants or seeds will have room to become established in an existing prairie. Let the area lie dormant for a year and mulch to keep weeds from growing. Various weed-free, natural mulches as well as black plastic are effective. Then replant the area.

When interseeding a large area, clear the weeds by burning, spot treating with Roundup, or mowing with a rotary or flail mower before seeding. The flail mower works well on a prairie where the sod has not become thick. Use straight renovating blades adjusted low to dig into the soil 1/2 to 3/4 inch. Or you may disk or rototill very lightly so as not to disturb the existing prairie plants. Then seeding can be done by hand or with a drill, followed by dragging to pack the seeds for soil contact. No-till is another choice, and an additional method to encourage soil contact is casting a layer of sand over the newly seeded prairie. It is sometimes beneficial to do the seeding following a fall burn, and ideally a late snow will work the seeds into the soil.

Fertile land presents more problems with weed infestation and domestic cool-season grasses. Continue to use the methods described previously to combat the weed infestation so that the prairie plants can become established. Roadside managers, soil conservationists, and chemical dealers can help prevent these problems. Natural disasters can be prevented with conservation management.

Long-lived perennials will now start to compete, and your prairie should be well on the way to establishment and holding its own against the weeds. You will find evidence of big bluestem, little bluestem, switchgrass, Indian grass, side-oats grama, and rattlesnake master. Purple coneflower, compass plant, and white and purple prairie clover will begin to flower. Annual fleabane disappears the fourth or fifth year.

Sixth Year

By the sixth year, the root mass should be adequate so that weeds have no room to establish themselves. Long-lived perennials that are slow to establish but have staying power will be prairie dropseed, compass plant, prairie cinquefoil, sky-blue aster, New Jersey tea, wild indigo, and Culver's root. Once established, the prairie requires no fertilizing, no spraying, no watering, and little weeding. Now you can put up that hammock and look forward to sipping your lemonade and enjoying the prairie. But your management does not end. Burnings must continue and the area watched for problems of alien encroachment.

This succession of growth is interesting to observe at Carl Kurtz's farm at St. Anthony, Iowa. He has planted a large area of native seeds at a rate of 20 pounds per acre, with 75 percent forbs and 25 percent grasses in each planting. Each area has a definite appearance, with the number of weeds decreasing each year. He has diligently followed the techniques of preparation, mowing, and management as described, and his beautiful farm is evidence that it really works when done correctly.

Long-term Adjustment Stage

Lead plant and prairie dropseed finally begin to flower and make a real show in the final stage, which can take from thirteen to even forty or more years. Seeds from the original planting can lie dormant or remain insignificant in the more vigorous growth and appear up to twenty years later. Because of the many variables the succession will vary from one restoration to another, but stages do exist and give an indication of the health of a prairie. Different species of prairie plants have been known to live from twenty-five to one hundred years.

Disturbances vary in the impact they have on the natural succession of the prairie. Windblown soil generated by fall plowing can bring in weed seeds from neighboring fields. Improper use of herbicides in the area can also selectively kill some vegetation and stress other types. During a heavy rain, bare soil with herbicide buildup can be washed into prairies where it can disturb native forbs. A weakened stand will allow the annual and noxious weeds to invade.

Maintaining the Native Border

When native plants are introduced into your border, they require the same care as any perennial bed. If you want to eliminate some of your lawn and increase your native plants, the quickest way is to remove the top three inches of grass and soil using a sod cutter. If you choose to eliminate the grass with herbicides, apply them in fall or spring, when the lawn is growing, and cultivate after everything has turned brown. A third choice is cultivation alone. This will need to be done two or three times, about one week apart or until all persistent grasses such as quack grass or Johnson grass are eliminated. This may take a year.

It is easier to start the border from plants rather than seeds. Plants may be started indoors about three months ahead of the last frost or purchased from reputable dealers. Refer to the species section to see if stratification or other treatment is necessary for germination.

Spring clean-up of the established border consists of removing cover mulch, pruning last year's stalks, and repositioning plants by division that have overgrown or heaved from the frost. Regular thinning and outright weeding of some of the native plants need to be done. Spiderwort and goldenrod tend to get into areas where they are not wanted and have to be pulled before the roots get entrenched. Plant aggressives in containers such as a large tin with both ends cut out. Plastic dividers planted between areas are helpful barriers. Dividing individual plants needs to be done while they are in their winter condition before shoots appear in the spring. Seedlings may be repotted. Eliminate the weaker specimens with a cultivating tool. Pinch back tops of fall-blooming composites to make them bushier. Fertilizing is done only when plants show the need.

Water newly established seeds or plants in the coolness of the evening or morning. Plants with shallow root systems, such as wild bergamot and rudbeckias, will need more water. Watering thoroughly with a hose is preferred to a sprinkler. A soaker hose will allow you to water slowly and steadily, so the water is absorbed by the roots. It dispenses just 1 gallon of water per foot per hour, and water is not lost to the atmosphere as it is with a sprinkler. Once established, the border will need little watering but will benefit from occasional watering during extremely dry periods for maximum bloom and color.

Weed by hand, with tools, or with spot herbicides following a rain when the soil is moist but not wet and muddy. Eliminate the weeds before they go to seed. Mulching with a natural material will help control weeds. Mulch should not touch the leaves of basal rosettes or flowering stems. Some plants, like butterfly weed, do not do well with mulching because they like well-drained soil during the growing season. However, butterfly weed, lead plant, and purple prairie clover should be mulched in the winter to prevent frost heaving. Clumping plants that are low and have shade tolerance can be planted in between larger plants for a ground cover and natural weed control.

Prune in small amounts. Begin early in the year. In the late summer do not remove large portions of new growth or the plants will be less hardy.

Removal of flowers after they bloom (deadheading) early in the season will bring more bloom. Cuttings may be made in the summer for fall planting.

Controlling insects the organic way can be done with integrated pest management (IPM). This method stresses minimal adverse side effects with the following course of action: evaluate if you need to do something, what you need to do, where you need to do it, when to do it, and which tactics to use. Learn to recognize pests and know their life cycles so you can attack them at the right time before damage occurs. When the cause and injury level are determined, you can then evaluate the type of treatment and cost effectiveness of the solution.

The types of control are cultural, mechanical, biological, and chemical, listed in the order they should be used. As a first defense, cultural control limits pest populations in the site preparation with the use of organic mulches for fertility and earthworms to aerate the soil, proper choice of plant varieties, and removal of diseased parts. Sometimes the mechanical means of picking off bugs and using the two-brick-smash method or preventing the predators' access by using collars, nets, sticky strips, or beetle traps will prevent the problem. Predators, parasites, and pathogens are used in the biological method. Beneficial insects can help rid your garden of destructive insect pests. Green lace wings, ladybeetles (ladybugs), praying mantis, trichogramma wasps, predatory mites, aphidoletes, fly parasites, and other beneficial insects are available in many catalogs, with tables of release rate recommended by square foot of coverage. Trichogramma wasps, *Bacillus thuringiensis*, and ryania are organic pest controls that should be used selectively for harmful leaf- and fruit-eating caterpillars, as they will kill beneficial butterflies. Beneficial insects will be absent from your property if wide-spectrum herbicides have been used. Botanical sprays and dusts derived from plants and minerals avoid the harshness of destructive chemicals. Diatomaceous earth (DE) is made from one-celled aquatic plants called diatoms, which lived millions of years ago. Their microscopic needles of silica puncture the insect's breathing system, disrupt its soft shell structure, and cause quick death by dehydration. Aphids, slugs, and other soft-bodied sucking insects can be sprayed with a mixture of 2 tablespoons of laundry soap in 1 gallon of water. The use of an insecticidal soap containing potassium salts of fatty acids and citrus aromatics is also a gentle method that has little effect on beneficials such as ladybugs, soil bacteria, honeybees, or animals. The soap kills many newly hatched insect pests including aphids, mealybugs, thrips, fungus gnats, whiteflies, and mites. Many catalogs now carry an insecticidal soap with or without pyrethrin,

Maintenance

ryania, and rotenone and also nicotine sulfate, aphid-mite attack, and tobacco dust. Rotenone is refined from a tropical plant. When it is combined
with the fungicide copper, insects and disease are controlled at the same
time. Pyrethrum, ryania (which comes from the stems of a woody South
American shrub), and sulphur are also organic controls. These are hard-
hitting pest controls made from plants with broad pest-killing properties
that degrade quickly. Study and use the organic methods of IPM that are
harmless to animals, plants, and the environment. As with any pest control,
follow directions and apply only in recommended amounts.

Staking will be necessary in the border when there is less support from
the prairie grasses. It can be done with a metal ring around a clump, individual stakes of metal or natural sticks, or in a row with stakes joined by a
natural cord. Keep staking as unobtrusive as possible for a natural look.
Some wildflowers become tall and weak stemmed from soil that is too rich.

Fall clean-up includes removing leaves with a rake or leaf vacuum. Chop
them and replace them lightly on the bed with a pitchfork for a mulch. To
prevent plants that spread quickly by seed, remove the seed heads after
the flower fades but before the seeds mature. Seeds can be harvested and
planted in another area. Wait to completely clear your wildflower border
until all the desirable species have gone to seed. When possible, leave plants
until spring to encourage beneficial insects, including butterflies. Plants can
be removed with a weed whip or sickle in the fall or spring. Dividing and
transplanting may also be done in the fall. If sufficient room was allowed
when the border was planted, division will not have to be done as often.
You now have enabled your wildflowers to complete their life cycle, and
they will reward you with an array of beauty the following year.

II

Prairie Species

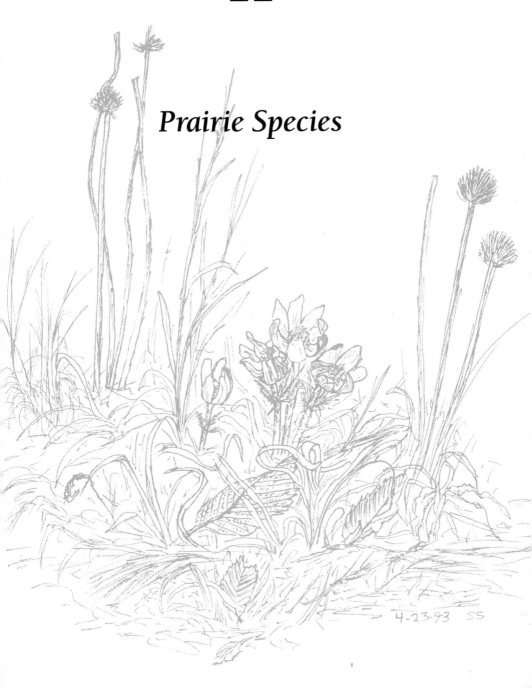

4-23-93 SS

8

Wildflowers

WILDFLOWERS WITH THEIR showy blooms give enjoyment and visual beauty to your prairie. The following information will show you how to use the species information.

Name and classification: So that plants may be compared for their similarities, they are arranged first by family, then by scientific name of genus and species. Common names are given, with the first one listed according to L. J. Eilers. Family characteristics are described in the appendix. Dicotyledonous forbs are presented first, with monocotyledonous forbs following. All plants presented are native. All are herbaceous (soft stem) except for the following shrubs (woody stem): lead plant, New Jersey tea, sunshine rose, and meadow sweet. All are perennials except partridge pea (an annual) and black-eyed Susan, gaura, and sand primrose (biennials).

Location: Areas are representative of Iowa locations according to L. J. Eilers. Soil, moisture, sun, and pH requirements of each species are given for site selection (border, meadow, or roadside). Wet soil stays wet all year. Wet mesic soil is wet in the spring and fall but often dries in the summer. Mesic soil absorbs water with no runoff, holding medium moisture. Dry mesic soil is well drained and loses moisture readily. Dry soil drains rapidly.

Plant description: Size, blooming time, color, and plant structure are given. Size will vary according to moisture, soil content, and competition. Time of bloom will vary according to location and seasonal changes. A drawing of each blooming plant, seedling, fruit, and seed is included. Use these drawings to select a prairie or border with complete diversity throughout the growing season. The appendix lists the order of blooming for all species. Catalog sources for seeds, plants, and equipment are given in the appendix. A pictorial glossary of parts of the flower follows the glossary.

Propagation: Layering, division, root or stem cuttings, and seeds are the main methods (do not remove plants from the wild for root or stem propagation). These methods can be advantageous after establishing your own plants.

Layering: The plant stem must be supple. Scratch the stem with your fingernail or knife and treat with a root hormone powder. Leave the stem attached to the plant, bend it down, and cover it with dirt.

Rootstalk division: When many shoots form a clump, known as clump-roots, lift the whole plant out during its dormancy, when it is not in bloom. Make sure all the roots are attached. With a sharp knife or spade, cut the clump of rootstock so that the divided pieces have at least one bud or eye attached. The plant size will be determined by the size of the division. Plant at the same depth in well-drained soil (to prevent bacterial and fungal rot) in a holding bed for one year and then transplant when dormant.

Bulbs and corms produce offsets at the ends of the roots. Dig them up during dormancy when the plants become densely overcrowded and break or cut off the offsets. Replant 3 inches deep, with the roots down. The off-sets of bulblets and cormlets take several years to grow to blooming stage after replanting.

Runners or stolons above ground (as seen in the familiar strawberry) send up sterile plants which may be transplanted. Cut the runner with a sharp knife.

Rhizomes are underground runners. Cut the rhizome between adjacent rooted plants (each cutting must have one eye or shoot). Leave in a cool place overnight for the cut to heal before planting. Plant where drainage is good with the bud point up, at the same depth as found in the plant. Transplant when dormant.

Root cuttings from thick tuberous roots like butterfly weed may be propagated in the spring. Cut a piece of the root 2 inches long and plant in a mixture of coarse sand and peat. Insert the root cutting vertically.

Stem cuttings are done in the early morning following a rain. The section cut should be growing and not have flowering buds. Cut off the top, leaving at least two pairs of leaves on the stem and 2 to 3 inches on the bottom of the stem stripped of leaves, so you have a 6-inch stem. Dip the bottom in a root hormone and plant in sand and peat, sand and sphagnum moss, or perlite. Insert the stem to where the first leaves are just above ground in a 6-inch pot, placing cuttings at least 1 inch apart. Moisten the soil. Place the pot in a clear plastic bag and fasten. If moisture accumulates on the bag, open it to prevent mildew. Do not place the pot in the sun. A fishbowl is also a good container, as it can be covered easily to hold moisture. Wait until the cuttings go into dormancy and then transplant.

Germination: Seeds can be carried a long distance in the prairie from the plant that produced them, sometimes landing in a hostile environment. Also, weather conditions could be harsh and unfavorable for germination. Therefore, seeds have built-in mechanisms to help them germinate when conditions are favorable. Seeds can lie dormant many years. Dormancy is protected by physical and chemical barriers. The physical barriers are hard seed coats or waxy layers that keep water out of the seeds. These barriers are broken down naturally at different times so that all the seeds do not germinate at the same time when weather conditions may be unfavorable. They are broken down by microbial decay, fire, digestion by animals, mechanical rubbing, and freezing and thawing. Chemical barriers occur in the seed or seed coat and inhibit germination even when the seed is high in moisture content and ready to germinate. Chemical dormancy is broken down by a combination of moisture, sunlight, soil, and temperature. Various treatments are required.

Afterripening occurs when the seed falls to the ground and the embryo is not mature. The seed will not germinate for 3 to 6 months, until the next spring when conditions are more favorable for growth. A germination test will tell you if the seed is mature. Some seeds will need *no treatment*. However, all prairie forbs, except legumes, can benefit from moist-cold stratification, giving a higher rate of germination if treated.

Moist-cold stratification is done by mixing seeds with equal amounts or more of damp sterile sand, vermiculite, or other sterile media. Silica sand purchased at a building supply center works well. Place the mixture in labeled sealed plastic bags and store them in the refrigerator at 33 to 38 degrees F. One to two months is enough to break the dormancy of most seeds. Some require up to 120 days. Sand should be avoided for drill plantings. For large plantings 1 part water, by volume, to 50 parts seeds is adequate, and most prairie seeds have enough chaff to hold the moisture needed for conditioning. Small amounts of potting soil may be added if necessary for moisture retention.

Cool soil treatment requires planting in fall or early spring.

Natural stratification results when seeds are planted outside in the fall, provided the winter temperature remains at least 40 degrees F for 30 to 120 days, depending on the species. Predation by critters could be a problem with this method. Seeds planted outdoors in the fall may be planted in flats that are buried to the top of the flat. The best area for this is on the north side of the house away from the sun. If temperatures remain cold for long enough periods, the flats may be left outside on top of the ground and brought into the greenhouse in February.

Hot water treatment is done by soaking the seeds overnight in water that has been boiled and removed from the heat just before pouring it over the seeds. Set aside overnight and plant the next day or continue with moist stratification if needed.

Scarification to break a tough outer coating can be done by lightly rubbing the seeds between medium-grit sandpaper, lining a tin with sandpaper and shaking the seeds in it, or tumbling them in a rock polisher with moist sand. Do not crush the seeds. Scarification precedes moist stratification.

For *warm-moist followed by cold-moist stratification*, mix the seeds in moist sand and place them in a labeled, sealed plastic bag. Store at 80 degrees F for 60 to 90 days and then move them into a refrigerator for 60 to 90 days. Outdoors a full year of dormancy will give this stratification. Michigan lily is one of the few examples of plants that require this.

Double dormancy requires two years.

Light is required for some small seeds. Plant them on the surface and do not let them dry out. Water from below and provide enough shade to retain moisture.

Fresh seeds need to be planted soon after harvest.

Inoculation of legumes will encourage formation of root nodules where atmospheric nitrogen is converted into organic nitrogen. Rhizobium, a nitrogen-fixing bacteria, forms nodules on legume roots that transform atmospheric nitrogen to a form the plant can use. Inoculating seeds with the right type of rhizobium for the specific plant encourages formation of root nodules. Seeds are mixed with water at a rate of 1 1/2 teaspoons liquid for each 2.2 pounds of seeds and then mixed with inoculant. Apply only to seeds sown in the spring. The bacteria will winter-kill without the legume roots as a host. Legumes germinate better if hulls are removed. If they are not removed, they need scarification.

Less well known are the mycorrhizal fungi that are associated with the roots of most plants. They help the plant resist adverse effects of heat and increase water and nutrient uptake and absorption, growth rate and general plant vigor, disease resistance, and soil toxicity tolerance. The endomycorrhizal fungi are found mostly in herbaceous plants such as wildflowers and weeds. Plants that need specialized study for their growth are not included in this book. For example, if a rare fungus is not available in the soil of Indian pipe, ladies'-slippers, and most orchids, they will not grow. It is important that you do not try to transplant these species or they will die. Ladies'-slippers are difficult to propagate from seeds. It takes seven years to germinate a lady-slipper seed. Acidic soil and a good snow cover in winter months are both necessary. There are 30,000 or more seeds in each capsule, but not 1 seed in 10,000 germinates. Because of the abuse that people have given plants trying to transplant them unsuccessfully, many are now on the endangered species list.

Harvest: Time of harvest and description of how to recognize, gather, and process the seeds are given. A chart comparing fruits for seed collection is found in the pictorial glossary. Amounts given by weight can vary and are given for general use for seed-size comparison.

Attracts: For those interested in wildlife, information is given for the insects and animals the forbs attract. In the appendix more information is given for butterfly habitats with native plants. The higher orders of both forbs and shrubs are insect-pollinated, the lower orders wind-pollinated.

Comments: Suggestions are given on special locations, history, and additional species that are native to Iowa or aliens to avoid.

Ruellia humilis
Wild petunia, fringeleaf, hairy ruellia
Acanthaceae (acanthus family)

Location: Wide variety of habitats in western part of the tallgrass prairie, often found on prairie uplands and disturbed sites. Most frequent in southern half of Iowa. Sandy, gravelly soil. Dry mesic to dry. Full sun. pH: Neutral 6–7.5. Border, meadow, roadside.

Plant description: Height: 6–24 in., normally less than 12 in. Blooming time: July–August. Violet flower. Smaller and less flared than the cultivated petunia. Corolla up to 3 in. long with 5 shallow lobes fused into a tube. Flower from upper axil, usually solitary. Flower lasts only 1 day. Years before expected bloom: 2. Hairy stem, branched or simple. Single stem early in the season, branching later. Tends to recline on the ground. Leaves opposite, pointed ovals, less than 3 in. long, up to 12 pairs of leaves along the stem. Smooth margins, leathery texture, hairy, sessile. Several stems arise from the fibrous root system.

Propagation: Easy to establish by seed.

Germination: No treatment needed.

Harvest: September. Late-season flower does not open but still produces seeds (self-fertile). Break or clip the stem into a paper bag. Oval capsule less than 1 in. long contains several seeds, with calyx of 5 segments protruding beyond capsule. Remove seeds from capsule and dry before storing in sealed bag in refrigerator. Individual seed round, flat, slightly indented, dark rust, 1/8 in. Seeds per oz.: 4,500. Per lb.: 72,000. Lb. per acre: 25. Oz. per 1,000 sq. ft.: 10.

Attracts: Hummingbirds, butterflies, and hummingbird sphinx moths.

Comments: Low-growing ground cover.

Eryngium yuccifolium
Rattlesnake master, button snakeroot
Apiaceae (Umbelliferae) (parsley family)

Location: Moist to upland prairie remnants throughout state. Moist, well-drained loam, but tolerates dry to wet. Wet mesic, mesic, dry mesic. Full or partial sun. pH: Acidic to wide range 5–7.5. Border, meadow, roadside.

Plant description: Height: 2–3 ft. Blooming time: July–August. White-green flower. Thistlelike globular head 1 in. round with 5 very small green-ish petals. Slightly ovoid 3/4-in. floret has sweet aroma. Develops bluish cast with maturity. Years before expected bloom: 1–2. Good dried flower. Irregular branching stem smooth, rigid. Good winter foliage. Yucca-type leaf with soft spiney edges; up to 3 ft. tall, alternate, firm, linear. Thick, fibrous rhizomes with stout, knotty rootstock, numerous short branches.

Propagation: Best from seed. Add sand to the potting soil. Also by division in the late fall. Old plants should be left undisturbed. Mark small seedling when set outside to avoid pulling as a weed. Look for tiny spurs on foliage. Quick to establish and self-sows.

Germination: Plant fresh seeds in cool weather. Needs stratification 33–38° F for 60 days.

Harvest: September–October. Clip 3/4-in. head into bucket or paper bag when it is brown. Each fruit holds numerous seeds. Spines crumble off the head so chaff can be separated from the seeds. 2 small segments, 1/4 in., owl-shaped, slightly scaly. Seeds per oz.: 8,000. Per lb.: 128,000. Lb. per acre: 10. Oz. per 1,000 sq. ft.: 4.

Attracts: Bees and butterflies. Rabbits and deer like the young leaves.

Comments: Vigorous and showy. Especially interesting form and texture. An indication of a good-quality prairie. Fiber from leaves was used to make rope. Used for the treatment of rattlesnake bites and other medicinals. An aggressive seeder. Needs competition. To limit plants remove fruit before they reseed.

Zizia aurea
Golden alexanders, divided-leaf golden alexanders
Apiaceae (Umbelliferae) (parsley family)

Location: Moist to mesic prairies, roadsides, sedge meadows, frequent to common throughout state. Average loam. Wet mesic to mesic. Full to partial sun. pH: Acidic-neutral 4–6.5. Meadow, roadside.

Plant description: Height: 1–3 ft. Blooming time: May–June. Yellow, terminal flat-topped cluster, small flower, the middle flower of each umbel being stalkless. Compound umbel 2 in. wide. Years before expected bloom: 2. Good cut flower. Red-tinged stems branched. Leaves twice-divided into 3–7 leaflets 1–2 in. long, doubly compound, ovate.

Propagation: Seed or division in the spring.

Germination: Easy. Plant fresh seeds in the fall or early spring. Likes cool soil to germinate. Needs stratification 33–38° F for 120 days for spring planting.

Harvest: August–September. Clip umbel from plant and store in paper bag. Shake seeds from umbel in bag when dry. 1/16 × 3/16 in., tan, linear-lined seed. Seeds per oz.: 9,500. Per lb.: 152,000. Lb. per acre: 11. Oz. per 1,000 sq. ft.: 4.4.

Attracts: Butterflies.

Comments: Aggressive and somewhat weedy, but colorful in the meadow or roadside. Heart-leaved meadow parsnip (*Z. aptera*) found in northern Iowa is very attractive.

5-13-92

1½" 1"

Asclepias incarnata
Swamp milkweed, red milkweed, marsh milkweed, water nerve root
Asclepiadaceae (milkweed family)

Location: Prairie swales, potholes, wet ditches, or marsh edges, frequent to common throughout state. Will grow in drier locations if well-drained soil, but does well in regular moist soil and good garden loam. Wet, wet mesic, mesic. Full sun. pH: Acidic-neutral 5–7. Border, meadow, roadside.

Plant description: Height: 24–60 in. Blooming time: July. Pink to red flower. Small umbel. Years before expected bloom: 1–2. Attractive dried seedpod. Glabrous, solitary, or clustered stem; milky juice; alternate, narrow lance-shaped leaves 3–6 in. long extending from a sturdy crown. Rhizomes; good drainage is necessary or rhizomes will die.

Propagation: Easiest by seed. Transplants easily with first-year seedling. Divide in the spring up to 4 years. After 4 years, the lateral root system makes it more difficult. One of the fastest growing prairie plants.

Germination: Easy, sow in fall or spring. Needs stratification 33–38° F for 30 days for spring planting.

Harvest: Seeds shed in September. Seeds with silk in pod 2–4 in. long, papery and wrinkled, usually found in pairs. Plum attached to dark-red flat seed. Seeds per oz.: 4,500. Per lb.: 72,000. Lb. per acre: 25. Oz. per 1,000 sq. ft.: 10.

Attracts: Monarch butterflies.

Comments: Easily controlled if rhizomes spread. Aromatic with fragrance of vanilla. Often found growing near Joe-pye-weed. Eilers lists 17 native species of this genus growing in Iowa.

7-10-92

3"

2"

2"

1½"

73

Asclepias tuberosa
Butterfly weed, pleurisy root, orange milkweed
Asclepiadaceae (milkweed family)

Location: Dry open prairies to loess, sandy, rocky, limestone, or clay; roadsides, disturbed areas, and fields. Scattered throughout state. Well-drained soil but adapts to all soil. Mesic, dry mesic, dry. Full to partial sun. pH: Acidic 4.5–6.5. Border, meadow, roadside.

Plant description: Height: 2–3 ft. Blooming time: June–July. Orange 2-in.-wide cluster, with individual flower 3/8 in. wide and 5 curved-back petals. Flowers increase in size and number as the plant grows older. Does not tolerate competition while establishing. Years before expected bloom: 2–3. Good cut flower and attractive dried seedpod. Hairy stem, but juice is watery rather than milky as in other milkweeds. Leaves alternate, oblong, and narrow 2–6 in. long. Deep taproots, a large tuberous rhizome with smaller fibrous roots. They often produce several stems from the crown.

Propagation: Easiest by seed. Long taproots do not transplant well. For rhizome cutting in May or fall, set rhizome upright just beneath the surface in sandy soil. Root cuttings from thick tuberous roots may be propagated in the spring. Cut a piece of root 2 in. long, treat with root toner, and plant 2 in. deep in a mixture of coarse sand and peat. Insert the root cutting vertically.

Germination: Plant fresh seed. Germination occurs with no treatment but benefits from 60 days of cold stratification.

Harvest: September–October. Golden spindle-shaped fruit, narrow, hairy erect pod 1 $\times$ 4 in. Seeds easily removed from pod. 1/4 $\times$ 3/16-in. seed flat with silk. Seeds per oz.: 3,500. Per lb.: 56,000. Lb. per acre: 25. Oz. per 1,000 sq. ft.: 10.

Attracts: Bees, hummingbirds, milkweed tiger moths, and monarch and orange sulphur butterflies.

Comments: Larger rock garden plant. Prettiest milkweed for the border, beautiful bloom.

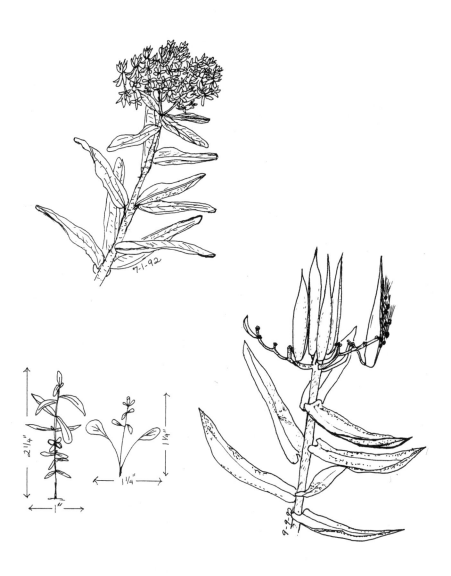

7-1-92

2¹⁄₄″

1″

1¹⁄₄″

1¹⁄₄″

9-2-

Asclepias verticillata
Whorled milkweed
Asclepiadaceae (milkweed family)

Location: Dry slopes, overgrazed pastures, fencerows, waste areas. Often grows in circular patches in roadsides. Common throughout state. Sandy, loam soil. Mesic, dry mesic, dry. Full sun. pH: Neutral 6–7. Meadow, roadside.

Plant description: Height: 16–30 in. Blooming time: July–August. Several white flowers in a cluster; umbel type. Years before expected bloom: 1–2. Whorls of leaves on a slender, sparingly branched stem containing milky juice. Leaves linear, sessile 3–6-in. whorls.

Propagation: Easy by seed.

Germination: No treatment needed.

Harvest: September–October. Pod slender 1/2 × 3 in. Dried seedpod attractive. Oval reddish brown seed 1/8 × 3/16 in. attached to 1-in.-long silk. Seeds per oz.: 4,300. Per lb.: 68,800. Lb. per acre: 25. Oz. per 1,000 sq. ft.: 10.

Attracts: Monarch butterflies.

Comments: Can be aggressive. All aboveground parts are poisonous. Sheep are most affected, but cattle and horses are also susceptible. Do not grow where animals are grazing or have access to little other forage. Considered, therefore, a pest to herders.

7-6-92

1 1/2"

1/2"

Antennaria neglecta
Pussytoes, everlasting, ladies'-tobacco, one-nerved pussytoes
Asteraceae (Compositae) (sunflower family)

Location: Driest prairie sites, loess bluffs, often clay or rocky ridges. Infrequent southwest, frequent to common elsewhere. Sandy, clay, or calcareous soil. Dry mesic to dry. Full sun. pH: Neutral 6–7. Border, meadow.

Plant description: Height: 4–16 in. Blooming time: Late April–early May. White clusters of tight flower beads on short stalk usually only 6 in., rayless and look like a pussy's toes. The flower is covered with silky hairs. Good dried flower. Basal leaves are covered with fine woolly hairs that give a gray appearance. Basal leaves appear after bloom and retain moisture. Leaf shape similar to plantain rosette, with 1 vein or nerve. The roots form mats underground.

Propagation: Difficult by seed. Reproduces more easily by the leaf-bearing stolon or rhizome (each section must have a bud and root) which forms dense colonies.

Germination: Low germination; seed is very tiny. Stratify 33–38° F for 30 days.

Harvest: Late May. Single, scaly stalk rises above the basal leaves about 1 ft. with the achene and pappus in a star-shaped receptacle. Similar in appearance to a fluffy dandelion. Pull achene from receptacle with fingers. Tiny black seed attached to hairy pappus used for dispersal. Seeds per oz.: 800,000. Per lb.: 12,800,000. Lb. per acre: 0.5. Oz. per 1,000 sq. ft.: 0.1.

Comments: Flower is not showy but interesting. Good rock garden plant. Leaves make nice ground cover and stay alive into winter. When moved from a sterile soil to a soil with nutrients, plants increase greatly in size. A larger variety of pussytoes, *A. plantaginifolia*, grows 2 ft., has 3-nerved veins on leaf.

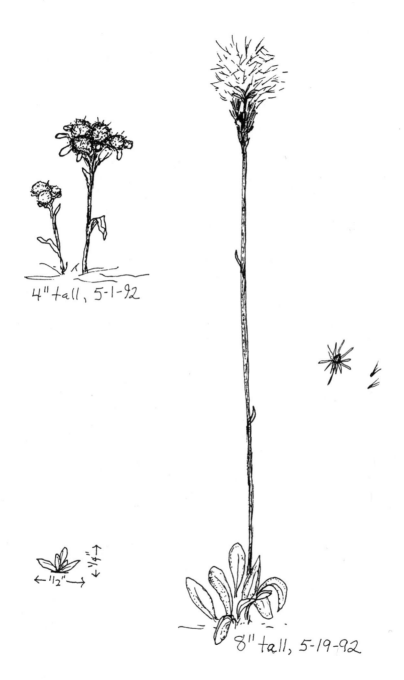

4" tall, 5-1-92

← 1/2" → ↓ 1/4" ↑

8" tall, 5-19-92

Artemisia ludoviciana
White sage, prairie sage, mugwort
Asteraceae (Compositae) (sunflower family)

Location: Wide range of tallgrass prairie and semidisturbed sites. Mainly sandy prairie remnants. Probably introduced from the west. Frequent to common throughout state. Rocky, sandy, or gravelly loam soil. Mesic, dry mesic, dry. Full or partial sun. pH: Acidic-neutral 5.8–7. Border, meadow, roadside.

Plant description: Height: 1–3 ft. Blooming time: August–October. Greenish white 1/8-in. flower formed on stem from the leaf axil on the upper branches. Each head contains numerous, inconspicuous tubular florets. Many clustered stems, multibranched, covered with a thick mat of grayish hairs. Leaves alternate, lanceolate, up to 3 in. covered beneath with a mat of whitish hair. Creeping slender rhizomes form a dense mat near the soil surface.

Propagation: By seed. Plants spread by cloning. Also propagated by division or cuttings taken in early summer.

Germination: Easy by seed. No treatment needed. Plant in fall or early spring.

Harvest: October. Break fruit off stem of plant. Seeds in small pod. Remove seeds from pod. Dry, smooth, broadly cylindrical seed. Seeds per oz.: 227,000. Per lb.: 3,632,000. Lb. per acre: 1. Oz. per 1,000 sq. ft.: 0.4.

Comments: Aggressive. Attractive foliage. Aromatic in the garden. This species is not used for sage seasoning. A member of the mint family is used in cooking. Traditionally burned in bundles by North Americans for ceremonial incense. Eilers lists 10 species of this genus growing in Iowa.

8-14-92

←½"→ ←½"→

ρ.

Aster azureus

Sky-blue aster, azure aster

Asteraceae (Compositae) (sunflower family)

Location: Wood edges, fields, roadsides, dry to mesic prairies. Infrequent northwest and some central counties. Wide range of soil. Mesic, dry mesic, dry. Full sun. pH: Neutral 6–7. Border, meadow, roadside.

Plant description: Height: 1–4 ft. Blooming time: September. Smooth flower with bright azure-blue rays. Years before expected bloom: 1–2. Cut flower or dried seed head attractive. Flowering branches narrowing into long stalks, with many tiny leafy bracts. Rough, mostly toothless leaves, lower basal leaves long-arrowhead shaped. May be slightly indented at base.

Propagation: Best by seed, self-sows easily. Also by division in fall.

Germination: Slow. No treatment needed.

Harvest: October. Clip fruit off stem, remove seeds from bract. Small achene with pappus. Seeds per oz.: 82,000. Per lb.: 1,312,000. Lb. per acre: 1.5. Oz. per 1,000 sq. ft.: 0.6.

Attracts: Birds and crescentspot butterflies.

Comments: There are 65 species of asters. Eilers lists 30 native species in Iowa.

9-9-92

← 1/3" →

← 1/4" →

Aster ericoides
Heath aster, frost weed, Michaelmas daisy
Asteraceae (Compositae) (sunflower family)

Location: Dry to mesic prairies, roadsides, and open grassy areas. Frequent to common throughout state. Well-drained soil. Mesic, dry mesic, dry. Full or partial sun. pH: Acidic-neutral 5.5–7. Border, meadow, roadside.

Plant description: Height: 1–3 ft. Blooming time: September–October. White starlike flowerhead is usually dense; some take the plumelike shape of goldenrod. Years before expected bloom: 1. Cut flower or dried seed head attractive. Alternate, panicle. Tiny heathlike leaves, numerous, linear, with no basal leaves. Rhizomes.

Propagation: Seed or good by division with easily separated rhizomes.

Germination: Low percent. No treatment needed.

Harvest: October. Clip stem into bucket or paper bag; achene removes easily from receptacle. Achene with attached pappus. Seeds per oz.: 82,000. Per lb.: 1,312,000. Lb. per acre: 1.5. Oz. per 1,000 sq. ft.: 0.6.

Attracts: Honeybees and butterflies.

Comments: This aster is unique with its tiny white bloom. This species varies greatly in size and vigor.

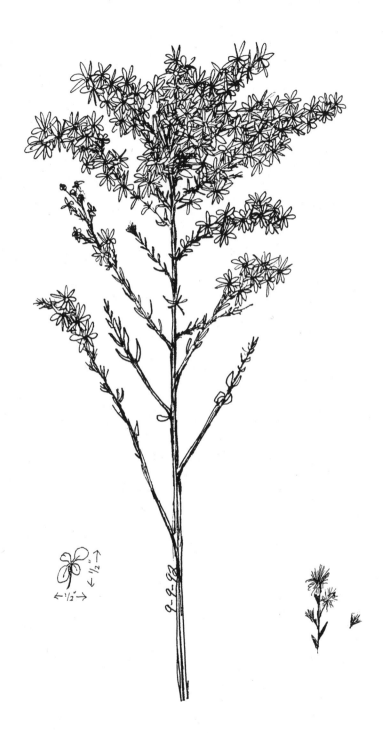

Aster laevis
Smooth aster, smooth blue aster
Asteraceae (Compositae) (sunflower family)

Location: Roadsides, prairies, and dry open soil. Frequent to common throughout state. Average loam. Wet mesic, mesic, dry mesic. Full or partial sun. pH: Acidic-neutral 5–6.5. Border, meadow, roadside.

Plant description: Height: 3–5 ft. Blooming time: September. Rich lavender-blue ray and yellow disk flower, about 1 in. wide. Years before expected bloom: 1–2. Cut flower or dried seed head attractive. Very smooth stem and slightly clasping leaves. Alternate becoming progressively smaller at top. Bright green foliage that is smooth to the touch, 1/4 in. long, thick, slightly toothed, elliptic or lanceolate. Lower leaves stalked and upper unstalked.

Propagation: By seed.

Germination: Easy. No treatment needed.

Harvest: October. Clip stem into bucket or paper bag, thresh and separate seeds. Small achene with pappus. Seeds per oz.: 48,000. Per lb.: 768,000. Lb. per acre: 3.5. Oz. per 1,000 sq. ft.: 1.4.

Attracts: Orange sulphur butterflies.

Comments: One of the most attractive asters. The leaves of all asters are alternate and numerous, but they vary in size and shape with the species. Aster is from the Greek word "star," referring to the shape of the flower and dried bracts and receptacles. Aster and goldenrod seeds have a similar appearance, but in general asters tend to be smaller and often their flowers are borne singly. Asters have several circles of bracts around the flower head, while annual fleabane (*Erigeron annuus*), which flowers earlier in the season, has only one circle, plus more numerous rays (40–70).

← 1/2" → ← 1/2" →

9-9-92

Aster novae-angliae
New England aster
Asteraceae (Compositae) (sunflower family)

Location: Mesic prairies, disturbed sites, prairie swales, wide range of adaptability. Frequent to common throughout state. From rich, mineral soil to disturbed sites with adequate moisture. Also excellent in clay soils once established. Wet, wet mesic, mesic. Full sun. pH: Acidic-neutral 5.5–7. Meadow, roadside.

Plant description: Height: 24–54 in. Blooming time: September–October. Deep violet, blue, or white 35–45-ray flower 1–2 in. wide in clusters with orange disk. Years before expected bloom: 1. Cut flower and dried seed head attractive. Hairy, sticky-glandular, large rough stem. Numerous narrow clasping, alternate leaves, toothless, lanceolate 2–5 in. long.

Propagation: Best by seed. Also by division in fall. Place top of rhizome at surface of soil. Benefits by division every 2–3 years to maintain its vigor.

Germination: Low germination rate, sow freely. Needs stratification 33–38° F for 30–60 days.

Harvest: Early November. Clip fruit off stem with golden fluffy balls, larger than most asters. Remove seeds from bract. Individual seed 1/8-in. achene with pappus. Seeds per oz.: 76,000. Per lb.: 1,216,000. Lb. per acre: 2. Oz. per 1,000 sq. ft.: 0.8.

Attracts: Bees, hummingbirds, birds, and painted lady, crescentspot, monarch, and orange sulphur butterflies.

Comments: Showiest aster. Fast growing. Striking roadside plant. Needs staking in border. Pinch back until August 15 to prevent plant from falling over when heavily laden with bloom. Can be identified by stickiness and turpentine smell when leaves are crushed. Somewhat aggressive with disturbance, reseeds itself. Dried plant resembles goldenrod.

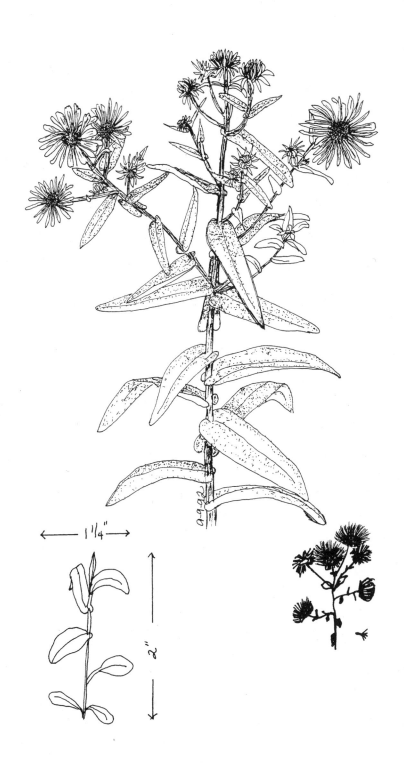

1¼"

2"

a-992

Coreopsis palmata
Prairie coreopsis, tickseed, stiff coreopsis, stiff tickseed
Asteraceae (Compositae) (sunflower family)

Location: Mesic to dry prairies throughout state. Medium to sandy, gravelly soil. Mesic, dry mesic, dry. Full to partial sun. pH: Acidic 4.5–6.5. Meadow, roadside.

Plant description: Height: 18–30 in. Blooming time: June. Many large yellow flowers on individual stem, 2 in. diameter, 8 rays. Disk flower slightly darker. Years before expected bloom: 1–2. Deadhead to produce longer blooming period. Good cut or dried flower. Smooth, slender stem, infrequently branched, leafy near ground. 3 narrow-lobed leaves, crow-foot-like, lance shaped. Spreading rhizomes; good soil holders.

Propagation: Good directly seeded in spring, also by division of rhizomes in spring. Plant the division with bud horizontally 1 in. deep. Plants are very easily divided and transplanted. Spreads vegetatively.

Germination: Easy. No treatment needed.

Harvest: October–November. Fruit found in dried bract formed into a flat-bottomed cup around the dried receptacle in only the outer flowers in the head; seeds crumble out of 1/4-in. head. Loosen the seeds by moderate beating or crushing (threshing). Individual seed 1/8 in. oblong with 2 short spines at tips (tick). Seeds per oz.: 12,500. Per lb.: 200,000. Lb. per acre: 10. Oz. per 1,000 sq. ft.: 4.

Attracts: Birds and butterflies including painted lady.

Comments: Tolerates drought. Keep in light soil to prevent spreading or needs competition. Aggressive. Good border or roadside plant, foliage attractive all year. Pioneers referred to it as an ocean of yellow. Lance-leaved coreopsis (*C. lanceolata*) is native, but not of Iowa.

6-29-92

2½"

⟵—— 3" ——⟶

Echinacea pallida
Pale coneflower, pale purple coneflower, black Sampson
Asteraceae (Compositae) (sunflower family)

Location: Loess bluffs, dry prairies, roadsides. Common and frequent throughout state. Sandy to clay soil. Mesic, dry mesic, dry. Full or partial sun. pH: Acidic-neutral 4.5–7.5. Border, meadow, roadside.

Plant description: Height: 24–40 in. Blooming time: June–July. Lavender-pink daisylike head 2–4 in. with 12–20 drooping narrow rays nearly 2 in. long. Disk is golden purple iridescent with a 1-in. dome. Years before expected bloom: 2. Cut flower or dried seed head attractive. Smooth, sturdy, elongated stem. Coarse foliage 3–8 in. toothless, lanceolate, 3 parallel lengthwise veined. Strong taproot, making it hardy.

Propagation: Best by seed. Also division in the spring. The crown can be divided into 2–5 plantlets. Divide every 3–5 years. Long-lived plant. If seed isn't needed, cut flower off after blooming.

Germination: Plant in fall or early spring. Needs stratification 33–38° F for 90 days.

Harvest: October–November. Fruit often stays in the head until spring. Sharp-spiney cone, shaped like a tiny pyramid, 1 1/4 × 1 1/4 in. Clip into bucket when seeds are ripe enough to shake out of receptacle when tapped. Crush seed head and separate chaff. Many nutlets are not viable. Individual seed 1/8 × 3/16 in., 3-sided, shaped like tiny pyramid. Seeds per oz.: 5,000. Per lb.: 80,000. Lb. per acre: 24. Oz. per 1,000 sq. ft.: 9.

Attracts: Hummingbirds; ottoe skipper, red admiral, and painted lady butterflies for their flowers. Goldfinches and other birds love the seeds.

Comments: Vigorous and showy. Plant in groups of 3–5. Aggressive. Pretty planted with grasses. Coarse and needs competition. Seed head is so stiff that it was used by Native Americans to comb their hair. Purple coneflower (*E. purpurea*) has wider ray flowers and is found in only 5 southeast counties. Purple coneflower (*E. angustifolia*) is a pink variety growing 18–30 in. in dry soil, most common in the Loess Hills.

5-13-92

6-26-92

4

Seedhead went thru the winter

↑ 1/2 " ↓

← 3/4 " →

Eupatorium maculatum
Spotted Joe-pye-weed
Asteraceae (Compositae) (sunflower family)

Location: Damp meadows, open marshy places, fens, moist ditches along roadsides. Common to infrequent north-central and south-central. Rich loam or calcareous soil. Wet, wet mesic. Full sun. pH: Acidic 4.5–6. Border, meadow, roadside.

Plant description: Height: 4–6 ft. Blooming time: July–August. Deep rose-colored, flat-topped 4–5-in. cluster with fuzzy 1/3-in. flower head. Flower buds are in a flat cyme. Years before expected bloom: 2. Stem is deep purple or purple spotted, sturdy. Structures in broad, opposite-branching clusters. Leaves in whorls of 3–7 around stem, toothed and coarse, 2–8 in. long, lanceolate, rough, pointed, ovate toothed.

Propagation: Seed is best. Division in spring only, every 2–4 years.

Germination: Easily grown, but spotty germination. No treatment necessary. Plant in fall or early spring when ground is cool. Fine seed, plant on surface.

Harvest: September–October. Dried stems grouped closely appearing as whorls, with fluffy fruit on the tip of each stalk. Total head gives rounded appearance. Pull off achene with fingers from receptacle. Individual seed 1/8-in. shiny black achene with pappus. Seeds per oz.: 85,000. Per lb.: 1,360,000. Lb. per acre: 2.5. Oz. per 1,000 sq. ft.: 1.

Attracts: Monarch and other butterflies. Bumblebees are fond of roosting on the flowers during cool September nights.

Comments: Allow 3 ft. if planted in border. Very showy in large stands. Aggressive. Looks a lot like ironweed, but leaves are alternate. Vanilla scented. Tall thoroughwort (*E. altissimum*) grows in the loess bluffs and prairie remnants.

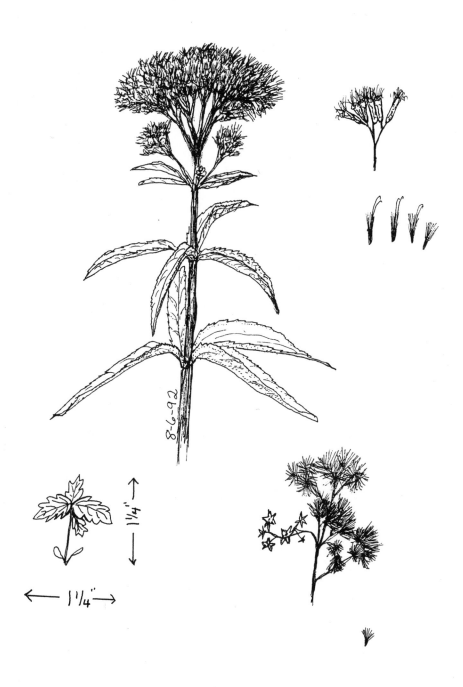

8-6-92

1 1/4"

1 1/4"

Eupatorium perfoliatum
Boneset, thoroughwort, feverwort
Asteraceae (Compositae) (sunflower family)

Location: Wet meadows, marsh edges, fens, prairie swales, open alluvium. Infrequent southeast but frequent elsewhere in state. Rich loam. Wet, wet mesic, mesic. Full sun. pH: Neutral 6.5–7. Meadow.

Plant description: Height: 3–4 ft. Blooming time: July–August. White 1/4-in. flowers in clusters, flat-topped, small fuzzy head. Stem structure is broad, opposite-branching clusters. Very hairy, opposite leaves, completely surrounding base of stem, lanceolate, wrinkled, toothed, and veiny. Fibrous, stout rhizomes.

Propagation: Seed or division of the rootstalk in fall or spring.

Germination: Easy. No treatment needed. Fine seed, plant on surface.

Harvest: September. Clip stem into bucket or paper bag. Remove seed from receptacle. Very tiny, 5-angled achene with pappus. Seeds per oz.: 200,000. Per lb.: 3,200,000. Lb. per acre: 1. Oz. per 1,000 sq. ft.: 0.4.

Attracts: Butterflies.

Comments: Pioneers wrapped its leaves in bandages with splints to heal broken bones. In an old recipe book a cough syrup was made by steeping 3 handfuls of boneset in a tin of water; strain off, add 1 pint molasses, and boil down until quite thick. Also used as a tea for upper respiratory infections and fevers. It was considered a cure-all by the pioneers.

8-6-92

←1/2"→ ↓1/2"↓

Helenium autumnale
Sneezeweed
Asteraceae (Compositae) (sunflower family)

Location: Swamps, marshes, moist prairies, fens, sedge meadows. Frequent to common throughout state. Rich loam. Wet, wet mesic. Full sun. pH: Neutral 6–7. Border, meadow, roadside.

Plant description: Height: 2–5 ft. Blooming time: August–September. Yellow daisylike flower 1–2 in. with 10–20 rays, 3-tipped lobes. Disk is ball-like, greenish yellow. Years before expected bloom: 1–2. Winged stems are rough, erect, stout, branching. Long, alternate, lanceolate, toothed with base leaves up to 6 in. forming winged extensions down the stem. Upper leaves 1.5 in. and stalkless. Fibrous roots.

Propagation: Easy by seed. Can be divided and transplanted in spring.

Germination: No treatment needed.

Harvest: October. Clip fruit from stem. Seeds crumble off receptacle. Small, oblong, dark achene with pappus. Seeds per oz.: 100,000. Per lb.: 1,600,000. Lb. per acre: 2. Oz. per 1,000 sq. ft.: 0.8.

Attracts: Butterflies.

Comments: Large multiple blooms are very attractive. Name derived from making dried leaves into snuff, cause sneezing and supposedly ridding the body of evil spirits or clearing congestion. Considered a generally good tonic by the pioneers.

Seedhead 1/3"

Helianthus occidentalis
Western sunflower, naked sunflower
Asteraceae (Compositae) (sunflower family)

Location: Dry prairies, dry open sand. Frequent only in eastern part of state. Refer to other species below for propagating throughout state. Sandy soil. Mesic, dry mesic, dry. Full sun. pH: Neutral 6–7.5. Meadow, roadside.

Plant description: Height: 2–4 ft. Blooming time: July–August. Numerous yellow ray flowers on disks. Years before expected bloom: 1–2. Good cut flower. Long stalks nearly naked and leafless, with a few small opposite, single leaves near the flower. Leaves are few and small on long stalks; large basal leaves are 6–8 in. Excellent soil holder on dry sites. Rhizomes spread slowly.

Propagation: Seed or best by division.

Germination: Easy. No treatment needed.

Harvest: October. Solitary fruit on long stalks. Cut 3/8 × .1/2-in. head from stem. Thresh seed head and remove seeds from chaff. Individual seed 1/8 in. oblong, tan-colored. Seeds per oz.: 13,000. Per lb.: 208,000. Lb. per acre: 10. Oz. per 1,000 sq. ft.: 4.

Attracts: Goldfinch and other birds for seeds; butterflies for nectar.

Comments: One of the loveliest of sunflowers. All sunflowers are aggressive, but this is the least aggressive of the sunflowers. Best sown in back edges, patches, or drifts. To avoid aggressiveness, avoid moist soils and fertilizer. Tends to inhibit growth of other species around it. Aggressiveness is also controlled when there is a wide diversity of healthy plants. Good in open areas where weeds are a problem. Was worshipped by the Incas as a symbol of the sun. Some of the other sunflowers native to Iowa are common sunflower (*H. annuus*), saw-tooth sunflower (*H. grosseserratus*) which can be weedy, Maximillian's sunflower (*H. maximiliani*), and prairie sunflower (*H. rigidus*). Seeds have high nutritional value.

8-1-92

1 1/2"

1"

1/2"

1/2"

Heliopsis helianthoides
Ox-eye, rough ox-eye, false sunflower, early sunflower
Asteraceae (Compositae) (sunflower family)

Location: Dry woodlands, prairies, roadsides, loess bluffs, disturbed sites. Frequent to common throughout state. Wide range of clay, loam, or moist sand, but prefers well-drained soil with sand content. If soil is rich will become leggy. Wet mesic, mesic, dry mesic. Full or partial sun. pH: Neutral 6–7.5. Border, meadow, roadside.

Plant description: Height: 2–3 ft. Blooming time: June–July. Yellow-orange 2–4-in. heads, center disk of small florets, conical. Not a true sunflower. Years before expected bloom: 1. Good cut flower lasting up to 10 days. Paired, opposite, coarse, arrow-shaped leaves; smooth stems. Competes well with grass. Does not spread by rhizomes.

Propagation: Easy from seed; it will self-sow. Also division in spring.

Germination: Low but easy. Short-lived perennial. No treatment needed, or benefits from stratification 33–38° F for 30 days.

Harvest: October. Tan cone 1 × 3/4 in., soft bristles. Both ray and disk flowers form seeds, thus differing from the true sunflower, where seeds are formed in the disk only. Clip into bucket. Seeds shake from cone head, leaving cone in original form. May also be crushed and separated when head is well dried. Dried seed head attractive. Individual seed 1/8 × 1/16 in., grayish black; bullet-shaped and will stand on end. Seeds per oz.: 6,500. Per lb.: 104,000. Lb. per acre: 20. Oz. per 1,000 sq. ft.: 8.

Attracts: Birds and painted lady butterflies.

Comments: Vigorous and showy. Attractive foliage. Long grown in the cultivated border; often found in disturbed areas. Establishes and spreads quickly. May become aggressive. Deadhead to prolong bloom. It is the only heliopsis listed by Eilers. Do not confuse with ox-eye daisy (*Chrysanthemum leucanthemum*), an alien from Eurasia.

Hieracium longipilum
Hawkweed, false dandelion
Asteraceae (Compositae) (sunflower family)

Location: Dry, rocky, and sandy prairies. Scattered in eastern Iowa. Sandy soil. Dry mesic to dry. Full to partial sun. pH: Neutral 6–7. Border, meadow, roadside.

Plant description: Height: 2–5 ft. Blooming time: August–October. Yellow, 1-in. ray arranged in a cyme. Sessile leaves on ascending stem become progressively smaller as they reach the blossom. Leaves alternate, ovate, toothed. Fibrous roots.

Propagation: Seed. Seedlings have hairs on oval-pointed leaves.

Germination: Needs stratification 33–38° F for 30 days.

Harvest: October. Clip stem. Remove achene from receptacle. Small achene; seed with pappus hairs. Seeds per oz.: 85,000. Per lb.: 1,360,000. Lb. per acre: 2.5. Oz. per 1,000 sq. ft.: 1.

Comments: Hawkweeds are known by their flowers, which resemble dandelions, a highly variable group with 19 or 20 in North America. *H. canadense* and *H. umbellatum*, both found in the state, grow in moist to mesic prairies. *H. canadense* has longer and finer hairs on the leaves.

8-8-92

3/4"

3/4"

1"

1/2"

1 1/2"

2 1/2"

Liatris aspera
Blazing star, rough blazing star, tall gay-feather, button snakeroot
Asteraceae (Compositae) (sunflower family)

Location: Western tallgrass prairies, roadsides, upland prairies, ravines, banks. Common and frequent throughout state. Well-drained, sandy-deep loam. Mesic, dry mesic, dry. Full or partial sun. pH: Acidic-neutral 5.5–7.5. Border, meadow, roadside.

Plant description: Height: 2–3 ft. Blooming time: August–September. Purple flower on a spike along top of stalk, with 16–40 tubular disk florets and protruding styles. Not crowded in their spacing. Rounded bracts flaring with pinkish translucent margins at base of flower head form a cup. Flower head sessile or short-stalked. Years before expected bloom: from corms 1, from seeds 2–3. Good cut and dried flower. One or more erect and unbranching stem. Alternate leaves are numerous, becoming progressively smaller as they go up stem. Stiff hairs make the plant rough to the touch (*aspera* is Latin for "rough"). Leaves lanceolate to linear up to 8 × 1 in., end of leaves blunt or rounded; leaves have a distinct, whitish midrib. Knobby corm with fibrous roots.

Propagation: Best by seed, also by corm. Old corms can be divided with a sharp knife.

Germination: Needs stratification 33–38° F for 30 days.

Harvest: October. Strip fruit from stalk with gloved hand. Separate seeds from chaff. White bristly achene with pappus. Seeds per oz.: 13,500. Per lb.: 216,000. Lb. per acre: 10. Oz. per 1,000 sq. ft.: 4.

Attracts: Birds and orange sulphur butterflies.

Comments: Vigorous and showy. Needs companion plants to prevent lodging. *L. cylindracea* in the northeast, *L. ligulistylis* in the north, *L. punctata* and *L. squarrosa* in the west are other species of blazing stars found in Iowa.

8-6-92

Liatris pycnostachya
Prairie blazing star, thickspike gay-feather
Asteraceae (Compositae) (sunflower family)

Location: Native pastures, moist prairies, roadsides, along railroads. Frequent to common throughout state. Well-drained, deep, sandy-loam soil. Wet, wet mesic, mesic. Full or partial sun. pH: Acidic-neutral 5.5–7. Border, meadow, roadside.

Plant description: Height: 2–4 ft. Blooming time: August. Lavender bloom starts at top and works down the stalk. The flower disk is 1/2 in. wide with purplish tips spreading or bent backwards; crowded sessile. Years before expected bloom: 2–3 from seeds, 1 from corms. Can have from 10–42 blooms on a 4-year-old plant. Good cut flower, used by florists. Also good dried flower. Cylindrical, stalkless, densely crowded on a hairy, very leafy stem. Stem is rough. Leaves narrow, untoothed, alternate. Lower leaves are 4–12 in. long and narrow; upper much smaller and punctate linear. Woody corm.

Propagation: Best by seed, also by stem cutting in the spring or division of corm when dormant. Old corms can be divided with a sharp knife. Plant 2 1/2 in. deep.

Germination: Easy but slow growing. Seedlings look like onion tuft. After transplanting into pots, hold 8–10 weeks for root establishment before planting outdoors. Plant in fall or early spring with stratification 33–38° F 60–90 days.

Harvest: September–October. Clip light hairy stalk into bucket. The tan fluffy achene with pappus furs out into a circle, making a full head. Crush and separate seeds. Achene with pappus hair attached, 3/8 in. Seeds per oz.: 12,000. Per lb.: 192,000. Lb. per acre: 10. Oz. per 1,000 sq. ft.: 4.

Attracts: Bumblebees, hummingbirds, monarch and other butterflies. Birds for seeds. Rodents like the corms.

Comments: Grandest of the blazing stars. Vigorous and showy. Good for naturalizing.

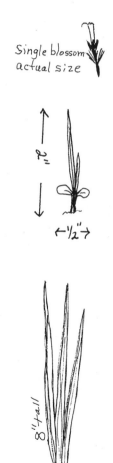

Single blossom
actual size

2"

←1/2"→

8" tall

8-8-92

Parthenium integrifolium
Feverfew, wild quinine, American feverfew
Asteraceae (Compositae) (sunflower family)

Location: Upland prairies, sandy bluffs, moist prairies. Frequent in eastern half of state. Sandy, loam soil. Wet mesic, mesic, dry mesic. Full sun. pH: Neutral 6–7. Border, meadow.

Plant description: Height: 18–36 in. Blooming time: June–August. White flat-topped, multibranched cyme clusters similar to the head of a cauliflower. Individual flower 1/4 in. high and globular. Flowers on the central disk are sterile, 5 tiny rays 1/12 in. Long-flowering, very attractive, but little known. Years before expected bloom: 2. Basal leaves on long petioles up to 4 × 12 in., rough and hairy. On the stem leaves are alternate, progressively smaller toward the top. Petioles on stem leaves become clasping at top. Long ovals, pointed at the tips with coarse, rounded teeth. On basal leaves they become so rounded they appear as lobes, some with toothed edges. Tuberous, short, and thick roots.

Propagation: Seed.

Germination: Easy. Needs no treatment or benefits from stratification 33–38° F for 30 days.

Harvest: Late September. Clip stalk into bag. Outer flowers of the head produce fruit. Crush and separate; seeds found on outer rim of disk only. Individual seed 1/8 in., black, flat with a ridge on one side. Seeds per oz.: 7,000. Per lb.: 112,000. Lb. per acre: 20. Oz. per 1,000 sq. ft.: 8.

Comments: The leaves have been used to reduce fevers, thus the common name feverfew. Flower insignificant but foliage interesting.

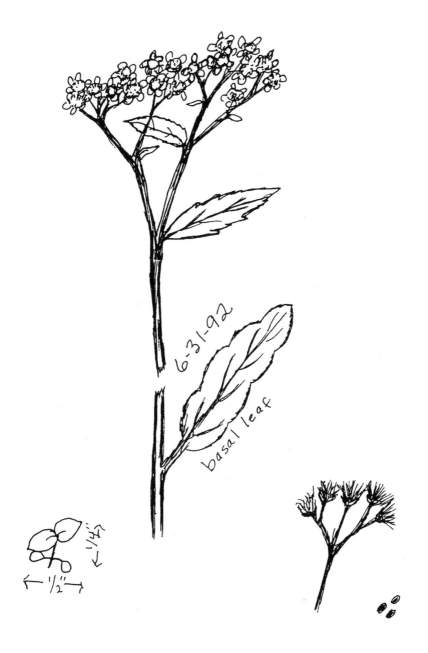

6-31-92

basal leaf

← 1/2″ →

← 1/4″ →

Prenanthes alba
Rattlesnake-root, white lettuce
Asteraceae (Compositae) (sunflower family)

Location: Moist woods, prairie remnants, roadsides. Infrequent in western and southern counties. Average, well-drained soil. Good for clay soils also. Wet mesic, mesic, dry mesic. Full sun. pH: Neutral 6–7. Border, meadow, roadside.

Plant description: Height: 2–4 ft. Blooming time: August–September. Pinkish flower, less bell-shaped and dangling than other rattlesnake-roots. Purple, hairy bud. Flowers 1/2-in. cluster in a narrow spike, 8–12 tiny rays with no disk. Stamens are prominent. Years before expected bloom: 2–3. Dried flower attractive. Milky juice in the purple stem. Hairy yellow bristles on the upper stem, smooth on the lower. Clasping, thick, elongated leaves on a nonbranching smooth stalk. Edges curling with purple outer edge and central vein.

Propagation: Seed.

Germination: Plant in fall, or in spring with stratification 33–38° F for 120 days.

Harvest: October. Clip stalk. Remove seeds from receptacle. Achene has pappus hairs attached. Seeds per oz.: 85,000. Per lb.: 1,360,000. Lb. per acre: 2.5. Oz. per 1,000 sq. ft.: 1.

Comments: Used as a remedy for snakebite. Similar to *P. aspera*, which has a rough, hairy stem and creamy flowers, growing in sandy soil on drier prairies.

8-28-92

←1/2"→ ←1/2"→

←1/2"→

113

Ratibida columnifera
Long-headed coneflower, Mexican hat, upright coneflower
Asteraceae (Compositae) (sunflower family)

Location: Dry prairies, sandy and disturbed areas, loess bluffs. Common northwest and southeast. Well-drained loam. Drought-tolerant when established. Mesic, dry mesic, dry. Full sun. pH: Neutral-alkaline 6–8. Border, meadow, roadside.

Plant description: Height: 2–3 ft. Blooming time: July–August. 5–10 yellow, 1/2 × 2-in. rays drooping down with dark central disk or upright cone 1/2 × 2 in. Clumps may have 50 blossoms. Years before expected bloom: 1. Good cut and dried flower. Several stems, alternate leaves. Dissected leaves, pinnately divided with linear segments. Diffuse taproots.

Propagation: By seed is best. One of the easiest to grow from seed. Establishes quickly, but is short-lived.

Germination: Easy with no treatment needed, but benefits from stratification 33–38° F for 60 days.

Harvest: October. Light gray, upright 1/3 × 1 1/4-in. fruit can be broken from stem. Seeds fall or crumble off head, leaving long, narrow spike. Individual seed dark brown 1/8 × 1/16 in., gray covering; flattened achenes are tipped with 1–2 bristles. Seeds per oz.: 32,000. Per lb.: 512,000. Lb. per acre: 5. Oz. per 1,000 sq. ft.: 2.

Attracts: Dakota skipper butterflies.

Comments: Gives a lot of bloom and color the first year. Pretty in borders while waiting for other plants to establish. Good with competition.

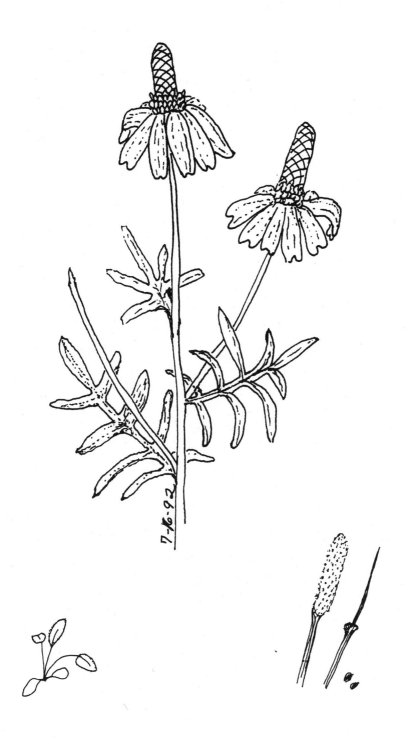

7-16-92

Ratibida pinnata

Gray-headed coneflower, yellow coneflower, prairie coneflower, pinnate coneflower

Asteraceae (Compositae) (sunflower family)

Location: Wide range of prairies, loess bluffs, sandy areas, railroad tracks, roadsides. Frequent and common throughout state. Calcareous soils, well-drained. Wet mesic, mesic, dry mesic. Full sun. pH: Neutral 6–7. Border, meadow, roadside.

Plant description: Height: 2–4 ft. Blooming time: July–August. Pale yellow drooping 2 1/2-in. rays with gray disk forming a cylindrical cone. Years before expected bloom: 1–2. Good cut flower and dried flower. Hairy stem and leaves, alternate, compound, pinnately divided. Basal leaves 8–16-in. diameter stay green late into fall and appear in early spring. Leaves are lance-shaped with coarse teeth, rough feeling. Vigorous, fibrous roots; good for stabilizing soil.

Propagation: By seed. Older plants can be divided but extensive root system difficult.

Germination: Fall or for spring planting, no treatment needed or stratify seeds 33–38° F for 30 days.

Harvest: October–November. Clip fruit from stem into bucket. Gray head 1/2 × 3/4-in. oval with dark spots. Clip stem. Seeds leave a small, hard, pointed tip on stem above bracts. Individual seed pyramid shape 1/8 in. Seeds per oz.: 27,812. Per lb.: 445,000. Lb. per acre: 6. Oz. per 1,000 sq. ft.: 2.4.

Attracts: Birds and butterflies.

Comments: Vigorous and showy. Can be aggressive, but good in large garden with competition. Often associated with disturbance. A long-lived perennial. Strong anise scent when crumbled from seed head, used like cedar chips by pioneers.

7-10-93

2"   1"   3|4'

Rudbeckia hirta
Black-eyed Susan
Asteraceae (Compositae) (sunflower family)

Location: Prairies, old pastures, roadsides. Common throughout most of state but rare in west. Likes poor soil lacking minerals; sand, gravel. Dry mesic to dry. Full to partial sun. pH: Acidic-neutral: 4.5–7.5. Border, meadow, roadside.

Plant description: Height: 1–3 ft. Blooming time: July–August. Golden ray, daisylike flowers with 10–20 petals 1 in. and brown disk 2–3 in. Years before expected bloom: 2, a biennial. Cut flower has 6–10 days vase life. Dried flower. Coarse, stiff, upright stem. The stem, bracts, and shriveled leaves are covered with rough hairs. Variable leaves, lanceolate to ovate, 2–7 in. long. Fibrous and extensive roots.

Propagation: Seed is best; division is difficult. Short-lived. Self-sows.

Germination: One of the easiest. No treatment needed.

Harvest: Late September–early October. Clip 3/4 × 3/4-in. conehead into bucket. Store in paper bag. Numerous tiny black seeds shake out of soft cone when pressed; head soft and retains its shape, lightens as it matures. Crush seed head, blow away chaff. Individual seed 1/5 in. long, black, dry. Seeds per oz.: 100,000. Per lb.: 1,600,000. Lb. per acre: 2. Oz. per 1,000 sq. ft.: 0.8.

Attracts: Crescentspot butterflies and beneficial insects that control garden pests.

Comments: The "sign of summer." This is a biennial and reseeds itself. Prolific. Remove seed head after bloom if you want to prevent seeds from spreading. Stems can become weak if planted in good soil and may need staking. Best sown in back edges, patches, or drifts.

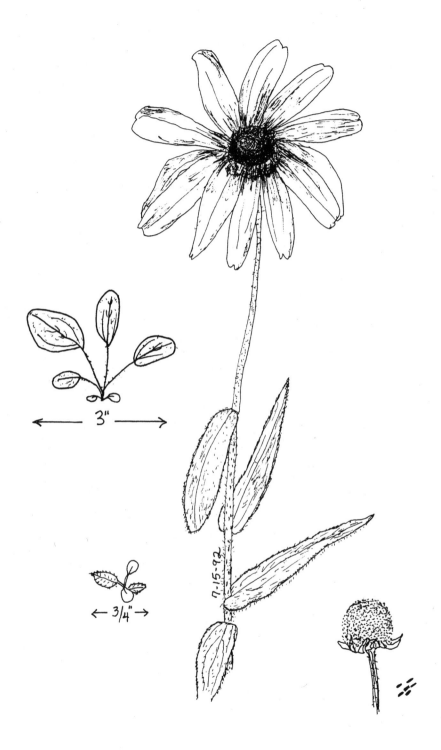

3"

3/4"

7-15-92

Rudbeckia subtomentosa
Fragrant coneflower, sweet black-eyed Susan
Asteraceae (Compositae) (sunflower family)

Location: Moist to mesic prairies, open grasslands. Absent northwest, infrequent elsewhere. Needs good, deep loam. Wet mesic, mesic, dry mesic. Full or partial sun. pH: Neutral 6–7. Meadow, roadside.

Plant description: Height: 4–5 ft. Blooming time: August–September. Yellow ray and brown disk, downy, large flower head. The showy blossoms open one-by-one over a period of many weeks. Years before expected bloom: 2. Cut flowers last 10 days. Dried flower also good. Stiff erect stem, branching, numerous 3-part leaves on lower part of stem. Forms large clumps with up to 50 stems. Lower leaves 3-cleft; downy; lanceolate to ovate.

Propagation: Establishes quickly from seed. A long-lived perennial. Seedlings have very rounded leaves. Also by division.

Germination: Easy. No treatment needed or benefits from stratification 33–38° F for 30 days.

Harvest: October. Clip medium brown seed head 3/8 × 5/8 in. into bucket. Seeds crumble off head, leaving a hard central point above the bracts. Individual seed 1/8 in., black. Seeds per oz.: 46,000. Per lb.: 736,000. Lb. per acre: 3. Oz. per 1,000 sq. ft.: 1.2.

Attracts: Birds and crescentspot butterflies.

1 ¹/₂"

Senecio plattensis
Prairie ragwort, groundsel
Asteraceae (Compositae) (sunflower family)

Location: Dry roadsides, prairies, woodland openings. Infrequent southwest and many central counties. Common elsewhere. Sandy soil. Dry mesic, dry. Full sun. pH: Acidic 5.5–6.5. Border, meadow, roadside.

Plant description: Height: 6–16 in. Blooming time: May–June. Dark yellow flower head is terminal with up to 10 individual flowers in flat-topped clusters. 8–12 rays and disk florettes. Years before expected bloom: 2. Good cut flower and dried flower. Basal, oval leaves; wooly on underside. Fibrous roots, sometimes stolons.

Propagation: By seed.

Germination: Easy, with no treatment needed.

Harvest: June. Aster-type seed, round tuft of white pappus on end of stem. Remove seeds with fingers from receptacle or clip stem. Small, white pappus hairs at an angle from the smooth achene. Seeds per oz.: 76,000. Per lb.: 1,216,000. Lb. per acre: 2. Oz. per 1,000 sq. ft.: 0.8.

Attracts: Butterflies.

Comments: Small bloom is nice when little else is blooming; an early composite. Similar to *S. pauperculus*, which grows in moist, rich loam.

5-16-92

5-22-92

⟵ 5/8″ ⟶

⟵ 1/2″ ⟶

⟵ 1/3″ ⟶

⟵ 1/3″ ⟶

Silphium integrifolium
Rosinweed, whole-leaf rosinweed, entire-leaved rosinweed
Asteraceae (Compositae) (sunflower family)

Location: Prairie remnants, old pastures, roadsides. Frequent to common southern 2/3 of Iowa. Sandy soil. Wet mesic, mesic, dry mesic. Full sun. pH: Acidic-neutral 4.5–7.5. Meadow, roadside.

Plant description: Height: 2–6 ft. Blooming time: July–August. Yellow ray and disk flower 1 1/2–3 in. across, enclosed by large, hairy-edged, green bracts. Years before expected bloom: 3–4. Rough, stalkless, opposite, paired leaves 3–5 × 1/3 in., with or without teeth. Grows from a caudex with fibrous roots, forming clumps or open colonies from short rhizomes.

Propagation: Easily by seed. 2-year-old plant roots become too long to transplant.

Germination: Sow untreated seeds in fall or stratify seeds 33–38° F for 30 days for spring planting.

Harvest: September–October. Cut head from stem. Seeds found only in the outer perimeter of disk. Shell from head. Flat, nearly oval, brown seed 1/4 × 1/8 in. Seeds per oz.: 4,000. Per lb.: 64,000. Lb. per acre: 25. Oz. per 1,000 sq. ft.: 10.

Attracts: Butterflies, songbirds, and deer.

Comments: Silphiums are large, coarse plants. Rosinweeds are named for their resinous juices. Most species of the sunflower family have disk florets, but the Silphium family contains ray florets, which are fertile and produce seeds. Each species has large leaves of different shape. Prairie dock (*S. tere-binthinaceum*) is a native of the U.S. but not Iowa. Its basal heart-shaped leaves reach up to 2 ft. in length, and plant reaches up to 10 ft.

7-3-92

1 1/4"

1"

⊢ 3/4" ⟶

Silphium laciniatum
Compass plant
Asteraceae (Compositae) (sunflower family)

Location: Open spaces, prairie remnants, roadsides, along railroads. Common throughout state. Very adaptable. Smaller plant in poor soil has advantages of sturdiness. Excellent in clay soils. Wet mesic, mesic, dry mesic. Full sun. pH: Acidic-neutral 4.5–7.5. Meadow, roadside.

Plant description: Height: 3–12 ft. Blooming time: July–August. Yellow ray flowers with 1-in. yellow disk progress down the stem and may last 2 months. Flowers are 3–4 in. across, with 20–100 per plant, facing east and west. Years before expected bloom: 3–4. Good cut flower. Stem is tall, bristly, and stout and exudes resinous juice. Leaves 6 × 12 in., facing north and south. Irregular-lobed basal leaves shaped like giant white oak leaves. Smaller vertical leaves clasping stem unstalked or short-stalked with fewer lobes. Taproot may reach 8–15 ft. Much energy goes into development of roots.

Propagation: Very successful from seed, roots too massive to move. Seedlings have fine hairs. Take care not to break taproot when transplanting seedlings.

Germination: Easy. Large seeds, plant 1/2 in. deep. Needs stratification 33–38° F for 60 days.

Harvest: Early October. 1 1/2-in. diameter disk in several cycles on the perimeter of the disk. Clip head and shell seeds from outer rim of disk. Individual seed flat, brown, 1/2 × 3/8 in., covered by tough seed coat. Seeds per oz.: 650. Per lb.: 10,400. Lb. per acre: 25. Oz. per 1,000 sq. ft.: 10.

Attracts: Songbirds, butterflies, and deer.

Comments: Young plants may need protection. Slow growing. May grow only 1 linear, rough leaf the first year. Unique plant of the prairie referred to in Aldo Leopold's famous quote about the silphiums that tickled the bellies of the buffalo.

3½"

6" Seedling

Silphium perfoliatum
Cup plant, square weed
Asteraceae (Compositae) (sunflower family)

Location: Moist alluvial woods and woodland edges, prairie swales, roadsides. Frequent to common throughout most of state except northwest. Excellent in tough clay soil. Wet mesic, mesic. Full to partial sun. pH: Acidic-neutral 5.5–7.5. Meadow, roadside.

Plant description: Height: 3–8 ft. Blooming time: July–August. Yellow 2–3-in. ray flowers and disk surrounded by large bracts. Years before expected bloom: 3. Good cut flower. Stem smooth, square. Opposite leaves, rough, perfoliate form a cup at the stem. Spreading fibrous roots.

Propagation: Best by seed. Plants up to 2 years old can be transplanted, but after that it is difficult because of large roots.

Germination: Easy. Needs stratification 33–38° F for 30 days.

Harvest: September. Cut 1 1/2-in. seed head from stem. Remove seeds on seed head from outer rim of disk. Large seed in shell similar to sunflower seed. Seeds per oz.: 1,400. Per lb.: 22,400. Lb. per acre: 25. Oz. per 1,000 sq. ft.: 10.

Attracts: Hummingbirds, other birds, and butterflies.

Comments: The leaves form a cup that collects rainwater and attracts birds.

7-17-92

2"

seed 1/4"x3/8"   head 1"

129

Solidago missouriensis
Missouri goldenrod
Asteraceae (Compositae) (sunflower family)

Location: Upland to sandy prairie remnants, loess bluffs, roadsides. Common western 2/3, infrequent to rare east. Sandy soil. Mesic, dry mesic, dry. Full or partial sun. pH: Acidic-neutral 5–7. Meadow, roadside.

Plant description: Height: 1 1/2–2 1/2 ft. Blooming time: July–August. Small yellow flower head arranged along upper side of branches in a plume-shaped, nodding inflorescence. Years before expected bloom: 2–3. Erect stem, single or in clusters; smooth, not hairy; often reddish. Lower leaves mostly shed before flowering. Numerous stem leaves, alternate, without stalks, broadly linear to narrowly elliptic, 2–4 × 1/2–1 in., some margins toothed. 3 parallel veins, thick, somewhat rigid. Spreading caudex or creeping rhizome.

Propagation: Easily by seed or division.

Germination: Plant in fall or spring in cool soil. Needs stratification 33–38° F for 30 days.

Harvest: September. Clip fruit into bucket several weeks after bloom. Remove achene with pale pappus from receptacle. 1/4-in. triangular achene with light-colored pappus. Seeds per oz.: 92,000. Per lb.: 1,472,000. Lb. per acre: 2. Oz. per 1,000 sq. ft.: 0.8.

Attracts: Butterflies.

Comments: Earliest of goldenrods to bloom.

Solidago nemoralis
Field goldenrod, gray goldenrod, Dyer's weed
Asteraceae (Compositae) (sunflower family)

Location: Dry rocky prairies to ridge-top prairies. Frequent to common throughout most of state. Sandy soil. Dry mesic, dry. Full sun. pH: Acidic-neutral 5.5–7. Border, meadow, roadside.

Plant description: Height: 6–36 in. Blooming time: August–September. Bright yellow-gold flower, 5–9 rays, slender, 1-sided plumes. Flower pungent. Dries well. Years before expected bloom: 1–2. Grayish stem is densely covered with fine hairs as are the rough green-gray leaves. Tiny leaflets in the axils of the leaves where they join the stem. Leaves are feather-veined.

Propagation: Easily by division. Also by seed. When dividing plant each section must have a bud and a root.

Germination: Plant seeds in fall or stratify 33–38° F for 30 days and plant in early spring.

Harvest: September–October. Clip fruit into bucket several weeks after bloom. Remove achene with pale pappus bristles from bract. Individual seed 1/4-in. triangular nutlet with light-colored pappus. Seeds per oz.: 82,000. Per lb.: 1,312,000. Lb. per acre: 1.5. Oz. per 1,000 sq. ft.: 0.6.

Attracts: Birds and butterflies.

Comments: Individual plants of this species bloom at various times, extending blooming season. They are small enough for small areas and tall enough to rise above competitors. Goldenrods are insect pollinated and not the cause of hayfever. They bloom at the same time as ragweed, the real culprit, which is air-borne pollinated. The different species of goldenrods vary greatly in their flower and leaf shape. Flowers vary from plumelike, elm-branched, clublike and showy, wandlike and slender, to flat-topped. Leaves can be parallel-veined (or nerved) or feather-veined, smooth or toothed, lanceolate to oval.

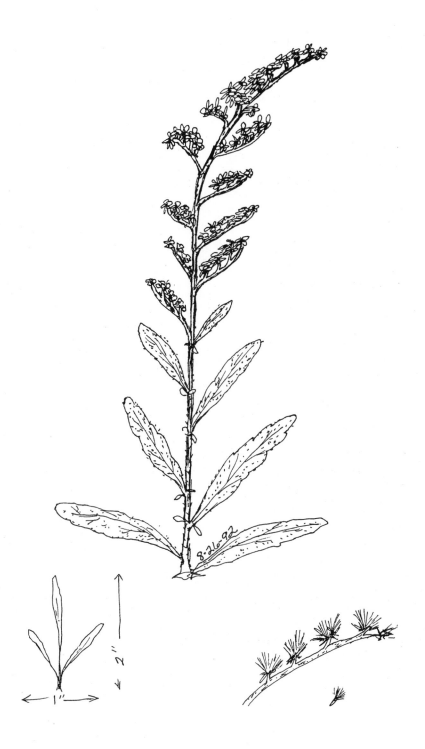

8-26-92

Solidago rigida
Stiff goldenrod, rigid goldenrod, gray goldenrod, hard-leaved goldenrod
Asteraceae (Compositae) (sunflower family)

Location: Wide range of prairies, loess bluffs, abandoned fields. Scattered throughout state. Wide range from moist clays to dry sands, even thin-poor soil. Mesic, dry mesic, dry. Full sun. pH: Wide range. Border, meadow, roadside.

Plant description: Height: 1–5 ft. Blooming time: August–October. Yellow, large, dome-shaped bloom, rounded or flat top. The terminal group of large 20–30 flowers are bell-shaped, 1/3 in. long, with 7–10 rays each. Dried plants resemble asters, but flowers are smaller and tightly clustered. Years before expected bloom: 2–3. Good cut and dried flower. Hang bloom to dry. Conspicuous, toothed, rough, long-stemmed. Basal leaves smaller, oval; rigid upper leaves oval, clasping, rough. Rosette leaves appear in fall for next year's growth.

Propagation: Best by seed sown; also by division in spring every 2 years.

Germination: Easy and quickly established. Plant in fall or early spring when soil is cool. If planted in spring, needs stratification 33–38° F for 30–60 days.

Harvest: October–November. Tan fruit, 1/2 in. in diameter, fluffy with gray leaves and stems. Recognized by total shape of plant arching across top and rigid oval upper leaves, which slightly clasp the hairy stem. Clip into bucket 1–2 weeks after bloom. Attractive dried seed head. Remove achene with pappus from receptacle. 1/4-in. triangular achene with light-colored pappus. Seeds per oz.: 46,000. Per lb.: 736,000. Lb. per acre: 3. Oz. per 1,000 sq. ft.: 1.2.

Attracts: Bees and painted lady butterflies.

Comments: Prettiest of goldenrods along with showy goldenrod. Vigorous and showy. Inhibits the growth of other species around it. A heavy seeder, aggressive and needs competition. Plant in back edges of border in patches and drifts in the meadow. Pinch tops off plants in June and July for sturdier plants.

Solidago speciosa
Showy goldenrod, noble goldenrod
Asteraceae (Compositae) (sunflower family)

Location: Dry to mesic prairies, open woods. Common to scattered throughout state. Loam to sandy soil. Mesic, dry mesic, dry. Full or partial sun. pH: Acidic-neutral 5.5–7. Border, meadow, roadside.

Plant description: Height: 1–4 ft. Blooming time: September. Yellow flower with 5–6 rays in dense pyramidal or club-shaped terminal clusters. Flower heads 1/4 in. long. Years before expected bloom: 2. Mixes well with asters in fall bouquets and dries well. Stout, smooth below and rough above, reddish stem and smooth, elliptical leaves lacking strong teeth on the margins of lower leaves. These have irregular edges. Basal leaves 4–10 in. long, stalked, upper much smaller and unstalked.

Propagation: Easily from seed or division.

Germination: Sow unstratified seeds in fall or stratify seeds 33–38° F for 30 days and sow in early spring.

Harvest: October. Clip fruit into bucket several weeks after bloom when pappus is fluffy. Remove achene with pale pappus bristles from receptacle. 1/4-in. triangular achene with light-colored pappus. Seeds per oz.: 105,000. Per lb.: 1,680,000. Lb. per acre: 2. Oz. per 1,000 sq. ft.: 0.8.

Attracts: Birds and butterflies.

Comments: This is the most attractive goldenrod. Best grown in dry soil as it becomes aggressive in moist soil. There are 125 species of goldenrods in the U.S. Eilers lists 14 native species of goldenrods in Iowa. Tall goldenrod (*S. canadensis*) grows in dry to moist prairies, smooth goldenrod (*S. gigantea*) grows in moist to mesic prairies, and Riddell's goldenrod (*S. riddellii*) grows in low, wet prairies to marshes.

9-1-92

← 1" →

↕ 2"

Vernonia fasciculata
Ironweed, western ironweed
Asteraceae (Compositae) (sunflower family)

Location: Wet open bottomland fields and marshes, roadsides. Scattered throughout state, infrequent in most southern and western counties, heaviest in east. Rich loam; grows taller in loam but good in tough clay soil also. Wet mesic, mesic. Full to partial sun. pH: Acidic-neutral 5.6–7. Meadow, roadside.

Plant description: Height: 3–5 ft. Blooming time: July–September. Brilliant deep purple flat blooms of numerous heads, 30 or more, 5-lobed disk flower with rays absent. Bract surrounds the flower head. Cluster is corymb-shaped. Years before expected bloom: 2–3. Good cut flower. Erect red-purple, tough and wiry stems. Its name comes from the strong, fibrous stems. Leaves narrow, smooth lance-shaped, alternate, sharply toothed. Heavy root system sends up clusters of stems.

Propagation: By seed, division in the spring only and cuttings in summer.

Germination: Easily grown from seeds, self-sows. Slow to germinate. Sow seeds outdoors when the ground is warm. Plant with no treatment or use stratification 33–38° F for 30 days.

Harvest: October. Clip stem with multiple heads 1/4 × 3/8 in. Total cluster 8–10 in. across. Dry and remove achene from receptacle. Rust or dark brown pappus on achene 1/4 in. long. Seeds per oz.: 20,000. Per lb.: 320,000. Lb. per acre: 8. Oz. per 1,000 sq. ft.: 3.2.

Attracts: Butterflies.

Comments: Aggressive and large, needs competition. The flowers resemble Joe-pye-weed, its better-known relative. Missouri ironweed (*V. missurica*) and Baldwin's ironweed (*V. baldwinii*) grow in full sun in the southern half of Iowa and can tolerate dry mesic soil.

7-30-92

← 3/4" →

1"

← 1'1/2" →

2"

Lithospermum canescens
Hoary puccoon, Indian paint
Boraginaceae (forget-me-not family)

Location: Prairie and open hillsides, sandy areas. Common throughout state. Sandy soil. Dry mesic, dry. Full sun. pH: Acidic-neutral 4–6.5. Border, meadow.

Plant description: Height: 6–18 in. Blooming time: May. Orange, 5 flat petals 1/2 in. each with tube that flares and conceals the stamens. Blooms in cluster at top of plant. Years before expected bloom: 2. Short-lived. Branched stems. Hoary refers to the whitish color due to the presence of tiny white hairs on leaf and stem. Slender, toothless. Deep, straight taproot is reddish. Juice has a purple stain.

Propagation: Seed or cuttings in summer. Seedlings are weak and often die. Difficult to transplant. Puccoons are semiparasitic and require a host plant. Low-growing grasses such as June grass are good hosts. Cut knife through soil 2 in. deep to cut grass roots before planting seed 3/8 in. deep, or plant grass and puccoon seeds at same time.

Germination: Difficult by seed. Needs stratification 33–38° F for 7–30 days and scarification. Plant fresh seeds or plant in fall after stratification with host plant.

Harvest: June. Fruit at axil of plant; will throw seeds when ripe. Few seeds mature. Clip stem into bucket before seeds are fully dried and lost. 4 nutlets are produced by each flower. Store seeds in paper bag and they will separate from pod when dry. Black, hard seed, 1/8 in. long. Seeds per oz.: 25,000. Per lb.: 400,000. Lb. per acre: 6.7. Oz. per 1,000 sq. ft.: 2.7.

Comments: Rock garden plant. Showy for a small, early plant. Fringed puccoon (*L. incisum*), found in the northern two-thirds of Iowa, has very narrow leaves and toothed pale yellow petals. Hairy puccoon (*L. caroliniense*), mainly in eastern Iowa, has yellow-gold flowers and is very drought resistant because of its deep taproot.

Yellow puccoon (L. incisum)
toothed petals, narrow leaves, yellow flower

Opuntia humifusa
Eastern prickly pear, prickly pear cactus
Cactaceae (cactus family)

Location: Dry, rocky, sandy prairies. Scattered sparsely throughout state. Sandy soil with good drainage. Will grow in average loam if well drained. Dry. Full sun. pH: Acidic 4.5–6. Border, meadow, roadside.

Plant description: Height: 4–6 in. Blooming time: June–July. Yellow, showy, large cuplike flower remains open for 2 days. Each joint 4 in. long. Pads have bristles (glochids) that can penetrate the skin and tufts. Fibrous and branched roots.

Propagation: By seed, or by division of joints in the spring, which is the easiest.

Germination: No treatment needed. Sow fresh seeds indoors.

Harvest: August–September. Red, greenish, or purple fruit 1 1/2 in. long. Remove berry with gloves on. Seeds are bound together with a sticky purple substance. Split the berry and scoop out the seeds. Place in a sieve, scrub with soap, and rinse. Numerous, 12–36 small, flattened seeds in each. Seeds per oz.: 1,000. Per lb.: 16,000. Lb. per acre: 30. Oz. per 1,000 sq. ft.: 12.

Comments: The only widespread eastern cactus. Rock garden plant. Can become 3 ft. across in 3–4 years. Easily cut back, however. Little prickly pear (*O. fragilis*) and prickly pear (*O. macrorhiza*) appear rarely in Iowa. Mulch in winter.

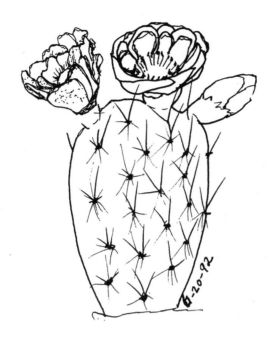

6-20-92

1/4"

3/4"

1 1/4"

Campanula rotundifolia
Harebell, fairy thimbles, witches' thimbles, bluebells of Scotland
Campanulaceae (bluebell or harebell family)

Location: Rocky prairies, limestone ledges, northern-facing wooded talus slopes. Common extreme east. Gravelly, sandy, or rocky soils. Dry mesic, dry. Full to partial sun. pH: Neutral 6–7.5. Border, meadow, roadside.

Plant description: Height: 4–20 in. Blooming time: June–September. Purple bell-like flower borne singly on nodding thin stalks; 3/4 in., 5-lobed. Years before expected bloom: 2. Alternate leaves on single, slender stems below bloom. Basal leaves broadly ovate; stem leaves linear 1–3 in. long. Grows from branched rhizomes, spreading by basal shoots to form clumps.

Propagation: By seed.

Germination: No treatment necessary, or stratify at 33–38° F for 30 days. Plant fine seeds on soil surface.

Harvest: September–October. Clip off stem with nodding capsules. Store capsules until dry in paper bag and separate seeds. Very fine, black seed. Seeds per oz.: 800,000. Per lb.: 12,800,000. Lb. per acre: 0.25. Oz. per 1,000 sq. ft.: 0.1.

Attracts: Hummingbirds.

Comments: Rock garden plant. Often found in open colonies. Tall bellflower (*C. americana*) is a 1–2-in. flat-shaped blue flower growing on spikes up to 6 ft. tall along shady roadsides and in woodlands. Marsh bellflower (*C. aparinoides*) grows in moist lowland prairies to marshes and sprawls over the ground.

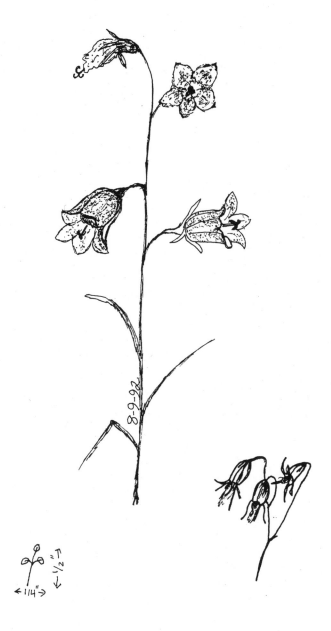

8-9-92

←1/4"→   ←1/2"→

Lobelia cardinalis
Cardinal flower
Campanulaceae (bluebell or harebell family)

Location: Wet, alluvial woods; moist, open prairies. Frequent northeast and southeast, infrequent south-central, rare north-central. Moist, rich loam. Wet, wet mesic, mesic. Partial shade. pH: Acidic-neutral 4−7. Border, meadow.

Plant description: Height: 2−4 ft. Blooming time: August. Red, 2-lipped, a slender spike of brilliantly beautiful flowers. Years before expected bloom: 1. Develops large basal rosette of leaves; some will bloom the first year. Basal rosettes. Alternate and toothed leaves on upper stem. Very shallow roots. Mulch in winter.

Propagation: Seed, stem cuttings in summer, or division in fall or spring. Wait 8−10 weeks for roots to establish before transplanting to pots. Then allow 4−6 weeks before planting outdoors. Plant seeds in fall or early spring outdoors. Take cuttings 6−8 in. long and lay them horizontally in sand and perlite, cover lightly, and keep moist. In 4−6 weeks rosettes will develop at the nodes. Pot individual rosettes.

Germination: Difficult by seed, very tiny and slow. Needs stratification 33−38° F 30−60 days. Germinates at 70° F. Fine seeds, plant on surface.

Harvest: September−October. Clip stalk when mature before seeds explode. Pods are short, 2-celled, shaggy, 1/4-in. spherical capsules, attached to the apex of the main stem. Shake stalk in paper bag after seeds have dried. Pods may also be crushed with a rolling pin and separated from chaff in sieve. Brown 1/16-in. seed. Seeds per oz.: 542,562. Per lb.: 8,681,000. Lb. per acre: 0.5. Oz. per 1,000 sq. ft.: 0.2.

Attracts: One of the best for hummingbirds.

Comments: Good naturalized in low, wet areas. Beautiful flower. Short-lived perennial. Stand maintained by new seedlings and offshoots. Can be grown in wide range of soils but roots must never be allowed to dry out completely.

8-9-92

↕ 3/4"

← 3/4" →

Lobelia siphilitica
Great lobelia, giant lobelia, great blue lobelia
Campanulaceae (bluebell or harebell family)

Location: Wet prairies, sandy marshes, streambanks. Infrequent northwest, frequent to common elsewhere in state. Moist, rich soil; will adapt readily to garden soil. Wet, wet mesic, mesic. Full sun. pH: Neutral 6.5–7. Border, meadow, roadside.

Plant description: Height: 1–3 ft. Blooming time: August–September. Purple-blue flower with persistent calyx segments, 2-lipped with 3 lower lobes. White stripes on lower lobes. Years before expected bloom: 2. Cut flowers do not last. Showy spike. Leaves pointed, irregular toothed.

Propagation: Seed, division, or layering.

Germination: Easily grown from seeds, self-sows freely. Needs stratification 33–38° F for 30 days. Fine seeds, plant on the surface.

Harvest: October. Short, 2-celled pod. Cut stalk off plant and store in paper bag. Shake seeds in paper bag after dried pods have opened at the top. Tiny golden-brown seeds. Seeds per oz.: 500,000. Per lb.: 8,000,000. Lb. per acre: 0.5. Oz. per 1,000 sq. ft.: 0.2.

Attracts: Hummingbirds.

Comments: Brilliant color along fencerows in September. It self-sows, so seedlings may be found near parent plant. Easier to grow than cardinal flower, but the contrasting colors make them pretty companion plants. Great white lobelia (*L. siphilitica alba*) is similar except for color. Indian tobacco (*L. inflata*) has the flower and fruit tucked into the axil of the leaf. Flowers are lavender, and fruit becomes inflated or balloonlike. Kalm's lobelia (*L. kalmii*) is a rare fen variety. The lobelias were used as medicinal cures for many ailments by pioneers.

8-9-92

← 1" →

← 3/4" →

Lobelia spicata
Spiked lobelia, pale spiked lobelia
Campanulaceae (bluebell or harebell family)

Location: Meadows, fields, thickets, moist prairies. Frequent to infrequent throughout state. Well-drained sandy soil, loam. Wet mesic, mesic, dry mesic. Full sun. pH: Neutral 6.5–7. Border, meadow, roadside.

Plant description: Height: 8–40 in. Blooming time: June–August. Lavender, pale blue, to white small flower in a narrow spike, sometimes crowded on upper part of stem. Good cut flower. Single spike stem, basal leaves, nearly toothless, ovate to lanceolate. Roots are fibrous.

Propagation: By seed or division in spring.

Germination: Needs stratification 33–38° F for 30 days. Fine seeds; plant on surface.

Harvest: September. Cut stalk with seed heads and store in paper bag. Shake seeds from seedpod. Individual seed very fine, dark. Seeds per oz.: 500,000. Per lb.: 8,000,000. Lb. per acre: 0.5. Oz. per 1,000 sq. ft.: 0.2.

Comments: The small flowers, less than 1/2 in. long, have a very delicate appearance. Over a dozen individual blooms appear on the upper spiked stem.

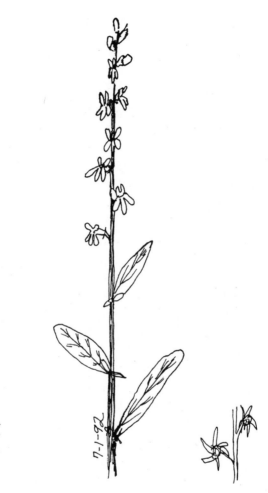

← 3/4" →

← 3/4" →

7-1-92

Silene antirrhina
Sleepy catchfly
Caryophyllaceae (pink family)

Location: Dry midwestern prairies, waste ground. Infrequent to frequent throughout state, mainly in southeast. Sandy soil. Mesic, dry mesic, dry. Full to partial sun. Border, meadow.

Plant description: Height: 24–40 in. Blooming time: June. Pink to white flower, 5 slender petals that are toothed or untoothed, short-stalked, calyx sticky. Good dried flower. Opposite leaves. A sticky substance is concentrated in zones between the nodes, which appear as swollen areas on the stem. Rounded at base, ovate, thick.

Propagation: Seed.

Germination: No treatment needed.

Harvest: August. Pretty pods with 6 teeth at the top of the calyx, paperlike covering. Clip pods from stem. Place seedpod in bag and shake. Small, hard, dark, somewhat irregular round seeds. Seeds per oz.: 10,000. Per lb.: 160,000. Lb. per acre: 10. Oz. per 1,000 sq. ft.: 4.

Attracts: Hummingbirds. Sticky hairs and exudate trap insects.

Comments: Starry campion (*S. stellata*) is an attractive native species found in moist prairies and upland woods and on shores. The alien white campion (*S. pratensis*) has 8–10 teeth on the fruit capsule and 20 veins on the calyx.

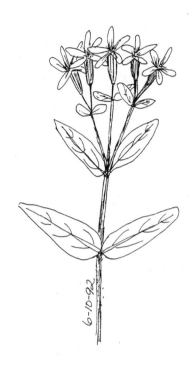

6-10-92

Pod
6-Teeth

← 1" →

← 2" →

153

Euphorbia corollata
Flowering spurge, white purslane, appleroot
Euphorbiaceae (spurge family)

Location: Dry open fields, disturbed areas, and roadsides. Common throughout state except for northwest and north-central. Dry, sandy soil, loam. Wet mesic, mesic, dry mesic, dry. Full sun. pH: Neutral 6.5–7. Border, meadow, roadside.

Plant description: Height: 2–4 ft. Blooming time: June–September. 5 white petal bracts that appear as 3/8-in. flowers in umbellate clusters. A delicate plant. Years before expected bloom: 2. Good cut flower. Stem smooth, may be spotted. Juice milky. Leaves linear to oblong, 1 1/2 in. long, mostly alternate but whorled below flowering umbel. Stout, brittle, deep root growing from a caudex.

Propagation: Best by seed, also by root cuttings using 2–3 in. of an upper section planted 2 in. deep, and by root division. Roots are brittle. Slow to establish.

Germination: Needs stratification 33–38° F for 30 days.

Harvest: August–September. When ripe the seed head snaps open, expelling the seeds. 3-celled capsule with 1 seed in each section. The fruit forms on a stem above the flower. Harvest when seed head turns from green to tan before seeds are completely dry. Pull from plant and place in paper bag. Seeds will open as they dry. Individual seed egg-shaped, 1/8 in., white, hard. Seeds per oz.: 10,000. Per lb.: 160,000. Lb. per acre: 10. Oz. per 1,000 sq. ft.: 4.

Comments: Pretty in rock gardens. Can become aggressive. Considered poisonous; milky juice can be irritating to the skin. Leafy spurge (*E. esula*), a nonnative, is a serious noxious weed problem in the central and northern Great Plains. Snow-on-the-mountain (*E. marginata*) is a native found in the loess prairies. *E. dentata* and *E. glyptosperma* are natives also found in Iowa in dry, sandy areas. The latter grows only 6 in. tall. The Christmas poinsettia (*E. pulcherrima*) is a relative but not found in this area.

Amorpha canescens

Lead plant, prairie shoestring, wild tea

Fabaceae (Leguminosae) (pea family)

Location: Prairie remnants, loess bluffs, dry, sandy, open habitats through-out state. Wide soil range but prefers dry, sandy, well-drained soil. Wet mesic, mesic, dry mesic, dry. Full sun. pH: Acidic-neutral 4.5–7.5. Border, meadow, roadside.

Plant description: Height: 20–42 in. Blooming time: June–July. Purple-orange iridescent flower. Dense colorful spike up to 6 in. long. Multiple 1/6-in. flowers with only 1 purple petal and 10 bright orange stamens. Good cut flower. Years before expected bloom: 3–4. Leaves 2–4 in. pinnately compound with 15–45 leaflets each 1/2 in. long. Entire leaf becomes hairy, giving a silvery green appearance with maturity. Branching taproots up to 15 ft. deep, drought-resistant.

Propagation: Moderately difficult by seed; also by greenwood cuttings of young stems or root cuttings 6–8 in. long. Mulch the first winter to prevent frost heaving.

Germination: Prone to damping-off. Needs stratification 33–38° F for 10 days and scarification. Remove boiling water from heat, pour over seeds, and allow to cool. Remove hull and apply Nitragin type EL rhizobium. Slow to germinate.

Harvest: September–October. Multiple spikes up to 6 in. long, with over-all dark purple cast. Strip seed by pulling up receptacle with fingers using gloves. Collect in paper bag. Thresh and separate seeds. Not all the 1/4-in. fuzzy pods contain seeds. Individual seed 1/8 in. with soft hull, 1/16 in. dark gold when hulled. Seeds sold either hulled or unhulled. Seeds resemble those of alfalfa but smaller. Seeds per oz.: 17,000. Per lb.: 272,000. Lb. per acre: 9. Oz. per 1,000 sq. ft.: 3.6.

Attracts: Marine blue butterflies.

Comments: One of the few prairie shrubs (woody stem). Growth and bloom are improved by burning. Requires little care once established. Foliage attractive. An indicator of a prairie in prime condition. Native Americans used leaves for tea. Seeds can be sprouted to eat.

Astragalus canadensis
Milk vetch, little rattlepod
Fabaceae (Leguminosae) (pea family)

Location: Ditches, wet to dry prairies, roadsides, woodland borders. Common western half, infrequent to frequent eastern half. Loam to sandy soil. Wet mesic, mesic, dry mesic. Full sun. pH: Neutral 6–7. Meadow, roadside.

Plant description: Height: 2–4 ft. Blooming time: July–August. Cream, slender, pealike flower, towering beautifully above plant and resembling lupine. Years before expected bloom: 1–2. Good cut flower and dried seedpods. Single upright stem. Pinnately shaped 7–15 leaflets of dark green leaves.

Propagation: Easiest by seed; division is difficult. Hard to transplant, except for seedlings in pots.

Germination: Slow, but grows rapidly once established in well-drained soil. Needs stratification 33–38° F for 10 days and scarification. Inoculate with astragalus-type rhizobium.

Harvest: August–September. Seedpods 3 in. long are easily removed. Clip into bag being careful not to spill seeds from open end. Best to wear gloves while harvesting as pods are rough. Shake seeds out of open end of pod into paper bag. 1/16-in. hard golden seed. Seeds per oz.: 16,000. Per lb.: 256,000. Lb. per acre: 9. Oz. per 1,000 sq. ft.: 3.6.

Attracts: Hummingbirds, birds, and butterflies.

Comments: An aggressive legume with attractive foliage. Needs competition. Often in disturbed areas. Another milk vetch (*A. lotiflorus*) found in dry prairies in the loess bluffs is only 3 in. tall, pale red, blooming in May. Eilers lists 7 native milk vetches of the *Astragalus* genus.

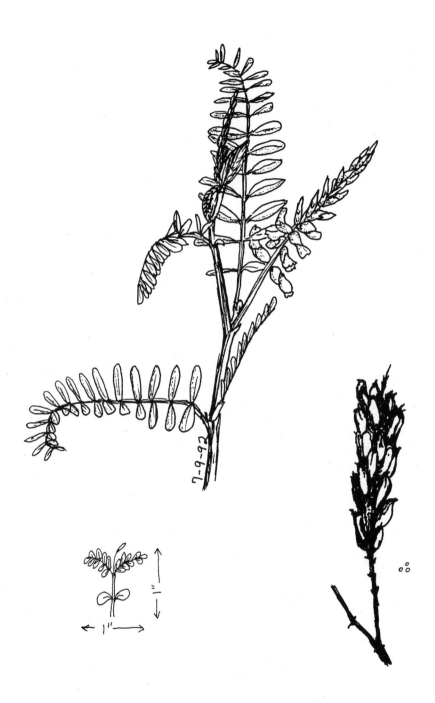

7-9-93

Astragalus crassicarpus
Ground plum, buffalo apple, buffalo pea
Fabaceae (Leguminosae) (pea family)

Location: West side of dry, gravelly, or sandy hillsides, loess prairies. Common northwest and north-central. Calcareous soil. Dry mesic, dry. Full sun. pH: Neutral-alkaline 6.5–8. Border, meadow.

Plant description: Height: 6–15 in. Blooming time: Early May. 8–10 pale purple to white, small pealike flowers borne on a central flower stalk. Sprawling close to ground with tips ascending, short hairy stems, alternate-pinnate leaves. The keel, the lowest petal, is short and rounded. Leaves small, smooth, slender ovals with tiny stiff hairs on underside. Branching roots, sending up new stems.

Propagation: Easiest by seed.

Germination: Needs stratification 33–38° F for 10 days and scarification. Inoculum for astragalus.

Harvest: July. Do not rush as seeds take about 2 months to mature, and they remain in the tough pod into the following year. Formation of fruit is the interesting part of the plant. In June it first forms a fleshy 1-in. edible plum, slightly oval, purple on the top and green on the bottom. The dried fruit becomes tough, with a thick, protective skin. When mature it is tan and wrinkled and resembles an English walnut. Seeds will rattle when you shake the fruit. The hard shell will open when tapped with a hammer into a 2-chambered pod, each side covered with a papery covering that contains about 12 black seeds. Remove sticky seeds with a toothpick. If white worms are present, store seeds with no-pest strip. Individual seed small, black, hard, kidney-shaped, 1/8 in. Seeds per oz.: 20,000. Per lb.: 320,000. Lb. per acre: 8. Oz. per 1,000 sq. ft.: 3.2.

Comments: Attractive small plant with early spring bloom. Fruit resembles wild indigo (*Baptisia lactea*) in size and inner structure but not color.

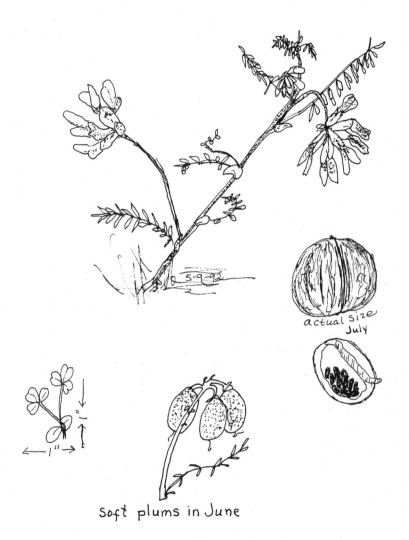

5-9-92

actual size
July

Soft plums in June

← 1" →

1"

Baptisia bracteata
Cream wild indigo, false indigo, cream false indigo, black rattlepod
Fabaceae (Leguminosae) (pea family)

Location: Upland prairies, roadsides, open woods. Infrequent to frequent throughout state. Well-drained, sandy to loamy soil; does poorly on open soil. Mesic, dry mesic, dry. Full sun. pH: Neutral 6–7.5. Border, meadow, roadside.

Plant description: Height: 18–30 in. Blooming time: June. Cream, downward-arching racemes up to 1 ft. long. Bloom is lush but brief. Years before expected bloom: 4–5. Slow to establish but worth the wait. Good dried flower. Coarse, hairy plant with spreading branches. Silvery sheen from silky hairs that cover stem and leaves. Leaf stipules are large and appear to be leaflets. They have 5 leaflets compared to 3 of *B. leucantha*. Foliage turns dark after frost.

Propagation: Best by seed.

Germination: Needs stratification 33–38° F for 10 days. Scarification needed. Inoculate with baptisia rhizobium.

Harvest: September–October. Pods 1 × 2 in., ovoid, downy, dark gray, narrow at base and end in a beak. Leaves the same color as the dried pods. Plant becomes separated from roots in dormancy and tumbles in the wind. Remove seeds from pod with toothpick. Store with no-pest strip. Individual seed roundish, golden, sticky, 1/8 in. Seeds per oz.: 1,700. Per lb.: 27,200. Lb. per acre: 27. Oz. per 1,000 sq. ft.: 11.

Comments: Yields an inferior indigo dye if steeped in water and allowed to ferment. Excellent garden perennial. Needs support from companions, particularly little bluestem.

Baptisia lactea
Wild indigo, white wild indigo
Fabaceae (Leguminosae) (pea family)

Location: Prairies, roadsides, open sandy soil. Infrequent to frequent throughout state. Wide range of dry to mesic prairies, best on dry sites but will grow in clay. Wet mesic, mesic, dry mesic, dry. Full or partial sun. pH: Neutral 6.5–7. Border, meadow, roadside.

Plant description: Height: 3–4 ft. Blooming time: June–July. White 1-in.-long flower in clusters to 12 in. long, erect raceme, flowering cluster. Flowers visible from a long distance. Years before expected bloom: 4–5. Good cut flower and dried pods. Smooth grayish white stems and semiwaxy rounded blue-green leaves palmately compound, divided into 3 oblong segments. They turn black when dry. Massive root system growing from a central core extending to 10 ft.

Propagation: Best by seed, also by division in early spring on young plants. Slow maturing, but long-lived and hardy once established.

Germination: Needs stratification 33–38° F for 10 days and scarification. Inoculate with Baptisia rhizobium. Slow; sow anytime. Soak in warm water the night before sowing. Let soil dry between waterings to prevent damping-off. Takes at least 2–4 weeks to germinate.

Harvest: September. Pod is black, drooping, oblong, and beaked; about 1 in. long. Store seeds with no-pest strip. Pod opens in 2 parts like a pea pod. Individual seed 1/8 in., round and golden. Seeds per oz.: 1,600. Per lb.: 25,600. Lb. per acre: 28. Oz. per 1,000 sq. ft.: 11.

Attracts: Hoary edge and sleepy dusky-wing butterflies.

Comments: Attractive plant. Allow 2 ft. for each plant. Most spectacular if surrounded by small species. The name comes from its inferior indigo dye. Attractive shrubby-looking plant. Well-established plant looks like asparagus when it emerges and grows to 4 ft. in less than a week. Blue wild indigo (*B. australis*) is rare but good for propagation.

a

Chamaecrista fasciculata
Partridge pea
Fabaceae (Leguminosae) (pea family)

Location: Prairie remnants, roadsides. Frequent to common throughout state. Dry, sandy soil. Dry mesic, dry. Full sun. pH: Neutral-alkaline 6.5–8.5. Border, meadow, roadside.

Plant description: Height: 6–36 in. Blooming time: July–September. 5 yellow unequal broad petals, up to 10 drooping dark red anthers; bloom 1 1/2 in. wide. Flower in leaf axil or slightly above. Years before expected bloom: 1, an annual. Good dried flower. Finely cut pinnate 14–30 leaflets, sensitive to touch. The leaves fold together when touched and at night, each tipped with a tiny bristle.

Propagation: By seed only. An annual, but reseeds itself.

Germination: Easy with high germination rate. No treatment needed except EL rhizobium.

Harvest: Late September. When pod dries seeds are cast out, so harvest needs to be done before this happens. Pull pods from stem. Open slender pod. Each seed has a section in the continuous pod. Tear-shaped, 1/4-in. dark seed. Seeds per oz.: 4,725. Per lb.: 75,600. Lb. per acre: 25. Oz. per 1,000 sq. ft.: 10.

Attracts: Birds; cloudless giant sulphur, little yellow, antillean blue, and hairstreak butterflies.

Comments: Good soil-builder and nurse plant to help cover bare ground while perennials are establishing. Wild senna (*Cassia marilandica*) is also yellow and grows 3–6 ft. in moist alluvial or open upland woods. The partridge pea can be distinguished by 1-in. stalk that attaches the pod to the stem. It also has larger stipules. The flowers of wild senna are smaller.

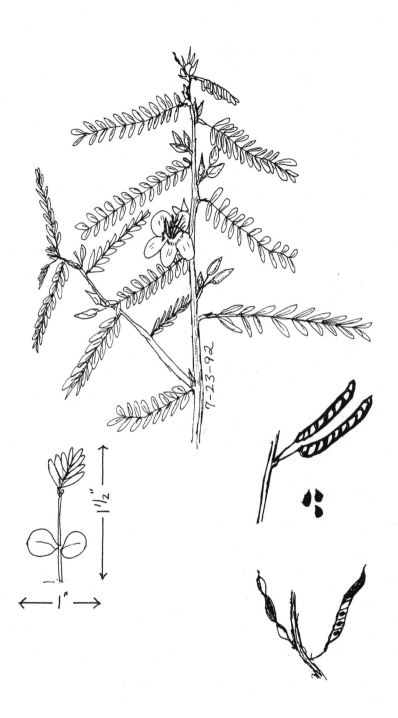

7-23-92

1½"

1"

Dalea purpurea
Purple prairie clover
Fabaceae (Leguminosae) (pea family)

Location: Prairies and dry hills. Very drought-tolerant when established. Frequent to common throughout state. Sandy soil. Mesic, dry mesic, dry. Full sun. pH: Acidic 5.5–6.5. Border, meadow, roadside.

Plant description: Height: 1–3 ft. Blooming time: July–August. Tiny purple flower 1/6 in. in cylindrical, headlike 2-in. clusters at end of stem. The corolla is not pealike, has 1 main heart-shaped petal (the standard) and 4 narrow petallike structures (modified stamens). Fragrant. The domelike center consists of disk, florets, and pointed bracts, all of equal length. Blooms progress from the bottom of the stem upward. Petals and stamens are joined. Buds are covered with silvery hairs. Years before expected bloom: 1–2. Good cut flower. Upright, wiry, pinnately divided 3–7 narrow segments, each 1/2–3/4 in. long. Deep taproot up to 6 ft. with extensive vertical branching. Nitrogen-fixing nodes on the taproots enrich the soil.

Propagation: Best by seed; division is difficult. Taproot reaches up to 20 in. by the first summer, so transplanting is not recommended.

Germination: Easy. Needs stratification 33–38° F for 10 days. Scarification is also needed. Remove hull. Inoculate with Saintfoin type F rhizobium.

Harvest: Late September–October. Strip fruit off by hand from long dark bluish-gray stem. The spike 1/3 × 1 3/4 in. that held the seeds remains when seeds are removed. Remove seeds from bluish flower heads 1/8 × 1/4 in. and separate chaff. 1–2 seeds in each pod. Individual seed golden pea, 1/16 in. Seeds per oz.: 18,312. Per lb.: 292,992. Lb. per acre: 8. Oz. per 1,000 sq. ft.: 3.2.

Attracts: Bumblebees, dogface and sulphur butterflies, beetles, and birds. Excellent forage.

Comments: Favorite of many, vigorous and showy, attractive with native grasses. Likes small companions. Mulch the first winter to prevent frost heaving. White prairie clover (*D. candida*) is a larger white species.

Desmanthus illinoensis
Prairie mimosa, Illinois bundle flower, pickleweed, false sensitive plant
Fabaceae (Leguminosae) (pea family)

Location: Prairies with both moist and dry soils, plains, prairies, loess bluffs, and riverbanks. Uncommon east of the Loess Hills. Average, well-drained loam to sandy alluvium. Mesic, dry mesic, dry. Full sun. pH: Neutral 6–7. Border, meadow, roadside.

Plant description: Height: 3–4 ft. Blooming time: July–August. Tiny, greenish white flower 1/2 in. across in a ball-shaped cluster on a single stalk 1–3 in. long. Flower has 5 petals each 1/8 in. and 5 long stamens giving a fuzzy look. Grooved stem without prickles; alternate leaves are bipinnate with 6–15 pinnae along each leafstalk. Each pinna has 20–30 pairs of leaflets along a central stalk. The total leaf is about 4 in. long. They are light- and touch-sensitive.

Propagation: By seed.

Germination: Scarification needed, and treat with inoculum for desmanthus.

Harvest: September. 20–30 curved dark brown pods 1 1/2 × 1/4 in. with 2–6 seeds in each. Pods borne in a cluster at the end of a stem forming a sphere; persists into winter. Remove seeds from pod. Individual seed rust-colored, flat, elliptical-shaped, 1/8 in. Seeds per oz.: 12,500. Per lb.: 200,000. Lb. per acre: 10. Oz. per 1,000 sq. ft.: 4.

Attracts: Butterflies.

Comments: The legume is high in protein and is being studied as a possible farm crop. Thought to be our most important native range legume. Decreases under heavy grazing. The only native *Desmanthus* species. Similar to prairie acacia (*Acacia angustissima*) but distinguished by its fruit of curved rather than straight pods.

7-5-92

1 1/2"

← 3/4" →

1"

1"

Desmodium canadense
Showy tick-trefoil, Canada tick-trefoil, tick clover, hoary tick clover
Fabaceae (Leguminosae) (pea family)

Location: Dry to moist prairies, open woods, roadsides. Common southwest in loess, infrequent to rare elsewhere. Wide soil range; does well in clay and loam as well as moist sand. Wet mesic, mesic, dry mesic. Full to partial sun. pH: Acidic-neutral 5–7.5. Border, meadow, roadside.

Plant description: Height: 30–40 in. Blooming time: July–August. Pink/purple elongated terminal cluster of pealike flowers 1/2 in. long on panicles to 1/3 in. long. One of the largest of the species. Good cut flower. Years before expected bloom: 1–2. Quick to establish. Bushy, hairy plant. Stipules at base of leafstalks. Pinnately compound leaves with 3 oblong untoothed leaflets each 3 in. long; cloverlike (trefoil). Slender, brown, branched taproots.

Propagation: Best by seed. Quick to establish and fast growing.

Germination: Moderately easy. No treatment needed or stratify 33–38° F for 10 days. Scarification needed. Remove hull. Inoculate with Nitragin type EL rhizobium.

Harvest: September–October. 1–3-in. segmented pod, 3–5 hairy joints resembling ticks that break apart and hitchhike, sticking to clothing and animal fur. Pod feels rough with hooks too small to be seen. Remove seeds from pod. Individual seed tiny bean 1/8 in. long, gold. Seeds per oz.: 4,500. Per lb.: 72,000. Lb. per acre: 25. Oz. per 1,000 sq. ft.: 10.

Attracts: Bees; birds; deer; eastern-tailed blue, hoary edge, and silver-spotted skipper butterflies.

Comments: Attractive, aggressive. Allow 18 in. in the border. Grasses hold it back in the prairie. Showiest flowers of the pea family. Illinois tick-trefoil (*D. illinoense*), native on dry soil, has white flowers and prominent stipules, is 3–6 ft. tall, and is flattened, with 3–7 jointed seedpods.

7-16-92

1"

Lespedeza capitata
Round-headed bush clover, tall lespedeza
Fabaceae (Leguminosae) (pea family)

Location: Dry and sandy prairies, loess bluffs, roadsides, and open places. Common throughout state. Sandy, well-drained, loamy soil. Mesic, dry mesic, dry. Full or partial sun. pH: Neutral-alkaline 6.5–8. Border, meadow, roadside.

Plant description: Height: 30–48 in. Blooming time: July–September. Cream/green flower has dense bristly clusters in the leaf axil. White and magenta-spotted corolla concealed by long sepals. Years before expected bloom: 2. Erect, simple, or branched stem. Many cloverlike leaves alternate, compound, nearly stalkless, hairy, each with 3 oblong leaflets. Taproots grow 5–8 ft. and appear indestructible.

Propagation: Best by seed; however, seedlings prone to damping-off.

Germination: Moderately easy. Needs stratification 33–38° F for 10 days and scarification. Inoculate with EL rhizobium. Valuable forage in pastures.

Harvest: October–November. Dried seed head attractive. Dried head is rust-colored and bushy, 3/4 × 1/2 in., containing fruit 1/2 × 3/4 in. in claw-shaped husk. Clip stem with heads into bucket. Crush fruit and separate seeds. The hulled seed is 1/16 in. and golden. Seeds per oz.: 10,000. Per lb.: 160,000. Lb. per acre: 11. Oz. per 1,000 sq. ft.: 4.4.

Attracts: Birds value the large seeds; eastern-tailed blue and hoary edge butterflies.

Comments: Vigorous and showy. Tends to decrease in numbers in undisturbed areas and is susceptible to herbicide drift. Sprouts can be grown and eaten like alfalfa or bean sprouts. Appears to lower blood cholesterol levels. Prairie bush clover (*L. leptostachya*) is rare on upland prairies and is on the endangered species list.

7-22-92

8-7-92

← 1/2" →

← 1/4" →

Pediomelum argophyllum
Silvery scurf-pea, silverleaf scurf-pea
Fabaceae (Leguminosae) (pea family)

Location: Dry uplands of western tallgrass prairies, loess bluffs. Common northwest and north-central, frequent southwest and south-central, rare northeast. Sandy-loam, well-drained soil. Dry mesic, dry. Full sun. pH: Neutral 6.5–7.5. Border, meadow.

Plant description: Height: 2–3 ft. Blooming time: June–July. Blue-whorled flowers on stalks from the axil of the upper leaves. 1–5 whorls on each stalk with 2–8 small flowers in each whorl, each 1/8 × 1/3 in. Few flowers are produced. Years before expected bloom: 2–3. The stem and leaves are the outstanding part of the plant. Compound, palmately divided into 3–5 short-stalked elliptic leaflets each 3/4 × 2 in. long, covered with soft whitish hairs, giving a silvery appearance. Very downy. Leaves are alternate and have about a 1-in. stalk. Woody taproot spreading from creeping rhizomes and root buds, growing from a caudex.

Propagation: By seed or by division of creeping rhizomes in the spring.

Germination: Easy. Needs stratification 33–38° F for 10 days and scarification. Inoculant not available.

Harvest: August, when the leaves are fading and the seeds are still present. By September the total plant aboveground is gone. Silky-ovate pod has only 1 seed, unusual for a legume. Clip stem into bucket. Remove seeds from pod when dry. Individual seed triangular, flat, reddish, 1/16 in. Seeds per oz.: 9,000. Per lb.: 144,000. Lb. per acre: 12. Oz. per 1,000 sq. ft.: 4.8.

Comments: Often found with little bluestem. Poisonous to cattle. Scurf-pea (*Psoralidium tenuiflora*) has smaller leaves that are not downy. Prairie turnip or prairie potato (*Pediomelum esculentum*) roots were eaten by pioneers.

6-15-92

Vicia americana
Vetch, American vetch, purple vetch
Fabaceae (Leguminosae) (pea family)

Location: Prairie remnants, loess bluffs, roadsides. Frequent to common in northern half of state, infrequent to rare southern half. Average loam. Wet mesic, mesic. Full sun. pH: Neutral 6.5–7. Border, meadow, roadside.

Plant description: Height: 15–30 in. Blooming time: May–August. Purple pealike flower in loose clusters of 3–9 flowers with 2 lips or lobes, the upper lip shorter, 10 stamens (9 forming a tube on the upper side and the 10th free in the opening). Years before expected bloom: 2–3. Delicate plant with slender, weak-smooth stems. 8–16 compound opposite leaves with tendril as terminal "leaf." Leaflets are oval and smooth; about 1 × 1/2 in.

Propagation: By seed.

Germination: Inoculate seed.

Harvest: July–September. Pea-pod. Strip from plant when pod feels full. Remove seed from smooth pod when dry. Individual seed round, dark, firm. Seeds per oz.: 5,000. Per lb.: 80,000. Lb. per acre: 24. Oz. per 1,000 sq. ft.: 9.5.

Attracts: Birds, deer, and orange sulphur butterflies.

Comments: A larger variety, hairy vetch (*V. villosa*), an alien, with more flowers and hairy stems, is found more commonly along the roadsides.

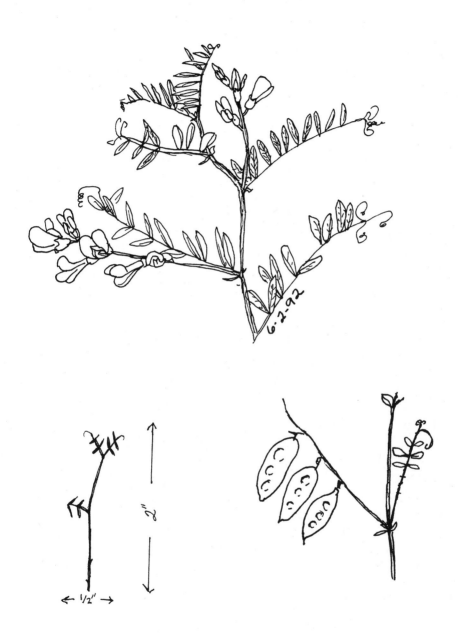

6.2.92

2"

← 1/2" →

179

Gentiana andrewsii
Bottle gentian, closed gentian, blind gentian, cloistered heart
Gentianaceae (gentian family)

Location: Wet prairies. Frequent in the north and east. Sandy loam rich in humus. Wet mesic, mesic. Full to partial sun. pH: Acidic-neutral 5–7.5. Border, meadow, roadside.

Plant description: Height: 18–30 in. Blooming time: September–October. Deep blue, cylindrical flower, nearly closed at top. 1 1/2 in. long, whitish plaits between the 5 corolla lobes are slightly larger than petals. Possibly self-fertile. Years before expected bloom: 3–4. Leaves whorled below flower cluster, opposite on lower stem. Smooth, 4-in. ovate or lanceolate.

Propagation: Best by seed, difficult. Slow, with only 1 leaf the first year, but faster thereafter. Try repeated plantings on location over several years. Can also be divided.

Germination: Delicate; needs protection such as a cold frame or shade the first year. Fine seeds, plant on surface. Mix 2 parts sawdust to 1 part fine clean sand and cover with 1/4-in. milled sphagnum moss. Add sand to the soil when set out and keep soil moist.

Harvest: Late October–early November. Husks become tan and papery, 2 × 3/8 in. Clip from stem. Turn husk upside down and shake tiny, fine, numerous seeds out. 1/16-in. light tan seed. Seeds per oz.: 227,000. Per lb.: 3,632,000. Lb. per acre: 1. Oz. per 1,000 sq. ft.: 0.4.

Attracts: Bees and bumblebees force their way into the closed flower to cross-pollinate.

Comments: Rock garden species. There are other erect, vaselike species of gentians worth propagating: fringed gentian (*Gentianopsis crinita*), pale gentian (*Gentiana alba* or *G. flavida*), downy gentian (*G. puberulenta* or *G. puberula*), and stiff gentian (*Gentianella quinquefolia*). Soapwort gentian (*Gentiana billingtonii* or *G. saponaria*) is similar to closed gentian but opens slightly. Bottle gentian and pale gentian are the easiest, with the other three being difficult. Fringed gentian and stiff gentian are biennials. Prairie gentian (*Eustoma grandiflorum*) is an annual.

←⅓"→ ←1⅓"→

9-892

Hypericum punctatum
Spotted St. John's wort
Hypericaceae (St. John's wort family)

Location: Open woods, prairie remnants. Frequent to common east and south. Loam. Wet mesic, mesic. Full to partial sun. pH: Acidic-neutral 5.5–7. Border, meadow, roadside.

Plant description: Height: 2–5 ft. Blooming time: July–August. Yellow 2-in. beautiful flower with very bushy stamens, 5 petals and 5 styles spreading from the base. Flower dotted with black glands. Most species have 3 styles. Opposite, sessile, toothless, elliptic leaves are 2–3 in. and also spotted with black glands. Rhizomes.

Propagation: By seed.

Germination: Fine seeds, plant on the surface. Needs stratification 33–38° F for 30 days.

Harvest: September–October. Dried seedpod attractive. Clip stem into bucket. Separate seeds from chaff. Small black seeds resemble pepper. Seeds per oz.: 200,000. Per lb.: 3,200,000. Lb. per acre: 1. Oz. per 1,000 sq. ft.: 0.4.

Comments: The name came from the legend that the bloodlike spots on the leaves appeared immediately after St. John was beheaded. It was smoked to ward off evil spirits on the eve of St. John's Day (June 24). Some authors place in Guttiferae. Eilers lists 11 *Hypericum* species. Giant St. John's wort (*H. pyramidatum*), a native, grows in marshes and on riverbanks, and shrubby St. John's wort (*H. prolificum* or *H. spathulatum*), a native, is found in the southeast on rocky streambanks and pastures. Common St. John's wort (*H. perforatum*), an alien, and round-fruited St. John's wort (*H. sphaerocarpum*), a native, are found in dry disturbed sites.

Monarda fistulosa
Wild bergamot, purple monarda, horsemint
Lamiaceae (Labiatae) (mint family)

Location: Dry fields, prairies, roadsides. Widely distributed. Common throughout state. Tolerant to wide range of soil, even clay. Wet mesic, mesic, dry mesic, dry. Full sun. pH: Acidic-neutral 5–7.5. Meadow, roadside.

Plant description: Height: 2–4 ft. Blooming time: July–August. Lavender, dense, rounded cluster of tubular irregular flowers. Each head on a single stem. 2-lobed upper lip and broader 3-lobed lower lip, 2 stamens projecting. Bracts under flower cluster are pink-tinged. Years before expected bloom: 1–2. Good cut flower. Dried flower is intricate. Square stem as in mint family, fuzzy. Opposite, 2 1/2 in. long, gray, hairy-green, lanceolate, coarsely toothed. Leaves are aromatic and used for tea. Roots form clumps from rhizomes.

Propagation: Easy by seed, division in spring, or cuttings of rhizomes in summer to be planted 1 in. deep. Avoid fall division because winter kill is likely.

Germination: No treatment needed. Slow. Allow roots to fill container before transplanting. Plant in fall or spring when soil is cool. Pinch out tops of plant.

Harvest: October. Head resembles wasp's nest. Clusters radiate outward from central point. Nice aroma. Fruit 3/4 × 5/8 in., tan and soft. Clip from plant into bucket. Shake fruit into paper bag. Individual seed 1/16 in., small, hard, black long oval (elliptical nutlet). Seeds per oz.: 78,000. Per lb.: 1,248,000. Lb. per acre: 2.5. Oz. per 1,000 sq. ft.: 1.

Attracts: Hummingbirds, birds, clear-wing sphinx moths, and many butterflies.

Comments: Vigorous and showy. Clumps can be encouraged by mulching. Needs competition to avoid aggressive spreading in landscapes. Oswego tea or bee-balm (*M. didyma*) has crimson flowers, and spotted horsemint (*M. punctata*) is an aggressive biennial.

Pycnanthemum virginianum
Common mountain mint, Virginia mountain mint
Lamiaceae (Labiatae) (mint family)

Location: Prairies, along railroads, roadsides. Common eastern 2/3 and infrequent to rare in west. Loam. Wet, wet mesic, mesic. Full or partial sun. pH: Acidic-neutral 5–7. Border, meadow, roadside.

Plant description: Height: 20–36 in. Blooming time: July–August. White flower with purple spots of heavy clusters with terminal flowers about 1 in. across, numerous and small; lipped corollas. Not showy. Aromatic. Good cut flower. Square stems of the mint family, freely branched. Narrow leaves, lance-shaped. Stolons become horizontal, branching underground.

Propagation: Best by cuttings and division in spring. Divide every 3–5 years.

Germination: Difficult and slow, but hardy once established. No treatment needed. Pinch off tops of young plants to make them more sturdy.

Harvest: October. Fruit produced only in heads where calyx/corolla remains open. The dense head of small calyx tubes is borne on the end of opposite gray-colored branches curving upward. Head pulls off. Strip with gloved hand from the stem. Easily recognized by its deep blue fruit and strong aroma. Fruit 1/2 × 1/2 in. Shake seeds in a paper bag and sieve. Tiny black seeds. Seeds per oz.: 284,000. Per lb.: 4,544,000. Lb. per acre: 1. Oz. per 1,000 sq. ft.: 0.4.

Attracts: Butterflies.

Comments: Can be invasive but not aggressive. Good backdrop for butterfly weed, cardinal flower, or pale beardtongue. Makes an aromatic tea. Slender or narrow-leaved mountain mint (*P. tenuifolium* or *P. flexuosum*) has extremely narrow leaves, grows in drier soil, and blooms August–September.

7-16-92

1/2"

←1/3"→

Sphaeralcea coccinea
Scarlet mallow, globe mallow
Malvaceae (mallow family)

Location: Dry sandy plains and loess prairies. Rare east. Restricted to sandy soil. Dry mesic, dry. Full sun. pH: Neutral 6–7.5. Border, meadow.

Plant description: Height: 6–12 in. Blooming time: July–August. Red, short, clustered, leafy racemes red/salmon with creamy yellow stamen columns. Petals 3/4 in. in length. Nice fragrance. Years before expected bloom: 2. Blooms over a long period. Alternate, creeping, starlike, palmately lobed, branching leaves with hairs giving the plant a grayish appearance. Develops a deep-growing divided taproot.

Propagation: Seed, with best results when seeds are sown outdoors in fall. Also by transplant in an early spring planting. Division is difficult. Spreads by creeping roots from the thickened taproot. Mature plants can spread to cover 3–4 ft. of ground.

Germination: Plant in fall or early spring with stratification 33–38° F for 30 days.

Harvest: September–October. Clip capsule from stem. Shake seeds out. Fruit is a spherical capsule with 10 or more densely hairy carpels containing 1 seed. Dark, hard, crescent-shaped seed. The case around it breaks off into 2 clear, plasticlike pieces. Store seeds with 3 in. of no-pest strip. Seeds per oz.: 6,000. Per lb.: 96,000. Lb. per acre: 20. Oz. per 1,000 sq. ft.: 8.

Attracts: Painted lady and common checkered skipper butterflies.

7-18-92

3/4" 1/2"

Mirabilis nyctaginea
Wild four-o'clock, umbrellawort
Nyctaginaceae (four o'clock family)

Location: Dry sandy or gravelly soil, roadsides, along railroads. Common throughout state. Average loam. Mesic, dry mesic. Full to partial sun. pH: Neutral 6–7. Meadow, roadside.

Plant description: Height: 1–5 ft. Blooming time: June–September. Pink or purple bell-shaped flower with 5-lobed green bracts up to 3/8 in. across facing upward in tight, flat-topped terminal clusters, arising from the leaf axil. No true petals, 5 showy sepals open in the afternoon, giving color. Years before expected bloom: 1. Nearly smooth, reddish, squarish stems are profusely forked especially near the top. Opposite leaves, heart-shaped, with smooth margins and short petioles. Upper leaves are smaller. Fibrous roots.

Propagation: Seed.

Germination: Easy. No treatment needed.

Harvest: July–September. Fruit found in a star-shaped umbrella husk-type covering hanging down from the axil on a stem. Hairy capsule contains nutlets. Pull from plant. Seeds easily removed from husk. Individual seed firm, dark, 5-ribbed, 1/6 in. long. Seeds per oz.: 6,500. Per lb.: 104,000. Lb. per acre: 15. Oz. per 1,000 sq. ft.: 6.

Attracts: Butterflies.

Comments: Aggressive for the border.

5-sided
fuzzy seed

2 seeds in each 5-star husk

Gaura biennis
Gaura
Onagraceae (evening primrose family)

Location: Prairie remnants, open woods, sandy areas, roadsides. Frequent to common southern half, infrequent to rare northeast quarter, rare northwest. Sandy soils. Wet mesic, mesic, dry mesic, dry. Full to partial sun. Meadow, roadside.

Plant description: Height: 3–7 ft. Blooming time: June–October. Pink and white downy cluster of small flowers. The petals do not go all the way around the flower. 8 stamens protruding, 4 petals with a cross-shaped stigma on the pistil. The long-tube flowers bloom 2 or 3 at a time in clusters on long wandlike spikes. Years before expected bloom: 2. Panicle arrangement of many-branched stems. Rough stem. Leaves alternate, broadly lanceolate, lightly toothed. Taproot.

Propagation: Seed. This is a biennial, as the name indicates.

Germination: Needs stratification 33–38° F for 30 days.

Harvest: October. Podlike 4-sided fruit 1/8 × 1/4 in., attached individually to main stem. Tan pod is closed and hard. Strip from stem. Similar to a nut, difficult to open, 2 seeds inside. Individual seed light gold, round, small. Seeds per oz.: 10,000. Per lb.: 160,000. Lb. per acre: 10. Oz. per 1,000 sq. ft.: 4.

Comments: Scarlet gaura (*G. coccinea*), a western species found frequently in the Loess Hills and all counties on the western border, is a native with flowers that turn from white to pink to deep scarlet. *G. parviflora*, found infrequently in Loess Hills, grows on crests of loess bluffs and on dry, upland prairies.

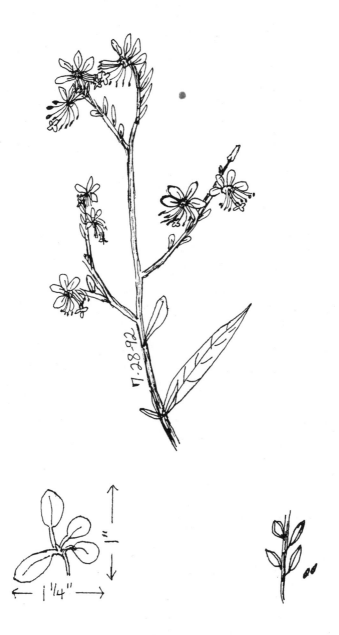

7.28.72

1"

1 ¼"

193

Oenothera pilosella
Prairie sundrops, tooth-leaved primrose, small primrose, sundrops
Onagraceae (evening primrose family)

Location: Dry hilly prairies, open sandy soil, margins of fens. Infrequent in east. Sandy soil. Dry. Full sun. pH: Acidic-neutral 5.5–6.8. Border, meadow, roadside.

Plant description: Height: 16–30 in. Blooming time: July–August. Yellow flower, 4 petals with wrinkled appearance. Stigmas are simple, unlike the 4-lobed stigmas in other of the oenothera genera. Years before expected bloom: 1–2. Good cut flower. Smooth reddish stem; narrow, serrate, alternate leaves.

Propagation: Easy by seed, cuttings in summer, or division in early spring.

Germination: Needs stratification 33–38° F for 30 days.

Harvest: July–August before seed capsules are dispersed and lost. Break 4-sided, 1-in.-long capsule from plant. Let elongated capsule dry in paper bag. Break open and shake out seeds. Individual seed small, dark. Seeds per oz.: 78,000. Per lb.: 1,248,000. Lb. per acre: 2.5. Oz. per 1,000 sq. ft.: 1.

Comments: Rock garden plant. Delicate flower, pretty in border at front. Evening primrose (*O. biennis*) is a native, weedy biennial but has a pretty flower June–September; seen along roadsides and in waste places growing up to 6 ft. tall. It attracts ground beetles, a beneficial beetle that eats moths and maggots. Ragged evening primrose (*O. laciniata*) is also under 2 ft., an annual found frequently in sandy soil. Gray evening primrose (*O. villosa*) is a biennial, 2–3 ft., growing in moist to dry prairies and common throughout state.

7-9-92

← 1/4" → ← 1/4" →

''

Oenothera rhombipetala
Sand primrose, small-flowered primrose, four-point evening primrose
Onagraceae (evening primrose family)

Location: Disturbed sites, roadsides, and low, rolling sandhills. Frequent east, infrequent to rare central and south-central. Sandy soil. Dry. Full sun. pH: Acidic-neutral 5–7.5. Border, meadow, roadside.

Plant description: Height: 16–40 in. Blooming time: June–September. Yellow flower on a crowded pyramidal spike 4–10 in. long at top of stem, roughly diamond-shaped (rhomboidal) petals spreading flatly. Stamens are prominent and longer than style with stigmas forming a cross shape 1–2 in. across. Years before expected bloom: 1 if fall planted, 2 if spring planted. Stems erect, usually not branched; alternate leaves, linear to narrowly lanceolate with pointed tips, stalkless, 1–3 in. long. Taproot.

Propagation: By seed. A biennial or winter annual.

Germination: Needs stratification 33–38° F for 30 days when spring planted.

Harvest: September. Clip stem. Remove pods from stem, break open pods, and shake out seeds. Small, rust-colored, tear-shaped seeds. Seeds per oz.: 102,000. Per lb.: 1,632,000. Lb. per acre: 2.4. Oz. per 1,000 sq. ft.: 0.9.

Comments: One of the first plants to reclaim sandy soils in the sandhills when the center-pivot irrigation systems are abandoned. Also, evening primrose (*O. biennis*) is weedy, but delicate bloom is staple food for goldfinches.

7-2-92

dk gold

Phlox pilosa
Prairie phlox, downy phlox
Polemoniaceae (phlox family)

Location: Prairie remnants, open sandy plains, moist ditch bottoms. Common throughout state. Sandy-loam soil. Wet mesic, mesic, dry mesic, dry. Full or partial sun. pH: Acidic-neutral 3.5–6.8. Border, meadow, roadside.
Plant description: Height: 1–2 ft. Blooming time: May–June. White, lavender, and rose terminal clusters, 3/4-in. round-lobed flower, 5 petals with elongated trumpet (corolla tube). Enclosed 5 stamens and 3 styles. Years before expected bloom: 1–2. Good cut and dried flower. Erect with slender, very hairy stems. Sharply tapered narrow leaves covered with soft hair. Diffuse and fibrous taproot with no basal runners.
Propagation: By seed, but best by division in the spring or 6-in. stem cuttings in late spring. Tops will wilt on stem cuttings. Plant in permanent location in the late summer. Set crowns at soil level 1 ft. apart.
Germination: Plant fresh seeds when collected or in the fall. Seeds lose viability the second year in storage. Benefits from stratification 33–38° F for 7 days.
Harvest time: June, before seeds are forcibly ejected from pod upon drying. Tan pod breaks open into 3 sections. Keep in a paper bag; seeds will break out of pod when dry. 1/8-in., slightly oval, black-hard seed. Seeds per oz.: 10,000. Per lb.: 160,000. Lb. per acre: 11. Oz. per 1,000 sq. ft.: 4.4.
Attracts: Hummingbirds, deer, monarchs and other butterflies, and hawkmoths.
Comments: Rock garden species. Mulch and deadhead to prolong bloom. Will dry back to its roots in dry summers but reappear in spring. Similar species: Dame's rocket (*Hesperis matronalis*), alien, is larger with 4 petals. Garden phlox (*P. paniculata*), alien, is stouter with wider and more veiny leaves. Wild sweet William (*P. maculata*) native of moist prairies in northeast Iowa with purple-spotted stems and long corolla tubes. Sweet William (*P. divaricata*) native of woodlands.

5-20-92

Dodecatheon meadia

Shooting star, midland shooting star, bird's bills, prairie pointer, American cowslip

Primulaceae (primrose family)

Location: Moist to dry, light, sandy prairies, open upland wooded bluffs. Found in eastern areas. Sandy loam. Wet mesic, mesic, dry mesic. Full to partial sun. pH: Neutral-alkaline 6–8. Border, meadow.

Plant description: Height: 8–24 in. Blooming time: late May. White or lavender flower nodding with 5 strongly backward pointing petals, 5 yellow protruding stamens that join to form a pointed beak. Flower on single stem, turns upward as fruit matures. Years before expected bloom: 3–4, slow to establish. Basal, rosette of elongated leaves. The foliage disappears in summer.

Propagation: By seed, best by division in July, or root cuttings in early spring or fall. Seed growth is so slow seedling cannot be handled until the third or fourth year. Young plants grow in the spring for a short time but become dormant in July. Chilling young plants for 10 days at 35° F in July before replanting increases growth the next spring. Label location since the plant is invisible from July until spring. Mulch bed the first winter.

Germination: Plant fresh seeds in the fall. Fine seeds, plant on the surface. Needs stratification 33–38° F for 60 days if planted in spring.

Harvest: July–August. Dried seedpod attractive. Wait until pod is firm and dry; pod breaks off. Shake seeds from pod that has opened at the top. Tiny, hard, rust-colored seed. Seeds per oz.: 75,000. Per lb.: 1,200,000. Lb. per acre: 2.5. Oz. per 1,000 sq. ft.: 1.

Attracts: Bees.

Comments: Likes small companions. Rock garden plant. Abundant when prairies were sensitive to spring fires. Now the species is scarce and should not be picked even though it is a good cut flower. Amethyst or jeweled shooting star (*D. amethystinum*) has a violet flower and grows in limestone, sandstone cliffs and ledges.

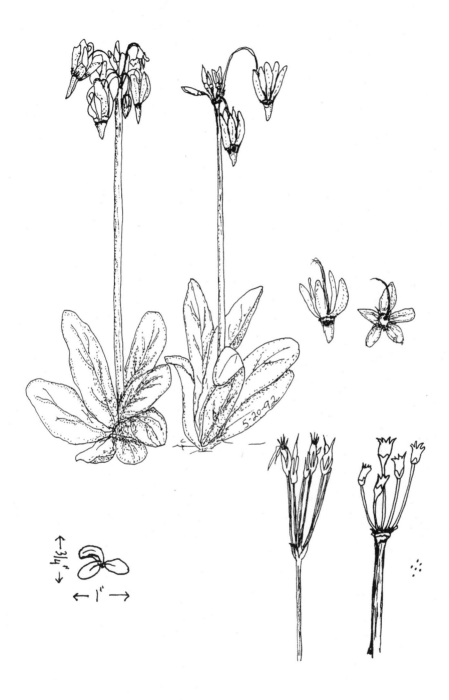

5-20-72

↑
3/4"
↓

← 1" →

Anemone canadensis

Canada anemone, Canada windflower, meadow anemone

Ranunculaceae (buttercup family)

Location: Low-lying areas, cool prairies, roadsides, alluvium. Frequent extreme east and south-central, common elsewhere. Humus soil. Wet mesic, mesic. Full to partial sun. pH: Acidic-neutral 5.5–7. Border, meadow, roadside.

Plant description: Height: 1–2 ft. Blooming time: May–June. White, 5 broad petallike sepals 1–1 1/2 in., petals absent, rich yellow stamens numerous, pistils yellow. Single flower on a stalk. Years before expected bloom: 2. Palmately 3-cleft leaves parted with whorled segments. The sessile leaves surround the stem. Rhizome, thick and fleshy, grows horizontally underground with buds on the top and roots on the bottom.

Propagation: Sow seeds as soon as ripe in spring. Colonies form quickly. One of the easiest to grow. Also by division in the spring or stem cuttings in the fall. Spreads by underground roots.

Germination: No treatment needed.

Harvest: July–August. Seeds begin dropping during this period. Clip stem when seeds turn dark. Seed head 1/3-in. round ball with spikes. Seeds easily crumble off the head when ripe. Individual seed flat, 1/4 in., dark rust, with hairy protruding tip. Seeds per oz.: 6,000. Per lb.: 96,000. Lb. per acre: 20. Oz. per 1,000 sq. ft.: 8.

Attracts: Bees.

Comments: Rock garden plant. Excellent ground cover but can crowd out other flowers in the border; quite invasive. Confine it with a 6-in. metal or plastic can open on both ends buried at soil surface.

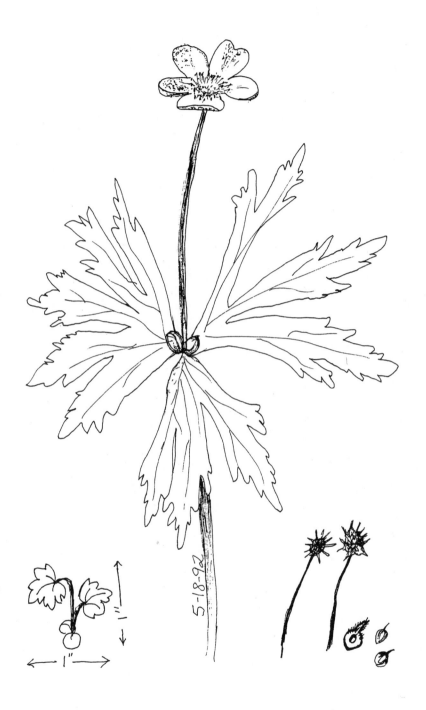

5-18-92

1"

Anemone cylindrica
Windflower, thimbleweed, candle anemone, long-headed thimbleweed
Ranunculaceae (buttercup family)

Location: Dry sandy prairies, loess bluffs. Common in most of state except southeast. Calcareous soil rich in humus. Mesic, dry mesic, dry. Full or partial sun. pH: Wide range 5.5–8. Border, meadow, roadside.

Plant description: Height: 2–3 ft. Blooming time: June–August. White flower, 5–9 petallike sepals 1 in. wide. Petals absent. Numerous stamens and pistils. Single flower on long erect stem. Years before expected bloom: 2. Harvest early for dried flowers. Single flower on stem, smooth, 8 in. from petals. Leaves are in a whorl at the base, palmately divided. Stem bulges at the nodes. Leaves deeply toothed, 3–10 leaves on a stem, compound leaves with 3 parts, wedge-shaped to oblong with lobed segments. Rhizomes.

Propagation: Easy by seed; older plants can be divided.

Germination: No treatment needed. Plant in fall or early April when soil is cool. In spring stratify 33–38° F for 60 days.

Harvest: October. Cottonlike fluffy covered seeds, attached upright in a spiral on top 1/2 × 1 1/2 in. hard, narrow receptacle. Strip off when pulled up the stem with fingers. Dark gray seed with tiny hook inside light gray fluffy material. Seeds per oz.: 35,000. Per lb.: 560,000. Lb. per acre: 5. Oz. per 1,000 sq. ft.: 2.

Attracts: Hummingbirds select cotton from fruit for nesting material.

Comments: Likes small companions. Vigorous and showy.

last years dried leaf

Last years Thimbleweed

new leaf

5-15-92

6-26-92

2"

⅛"

Delphinium virescens
Prairie larkspur
Ranunculaceae (buttercup family)

Location: Dry upland prairies. Infrequent south-central, rare southeast, frequent to common elsewhere. Average loam to sandy, well-drained soil. Mesic, dry mesic, dry. Full sun. pH: Neutral 6.5–7. Border, meadow, roadside.

Plant description: Height: 20–48 in. Blooming time: June. Blue-white spurred, narrow cluster with 1-in. flower, 4 inconspicuous petals. Flower on spike above leaves. Spur on flower gives it the name "larkspur." Good cut and dried flower. Downy stalk with alternate leaves, erect or clustered. Palmately divided with narrow leaf segments 1/4 in. wide. Fibrous roots.

Propagation: Seed is best, also by division in early spring or fall.

Germination: Easy to moderately difficult. No treatment needed. Plant in fall or early spring. Germinates best in cool weather. Benefits from stratification 33–38° F for 60 days when planted in the spring. Damping-off occurs if soil holds excessive moisture.

Harvest: July–August. Plant dries after seeds have formed. Collect before seeds are lost. The seed head dries for pretty winter arrangements. Triple seedpod, papery-tan, 3/4 in. long that splits open along a single seam, leaving an opening in the top. Turn upside down and shake from pod. Individual seed 1/8 in., irregular, black. Seeds per oz.: 30,000. Per lb.: 480,000. Lb. per acre: 6. Oz. per 1,000 sq. ft.: 2.4.

Attracts: Hummingbirds.

Comments: Cut back to basal foliage in midsummer for additional bloom. Mature plants sometimes disappear in hot weather, then reappear in cool weather. All parts of fresh plants are poisonous, except to sheep.

6-12-92

← 1" →

1"

Pulsatilla patens
Pasque flower, windflower, Easter flower, wild crocus, lion's beard, goslin weed
Ranunculaceae (buttercup family)

Location: Dry rocky prairies to upland prairies, loess bluffs, prairie knolls. Common to frequent in northern half of state. Rich humus, well-drained, to sandy loam soil. Dry mesic, dry. Full or partial sun. pH: Acidic-neutral 5.5–7.5. Border, meadow.

Plant description: Height: 6–16 in. Blooming time: March–April (Easter). White-lavender solitary flower, 2 1/2 in. wide, 5–7 petallike sepals, petals absent. Stamens and pistils numerous, with long styles. Flower appears before the leaf, sometimes following a snowstorm. Years before expected bloom: 2–3. Numerous soft hairs on stem with leaves whorled about 1 in. below flower. The delicate leaves, deeply cut, palmately finely divided into linear segments, give a fernlike appearance after the plant has flowered. Thick horizontal rootstock, fibrous with good regenerating ability. Buds can send up new shoots if the plant is damaged.

Propagation: By seed as soon as it is ripe in spring. Also by division in fall or root cuttings several inches long in late summer. Shallow planting is best for cuttings.

Germination: No treatment necessary. Plant fresh seeds in fall. Slow, so cover fresh seed with sand in flats and keep moist. Most growth in spring or fall; dormant in summer.

Harvest: May. Do not wait too long to collect, as they disappear early. Multiple seeds on head have long feathery plumes which pull off easily. Plume 1 in. or longer attached to each seed. Seeds per oz.: 18,000. Per lb.: 288,000. Lb. per acre: 8. Oz. per 1,000 sq. ft.: 3.2.

Comments: Announces the arrival of spring, the earliest of prairie wildflowers. Can't endure tall competition; needs small companions. Good rock garden plant. When once established, it should not be disturbed. Hairy, silky, or ghostly appearance of the plant accounts for some of the common names. Seed production is improved if the plant is protected from the wind. A delicate plant that can withstand the last snows of winter.

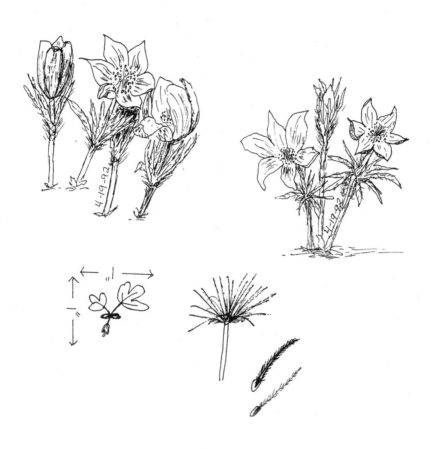

Thalictrum dasycarpum
Purple meadow-rue, maid-of-the-mist, meadow-rue
Ranunculaceae (buttercup family)

Location: Wet prairies and streambanks, roadside ditches, moist alluvium. Common throughout. Loam, high in organic matter. Wet mesic, mesic. Full or partial sun. pH: Acidic 5–6. Meadow.

Plant description: Height: 3–5 ft. Blooming time: May–June. Greenish white flower, each on its own stalk, multibranched with no true petals. 4–5 small greenish petallike sepals. Up to 20 whitish stamens dangle from flower, giving a feathery appearance to the plant. Up to 100 flowers on each plant. Male and female on separate plants. Years before expected bloom: 2. Dried flower attractive. Purple, branched stems, with lacy bluish green leaves closely resembling those of columbine. The tan stem becomes smooth and shiny in the winter. Leaves alternate, without petioles. Basal leaves in a rounded clump. Leaves divide into 3 segments and often subdivide into leaflets, each with its own stalk; tiny hairs on underside.

Propagation: By seed, plant in fall or early spring. Division in fall or early spring.

Germination: Sow in sandy soil to germinate, then transplant seedlings into loam when 1–2 in. high. Best planted in the fall. Needs stratification 33–38° F for 30 days.

Harvest: Late August–September. Dark brown fruit with leaves wilting. A very pretty and graceful fruit formation. Strips from stems. Point on tip of each firm pod is curved and sharp. Individual seed 1/4 × 1/12 in., narrow, pointed ovals with grooves, 1 brown seed in each pod. Seeds per oz.: 13,900. Per lb.: 222,400. Lb. per acre: 9.5. Oz. per 1,000 sq. ft.: 3.8.

Comments: Seeds were used as perfume by Teton Dakota and Pawnee, who mixed them with clay and rubbed them on horses' muzzles to stimulate them during long journeys.

6-14-92

← 1" →

↑
1 1/4"
↓

Ceanothus americanus
New Jersey tea
Rhamnaceae (buckthorn family)

Location: Dry upland prairies, rocky prairie hillsides, woodland edges, and roadsides. Frequent northwest, infrequent south-central, common elsewhere. Sandy soil. Mesic, dry mesic, dry. Full or partial sun. pH: Neutral 6.2–7. Border, meadow, roadside.

Plant description: Height: 18–36 in. Blooming time: June–July. White terminal oval cluster of bloom on new wood rising from leaf axils. Individual flower 1/5 in. wide, 5 petals. Years before expected bloom: 3–4. Good cut or dried flower. Leaves 1–3 in. long, 3-veined, toothed, ovate with sharp pointed end. Heavy, deeply branched taproots were given the name "rupture root" by early farmers.

Propagation: By seed is the best, also cuttings in early spring, and fall root division.

Germination: Difficult; scratch surface and soak in hot water overnight (bring water to near boiling, remove from heat, and pour over seed) and plant immediately. Seeds that sink are more likely to germinate; germination is slow. Needs stratification 33–38° F for 60–90 days.

Harvest: September–October. Seeds are thrown from plant when drying. Strip 3-lobed fruit, splitting into 3 parts from plant before seeds are lost. Remove the 3 individual seeds from receptacle. Dark brown, hard-round seed 1/8 in. Seeds per oz.: 7,000. Per lb.: 112,000. Lb. per acre: 17. Oz. per 1,000 sq. ft.: 7.

Attracts: Hummingbirds, deer, and mottled duskywing, spring azure, and Arcadian hairstreak butterflies. The subtle scent of the foliage attracts deer.

Comments: A durable small shrub once established. Makes a beautiful low hedge when planted 1–2 ft. apart. Tea was made from the leaves during the American Revolution. Gather leaves from the plant while it is in bloom, dry the leaves, and store them in an airtight container.

6-29-92

2"

←— 1½″ —→

Geum triflorum
Prairie smoke, purple avens, torchflower,
old man's whiskers, prairie avens
Rosaceae (rose family)

Location: Cool prairie remnants, roadsides. Infrequent northeast, rare northwest. Medium loam to dry, rocky soil. Wet mesic, mesic, dry mesic, dry. Full or partial sun. pH: Acidic-neutral: 5–7.5. Border, meadow.

Plant description: Height: 6–13 in. Blooming time: May. Burgundy flower, 5 oval petals erect to form a 3/4-in. cup. Narrow, linear 5 bracts alternate with 5 green sepals at the base. Years before expected bloom: 3–4. Good dried flower. Numerous, 4–9-in. compound basal leaves that are deeply cut. Pair of small leaflets halfway up the stalk. Soft hairs on stem and leaves. Rhizomes tend to form dense mats.

Propagation: Seed or rhizome division. Somewhat difficult by seed. Growth is good in early spring and during cool fall weather. Transplanting should be done in fall.

Germination: Low. No treatment is necessary but will have higher germination with stratification 33–38° F for 30 days. Plants are delicate; keep in flats the first winter.

Harvest: May–June. 2-in.-long, plumelike, grayish pink tails with hooks that stick tightly to clothing and fur. Remove plumes with feather-duster appearance with fingers. Achene with long, plumy, 2-in. grayish pink tails. Seeds per oz.: 34,000. Per lb.: 544,000. Lb. per acre: 4.5. Oz. per 1,000 sq. ft.: 1.8.

Comments: Similar to pasque flower but a totally different family. Dense, competing grasses will crowd it out. Good ground cover, border, or rock garden plant. Yellow avens (*G. aleppicum*) grows 2–5 ft. in wet areas in northwest June–August. White avens (*G. canadense*) found in moist prairies and woods, rough avens (*G. laciniatum*) in marshes, and spring avens (*G. vernum*) in moist upland woods. All these *Geum* species are native to Iowa.

Potentilla arguta
Prairie cinquefoil, tall silvery cinquefoil, potentilla
Rosaceae (rose family)

Location: Dry to mesic prairies, sandy soils. Frequent throughout most of state. Gravelly or rocky soil. Wet mesic, mesic, dry mesic, dry. Full to partial sun. pH: Acidic-neutral 5.8–7. Border, meadow, roadside.

Plant description: Height: 12–40 in. Blooming time: July–September. Cream clusters of flowers, clammy brownish hairs, lighter in color than other cinquefoils. Years before expected bloom: 1–2. Good cut flower. Stem and leaves typical of the rose family. Upper branches are opposite, but lower branches are alternate. Erect; pinnately compound with 7–11 deeply cut leaflets. Downy below. This species does not have the radially 5-parted leaves typical of cinquefoil, from which it gets its name. Long creeping stem roots.

Propagation: Seed is best. Establishes quickly, self-sows.

Germination: Easy. Plant in fall or early spring. Likes cool soil. Fine seeds, plant on the surface. Needs stratification 33–38° F for 60 days.

Harvest: October. Break off 2 × 2-in. fruit of multiple pods close to the main stem. Soft and brown early, becoming drab brown. The top of the pod opens into 5 sections. Seeds often remain in sepals until fall or over winter. Shake seeds out of open pod. Individual pod 1/2 × 3/8 in. 1/16 in. or smaller golden hard seed. Seeds per oz.: 113,000. Per lb.: 1,808,000. Lb. per acre: 2. Oz. per 1,000 sq. ft.: 0.8.

Attracts: Purplish copper butterflies.

Comments: Vigorous and showy. Its leaves have been used for tea. The pod is very attractive. Eilers lists 13 species of *Potentilla*; 10 are native.

new leaf on 5-14-92 with remaining seedhead, brown
from last year.
new green

7-6-92

← 1/2" →

← 1/2" →

217

Rosa arkansana
Sunshine rose, prairie rose, pasture rose
Rosaceae (rose family)

Location: Dry prairies, fencerows along roadsides and railroads. Infrequent to frequent throughout state. Sandy, loam soil. Wet mesic, mesic, dry mesic, dry. Full or partial sun. pH: Acidic-neutral 4.5–7. Border, meadow, roadside.

Plant description: Height: 2–3 ft. Blooming time: June. Pink solitary flower or clusters up to 2 in., 5 broad petals, yellow stamens, 5 green sepals join to form an irregular-shaped base. State flower of Iowa. Years before expected bloom: 3–4. Good cut or dried flower. Branches have thorns; 5–7 leaflets, ovate, sharply toothed, 1 1/2 in. long. Stolons, spreading, sending up new shoots from the stolons.

Propagation: Good by seed but slow. Division in late fall or early spring. Plant root crown at surface. Greenwood cuttings in the early spring after shoots of plant emerge. Cut 6–7 in. long and plant 3 in. deep, keep moist.

Germination: Keep seeds moist. Seeds often germinate second year. Sometimes difficult to propagate. Plant fresh seeds in the fall. Needs stratification 33–38° F for 90–120 days.

Harvest: October. Hips 1/2 in. and round, turn red when ripe. Clip hips from stem. Remove seeds by soaking and scrubbing hip. Small, hard, tan seed. Seeds per oz.: 54,650. Per lb.: 874,400. Lb. per acre: 3. Oz. per 1,000 sq. ft.: 1.2.

Attracts: Bumblebees and butterflies. Birds feed on hips in winter, aiding seed dispersal.

Comments: The rose is a shrub. Rose hips are high in vitamin C. Rose petal jam: 2 c. petals, 1 c. sugar, 2–3 T. water, 2 T. lemon juice; stir until sugar melts and then add rose petals. Stir frequently. Rose petal sandwiches: Spread bread with cream cheese and rose petals. Meadow rose (*R. blanda*) has few prickles. *R. carolina* or *R. grandiflora* is native, but *R. multiflora*, which is nonnative and can become aggressive, is considered noxious.

6-2-92

3/4"

1 1/2"

2"

Spiraea alba
Meadow sweet, queen of the meadow
Rosaceae (rose family)

Location: Marshy areas, fens, and low prairies. Common northeast quarter, frequent north-central and extreme east. Rich loam. Wet, wet mesic. Full sun. pH: Neutral 6–7.5. Border, meadow.

Plant description: Height: 3–4 ft. Blooming time: June–September. White branching cluster with numerous tiny flowers, 5 petals, and delicate protruding stamens giving a fuzzy appearance. Good dried flower. *Spiraea* can be found in a single stock or with branches becoming more bushy. Has a little bit of fuzz on the stem but not on the fruits. Since this is a shrub, the stem is green under the bark, and the buds along the stem will produce new shoots in the spring. It does not die to the ground in the winter. Leaves alternate, toothed, lanceolate, about 2 in. long. Running rootstalk; aggressive.

Propagation: By seed. Can be divided. Summer cuttings of mature or green wood keep best when put under glass.

Germination: Plant fresh seeds immediately or use stratification 33–38° F for 30 days as soon as harvested.

Harvest: Fall. Clip stem. Each tiny pod is in a group of 5 segments; tips split when dried, forming 10 points on top of capsule. Remove seeds from capsule by shaking. Long, narrow seed tapers toward the end. Seeds per oz.: 9,000. Per lb.: 144,000. Lb. per acre: 12. Oz. per 1,000 sq. ft.: 4.8.

Comments: A shrub with brown twigs.

← 3/4" →

← 1¼" →

Heuchera richardsonii
Alumroot, prairie alumroot, coral bells
Saxifragaceae (saxifrage family)

Location: Prairies, open rocky woods, limestone bluffs. Common northeast and southwest, infrequent to frequent elsewhere. Average garden loam, well-drained. Wet mesic, mesic, dry mesic, dry. Full sun is best or partial sun. pH: Acidic-neutral 5.5–7. Border, meadow.

Plant description: Height: 1–3 ft. Blooming time: May–June. Greenish white small flower 1/4–1/2 in. on spike, unequal, drooping, bell-shaped. Years before expected bloom: 2. Good cut or dried flower. Long-stemmed basal leaves; very hairy leaf stalk and under leaf surface. The leaf is the outstanding feature of the plant; maple- or geranium-shaped. Leaves develop bronze or burgundy cast in summer.

Propagation: Seed or division in spring, fall, or after flowering. Also by stem cuttings close to the crown in summer. Divide every third year; each crown contains several well-formed roots. Sowing too many seeds can lead to damping-off.

Germination: Moderately easy. Growth is slow the first month, then faster the next 3–4 weeks. Plant fresh seeds in the fall. Fine seeds; plant on surface.

Harvest: Late June–July. Clip stem with clusters of 1/8-in., light tan oval capsules protruding slightly from papery calyx. Crush pod with hard object to remove. Air dry 3–4 days. Individual seed tiny, black fleck the size of pepper. Seeds per oz.: 800,000. Per lb.: 12,800,000. Lb. per acre: 0.25. Oz. per 1,000 sq. ft.: 0.1.

Attracts: Hummingbirds.

Comments: Rock garden plant. Flower not showy but leaves make a nice ground cover in the border. *H. americana*, a native found rarely in southeast Iowa, has beautiful purple-red foliage.

5-26-92

Pedicularis canadensis
Lousewort, wood betony
Scrophulariaceae (figwort or snapdragon family)

Location: Marshes, fens, prairie swales, wet sand. Infrequent to rare west, frequent to common elsewhere. Sandy or thin soil. Mesic, dry mesic, dry. Full or partial sun. pH: Acidic-neutral 5–7.5. Border, meadow, roadside.

Plant description: Height: 4–18 in. Blooming time: May–June. Yellow, tubular, 2-lipped, 3/4-in. flower in short, dense, terminal cluster. Upper lip arched with 2 small teeth and shorter 3-lobed lower lip. Years before expected bloom: 2. A hairy plant with leaflike bracts present beneath flowers. Leaves 3–5 in. long, mostly basal, lanceolate-oblong, deeply divided into toothed lobes. Fibrous roots.

Propagation: By seed or division.

Germination: Needs stratification 33–38° F for 30 days. Parasitic species, needs a host plant. Low-growing grasses are good hosts. Place a knife in the soil next to the grass 2 in. deep and sow seeds 3/8 in. deep in this area, transplant grass to area, or sow grass seed when seed is sown.

Harvest: June. Pods form on upright stem. Clip stem into bucket and store in paper bag. Turn stem with pod upside down and shake. Individual seed brown, elliptical, 1/16 in. Seeds per oz.: 78,000. Per lb.: 1,248,000. Lb. per acre: 2.5. Oz. per 1,000 sq. ft.: 1.

Comments: It was thought to keep animals free of lice. Swamp lousewort (*P. lanceolata*) is found in wet places in the northeast quarter of the state and upper northwest.

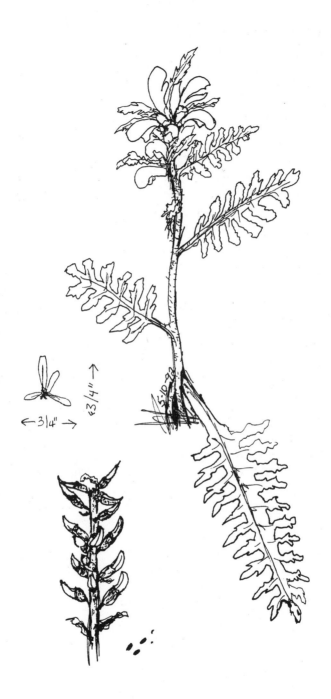

←3/4"→

←3/4"→

Penstemon grandiflorus
Large-flowered beardtongue, large-leaved penstemon
Scrophulariaceae (figwort or snapdragon family)

Location: Sandy soil, loess bluffs, dry slopes. Frequent to common in Loess Hills and sandy areas of east. Sandy, medium soil. Dry mesic, dry. Full sun. pH: Acidic-neutral 5–7.5. Border, meadow.

Plant description: Height: 24–40 in. Blooming time: May–June. Large 2-in. lilac to blue flower with a waxy look in terminal clusters, 2-lipped, with 2 lobes above and 3 below. Years before expected bloom: 2. Good cut flower. Stout, smooth stem with thick, broad, roundish, toothless, clasping, opposite leaves.

Propagation: Seed.

Germination: Needs stratification 33–38° F for 30 days. Difficult to establish from seeds but self-sows once established.

Harvest: August–September. Attractive dried seedpod. Capsule has 4 curved horns at tips. Clip stem into bucket or paper bag. Shake seeds from open capsule. Capsule may have to be crushed with rolling pin. Dark tan, oblong, flat seed. Seeds per oz.: 11,000. Per lb.: 176,000. Lb. per acre: 9. Oz. per 1,000 sq. ft.: 4.

Attracts: Hummingbirds.

Comments: Excellent garden plant. Other prairie species are foxglove penstemon (*P. digitalis*), frequent southeast on sandy prairies and roadsides with pretty white blooms but not as showy. White-flowered beardtongue (*P. gracilis*) rare in west-central and northwest, in mid-spring has 1–2-ft. plants, making a nice rock garden addition.

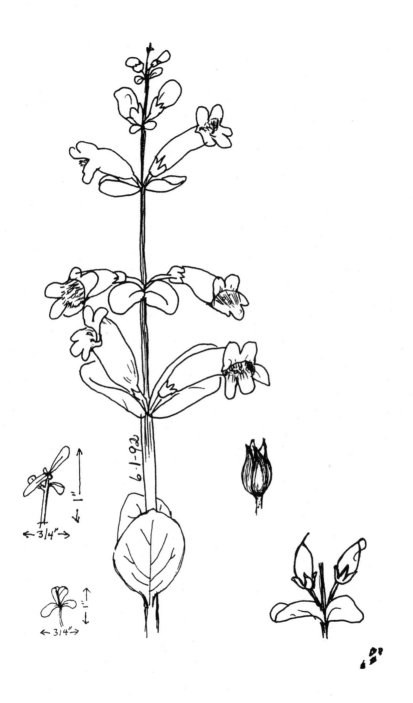

6-1-92

←3/4"→

←3/4"→

Penstemon pallidus
Pale beardtongue
Scrophulariaceae (figwort or snapdragon family)

Location: Eastern tallgrass prairies on roadsides and disturbed fields. Frequent southeast. Sandy soil. Dry mesic, dry. Full or partial sun. pH: Acidic-neutral 5.5–7. Border, meadow, roadside.

Plant description: Height: 8–36 in. Blooming time: June–July. Cream flower with faint purple lines inside. Up to 20 flowers arranged in a loose panicle, upper 2-lobed lip, lower 3-cleft lip, tufted sterile stamen. Attractive cut flower. Downy stem with sessile leaves; basal leaves have petioles; leathery and hairy, opposite, 1/2 in. wide. Fibrous roots.

Propagation: Seed.

Germination: Needs stratification 33–38° F for 30 days. Difficult to establish from seeds but self-sows once established.

Harvest: August. Attractive dried seedpod. Clip stalk with small capsules, 4 curved horns at tip, shake into bucket or paper bag. Crush capsule with rolling pin when dry and shake numerous seeds out. Small, dark seed. Seeds per oz.: 200,000. Per lb.: 3,200,000. Lb. per acre: 1. Oz. per 1,000 sq. ft.: 0.4.

Attracts: Bees and hummingbirds.

Comments: About 15 species of penstemons are found on the Great Plains. Eilers lists 7 natives of Iowa, but the others are quite rare.

← 3/4" →

229

Veronicastrum virginicum
Culver's root, Bowman's root, physic root
Scrophulariaceae (figwort or snapdragon family)

Location: Wet meadows, disturbed areas, woodland borders. Often found in colonies. Infrequent northwest, common elsewhere. Prefers loam with humus. Wet mesic, mesic, dry mesic. Full or partial sun. pH: Acidic to neutral 4.5–7. Border, meadow, roadside.

Plant description: Height: 3–7 ft. Blooming time: July–August. White or lavender flower resembling a white candelabra; beautiful spikes with 4-lobe trumpet-shaped flower and 2 brown stamens protruding. Spikes in an umbel. Years before expected bloom: 3–5 from seed, 1 from rootstock. Attractive cut flower. Erect over whorled leaves of 3–7 with whorls larger at the base. Lower leaves are opposite. Unbranched stems. Leaves 2–6 in. long, lanceolate, sharply toothed. The terminal bud of a segment produces the foliar-flowering shoot. Extensive yellow fibrous roots. Horizontal rhizomes have a root life of only 3 years.

Propagation: By seed, difficult to germinate but spreads reasonably well under natural conditions. Root division in fall is best when plants are dormant, planting buds of rootstalk on soil surface 1 ft. apart. By cuttings in summer, to be planted in fall. Plants stay small the first year.

Germination: Start outdoors. Fine seeds, plant on surface. Seeds need light to germinate.

Harvest: October. Attractive dried seedpod. Strip pods from stem with a gloved hand. Small-celled, oval capsule may be crushed with a rolling pin. Small, black seed. Seeds per oz.: 284,000. Per lb.: 4,544,000. Lb. per acre: 1. Oz. per 1,000 sq. ft.: 0.4.

Attracts: Bees and many butterflies.

Comments: Attractive; a nice texture in the back of the border. Prized for its pretty, clean lines. Annual additions of compost prove beneficial. Only species of this genus. Forms clumps but is not aggressive.

7-9-92

¼"

½"
← ½" →

231

Verbena hastata
Blue vervain, wild verbena, wild hyssop
Verbenaceae (vervain family)

Location: Moist prairies, streambanks, marshes, and roadsides. Common throughout state. Open, rich loam. Wet mesic, mesic. Full sun. pH: Neutral 6–7. Border, meadow, roadside.

Plant description: Height: 16–40 in. Blooming time: July–September. Blue, stiff, pencillike spikes up to 4 in. long with numerous 1/8-in. tubular flower, 5 flaring petals, 2 stamens, in pairs of different lengths; 1 pistil with 4-lobed ovary. Blooming starts at the bottom of the spike and works upward, providing a long blooming period. Years before expected bloom: 1–2, depending on when it is planted. Good cut flower. Square-erect stems; ovate, opposite, doubly toothed-paired leaves.

Propagation: Easy by seed and also self-sows. Division in spring. Cuttings in summer.

Germination: Needs light to germinate. Fine seeds; plant on surface. Needs stratification 33–38° F for 30 days.

Harvest: October. Fruit clustered several inches around spike. Clip off seed stalk; brown pods on the spiked stem. Fruit has 4 slender, reddish brown nutlets, each containing a single seed. Pods similar to Culver's root, but vervain has opposite leaves on square stalk, while Culver's root has whorled leaves on branching stalk. Avoid plantain on single stalk, basal leaves, and no branching on stem. Shake stalk in paper bag. Long, slender, greenish tan seed 1/8 × 1/16 in. Seeds per oz.: 100,000. Per lb.: 1,600,000. Lb. per acre: 2. Oz. per 1,000 sq. ft.: 0.8.

Attracts: Buckeye and monarch butterflies.

Comments: Easy, fast-growing. It tolerates disturbance and is somewhat weedy. When it grows in large colonies a violet mist is cast on the landscape. Cattle won't eat it because of its bitterness, and it tends to become weedy in pastures, increasing when it is heavily grazed. A good ornamental plant used in borders.

8-6-92

2"

1"

Verbena stricta
Hoary vervain, wooly vervain
Verbenaceae (vervain family)

Location: Dry prairies and roadsides, loess bluffs. Common throughout state. Dry mesic, dry. Full sun. pH: Neutral 6–7. Meadow, roadside.

Plant description: Height: 2–3 ft. Blooming time: July–September. Purple/rosy pink 1/2-in. flower, 5 petals on stalk blooming progressively upward. Years before expected bloom: 2. Good cut flower. Has whitish hairs with slightly squared stem. Leaves thick, coarse, almost stalkless, ovate-toothed, opposite, hoary with whitish hairs.

Propagation: By seed.

Germination: Easy. No treatment necessary or stratify 33–38° F for 30 days.

Harvest: October. Clip off spiked seed stalk with brown pods. Let dry in paper bag and shake seeds out. Small elongated dark-brown seed. Seeds per oz.: 32,000. Per lb.: 512,000. Lb. per acre: 5. Oz. per 1,000 sq. ft.: 2.

Attracts: Bees.

Comments: Aggressive, needs competition. Often associated with disturbance in pastures. Flowers are larger than blue vervain (*V. hastata*). Eilers lists 11 native vervains. *V. bracteata*, *V. simplex*, and white vervain (*V. urticifolia*) are also frequent to common throughout state.

Viola pedatifida
Prairie violet, larkspur violet
Violaceae (violet family)

Location: Prairie remnants, dry rocky ridges. Scattered to common throughout state. Well-drained, sandy soil. Mesic, dry mesic. Full sun. pH: Acidic-neutral 4.5–7. Border, meadow.

Plant description: Height: 4–8 in. Blooming time: May–June. Violet flower 1 1/2 in. wide, 5 petals, thick beard, lower petals grooved and spurred. 5 stamens with orange anthers are conspicuous in throat of flower. Years before expected bloom: 1–2. Good cut flower. Separate stalks for each leaf and flower. Mature plants have deeply cut or linear-toothed segments. The seedlings, however, do not have these segments and gradually indent. Rhizome.

Propagation: Seed or by division of root cutting of the rhizome, best done in the fall. Self-sows on open ground. Water heavily in fall to prevent winter freeze-out.

Germination: Easy, but sow immediately or refrigerate. Plant fresh seeds 1/2 in. deep in fall.

Harvest: June. Tie a net around the yellowish capsule as it will explode, ejecting seeds when dry, or harvest before seeds have been ejected. Seeds will eject from 3-sectioned capsule when stored in paper bag. Individual seed small, round, golden-tan to black, 1/16 in. Seeds per oz.: 22,000. Per lb.: 352,000. Lb. per acre: 7. Oz. per 1,000 sq. ft.: 2.8.

Attracts: Bees; fritillary, spring azure, and metalmark butterflies.

Comments: Tolerates only moderate competition. Good in rock garden. Bird's-foot violet (*V. pedata*) frequent in southwest; tips of orange stamens protrude conspicuously, with smaller, beardless flowers and less deeply cut leaves. Some are bicolored. Not to be confused with bird's-foot trefoil, the alien, with a yellow flower. Eilers lists 24 native violet species.

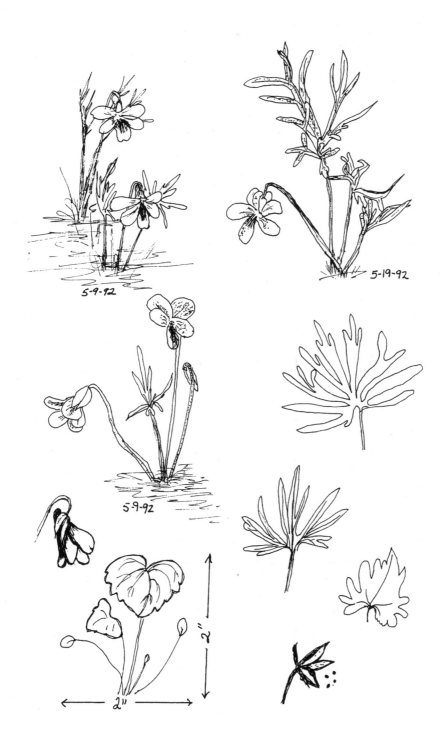

5-9-92

5-19-92

5-9-92

2"

2"

Tradescantia ohiensis
Spiderwort, widow's tears
Commelinaceae (spiderwort family)

Location: Open sandy prairies. Frequent to common east and south. Well-drained loam, will tolerate clay. Wet mesic, mesic, dry mesic, dry. Full or partial sun. pH: Neutral 6–7. Border, meadow, roadside.

Plant description: Height: 2–4 ft. Blooming time: June–July. Rose to blue flower, 3 petals 1–2 in. wide, terminal clusters above pair of long, narrow, leaflike bracts. 3 sepals, 6 stamens are hairy and resemble spider's legs. Flower lasts 1 day and then forms a sticky jelly that will drop a "tear" when touched in the late afternoon. Each day new ones open. Cut off flowers after blooming for second bloom. Years before expected bloom: 1–2. Good cut flower. Slender, straight, smooth stem, often branched; narrow, linear, up to 15 in.

Propagation: Easiest by seed, monocotyledon seedlings blue-green and hairy. Self-sows. Division in spring every 2 years, cuttings in summer, or nodes. Quick to establish.

Germination: Easy. Plant fresh seeds in fall or early spring in cool soil. Needs stratification 33–38° F for 120 days.

Harvest: August–September; 2–3 weeks after flower dies. Some seeds will be dropping while others flower. Use a net fastened over the seed head to catch the seeds or cut plant and put in water until seeds mature. Sow immediately or store in a dry, cool place. Oval capsule; 3 compartments will open in paper bag when dry. Gray oval seed, 1/8 in., pitted. Seeds per oz.: 9,000. Per lb.: 144,000. Lb. per acre: 12. Oz. per 1,000 sq. ft.: 4.8.

Attracts: Butterflies.

Comments: Foliage can become untidy in summer. Aggressive; avoid rich soils, or it will spread too fast. Can be controlled in border by dividing plants every second year and removing slumping stalks, which root at soil when nodes come in contact. Prairie spiderwort (*T. bracteata*) found commonly in low, sandy areas in western two-thirds also.

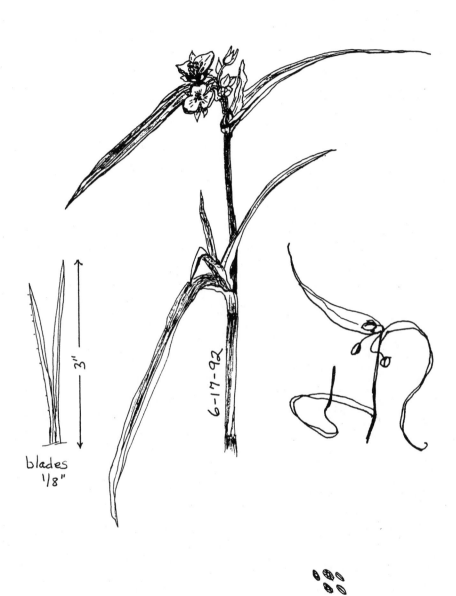

blades
1/8"

3"

6-17-92

239

Iris shrevei
Blue flag, wild iris
Iridaceae (iris family)

Location: Marsh and prairie pothole edges, prairie swales. Frequent to common throughout most of state. Light, sandy soil or loam that drains freely. Wet, wet mesic, mesic. Full to partial sun. pH: Acidic 5–6.5. Border, meadow, roadside.

Plant description: Height: 18–30 in. Blooming time: May–July. Blue flower 2 1/2–4 in. wide, 3 sepals boldly veined and nonbearded, 3 petals, and 3 narrower erect styles, giving the effect of 9 petals. The 3 stamens are hidden under the styles. Years before expected bloom: 2–3. Good cut flower. Single stem with several flowers branching off. "Flag" comes from the middle English "flagge," for rush or reed. Leaves are tall, swordlike, 8–32 × 1/2–1 in., wrap around stem. Lily leaves do not do this, as they are borne on whorls around the stem or opposite. Rhizomes spread rapidly.

Propagation: By seed. Best by rhizome division after flowering.

Germination: Iris, a monocotyledon seedling. Plant fresh seeds in the fall. Needs stratification 33–38° F 90–120 days.

Harvest: August–September. Capsule, 3-sectioned, 1/2 in. long, below flower. Flower withers above as capsule becomes larger and drops off in June. The capsule opens late in the winter, flaring at the top. In each of the 3 sections are seeds that resemble kernels of corn. Break off seed head and extract. Round, rust-colored, flat 1/4-in. seed. Seeds per oz.: 1,000. Per lb.: 16,000. Lb. per acre: 28. Oz. per 1,000 sq. ft.: 11.

Attracts: Hummingbirds and silver-spotted skipper butterflies.

Comments: Pretty on pond edges, streambanks, and other hard-to-landscape wet areas. Bearded iris (*I. germanica*) is a nonnative and is often found growing near cemeteries along with native flowers. Native iris are beardless.

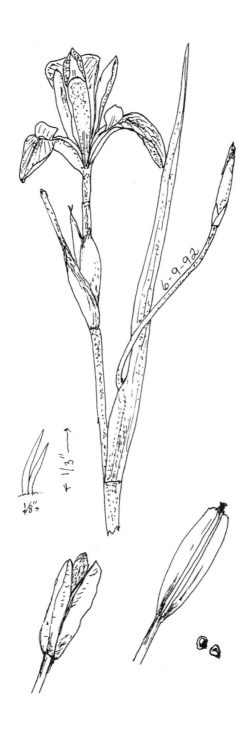

6-9-92

← 1/3″ →

1/8″

241

Sisyrinchium campestre
Blue-eyed grass
Iridaceae (iris family)

Location: Wide range of prairies, clearings in woods. Common throughout state. Sandy soil, or average garden loam. Mesic, dry mesic, dry. Full sun. pH: Neutral 6–7. Border, meadow.

Plant description: Height: 4–12 in. Blooming time: May–June. Blue flower, 6 petals, tipped with small point, yellow center 1/4–1/2 in. across. Flower comes out of little husk and is very delicate. Flower closes when picked. Years before expected bloom: 1–2. Stiff, grasslike stems, less than 1/8 in. across, flattened with 2 narrow ridges on wings. When pulled the stem separates from the plant base like a typical grass. Leaves smooth, linear, narrow, erect, taller than flower stems. The round stem has 2 wings running its complete length. Roots short and fibrous.

Propagation: By seed. Seedling grasslike, transplants easily. Also by division after the first growing season, when several buds and roots are present.

Germination: Easy monocotyledon seedling, reliable. Plant seeds in fall or early spring, when soil is cool. Need stratification 33–38° F for 90 days for spring planting.

Harvest: Early June. Collect when capsule begins to wrinkle, before it bursts open and seeds are gone. Small, round, pea-size pod; globose capsule 1/4 in. or less with 3 segments. Nearly 24 tiny seeds in each pod. Air dry a day before separating from pod with rolling pin. Tiny, black, round, hard seed, 1/16 in. Seeds per oz.: 473,000. Per lb.: 7,568,000. Lb. per acre: 0.5. Oz. per 1,000 sq. ft.: 0.2.

Comments: Delicate and needs freedom from competition. Excellent for rock gardens. Said to have been one of Thoreau's favorites. Yellow stargrass (*Hypoxis hirsuta*) is often found in the same area blooming at the same time. They are similar in size and go together well.

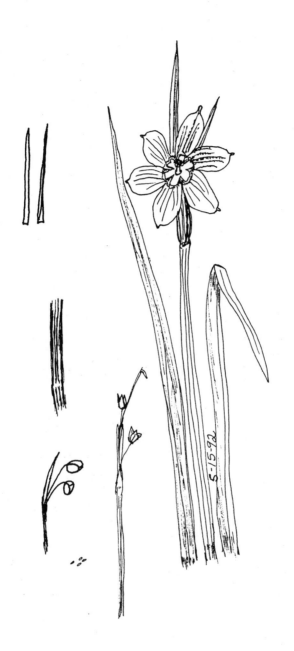

5-15-92

Allium cernuum
Nodding wild onion
Liliaceae (lily family)

Location: Prairies, roadsides, open woods, north-facing slopes. Rare. Rocky, moist, rich-to-medium soil with good drainage. Wet mesic, mesic, dry mesic. Full sun. pH: Acidic-neutral 4.5–7.5. Border, meadow.

Plant description: Height: 10–20 in. Blooming time: July–August. Rose, lavender, or white bell-shaped flower clustered in a nodding umbel. Years before expected bloom: 1 from bulb, 2 from seed. Leafless stalk. Leaves long, narrow, basal 4–16 in., flat and linear. Bulb.

Propagation: By seed or from offsets formed adjacent to the main bulb. Divide every 3 years or when 8–10 bulbs appear in the clump. Self-sows easily, also increases vegetatively. Competes better if started in a flat and transplanted before roots are crowded.

Germination: Monocotyledon seedling. Very easy to grow. Needs stratification 33–38° F for 30 days.

Harvest: September. Place bright yarn on stem while flowering to find fruit. Umbel about 2 × 2 in., with tan capsules, each attached to 1-in. stem that joins the main stem in an umbel. 3-lobed capsule opens with black seeds clinging. Clip off seed head when seeds turn black. Remove from open 1/4-in. capsule. Black seeds in each of the 3 segments. Individual seed hard, 1/8 in., 4-sided, black, irregular-pyramid-shaped. Seeds per oz.: 7,700. Per lb.: 123,200. Lb. per acre: 15. Oz. per 1,000 sq. ft.: 6.

Attracts: Butterflies.

Comments: Especially pretty when planted in groups of 12 or more. Does not do well against heavy grass competition. Edible. Other edible species are wild onion (*A. canadense*), wild prairie onion (*A. stellatum*), and wild leek (*A. tricoccum*). Wild garlic is earliest to bloom; nodding and prairie onions are later. All have the onion aroma, which the poisonous white camass does not have.

Hypoxis hirsuta
Yellow stargrass
Liliaceae (lily family)

Location: Prairies, woodland openings. Infrequent northeast, frequent to common elsewhere. Wide soil range. Wet mesic, mesic, dry mesic. Full or partial sun. pH: Neutral 6–7. Border, meadow.

Plant description: Height: 3–8 in. Blooming time: May–June. Yellow star-shaped, 3/4-in. flower has 3 petals and 3 sepals that are similar, giving the appearance of a 6-pointed star. Stamens are prominent. Years before expected bloom: 1–2. Erect, hairy, very fine stem. 2–7 flowers on each stem, with 1–2 opening at a time. Linear, basal, hairy, small, grasslike leaf below flower on stem. Hairy, small, brown, elliptic-shaped corm that is 1/4–1/2 in. in diameter, with numerous fibrous roots.

Propagation: Easy by seed. Also division of offsets of corms in early spring.

Germination: Easy, monocotyledon seedling. Needs stratification 33–38° F for 30 days.

Harvest: June before seeds are dispersed. Collect stem with capsules before they open. Remove seeds from capsule. Tiny, black, shiny seeds 1/16 in. in diameter are rough with short, hard points that can be seen when magnified. Seeds per oz.: 473,000. Per lb.: 7,568,000. Lb. per acre: 0.5. Oz. per 1,000 sq. ft.: 0.2.

Comments: Tiny, delicate. Good rock garden plant. Companion of blue-eyed grass (*Sisyrinchium campestre*). Only species of this genus appearing in Eilers. Appears as a fine grass unless the flower is noted. Related to the greenhouse bulb plant showy amaryllis (*H. stellata*).

5-13-92

Lilium michiganense
Michigan lily, Turk's-cap lily
Liliaceae (lily family)

Location: Wet meadows, swamps, or roadsides. Frequent to infrequent throughout state. Deep, fertile loam; evenly moist and cool. Wet, wet mesic, mesic. Full or partial sun. pH: Acidic-neutral 5–7. Border, meadow, roadside.

Plant description: Height: 3–4 ft. Blooming time: July–August. Orange bell-like, nodding flower with completely reflexed petals. Flowers up to 3 in. across. 6 rust-colored anthers each 1/2 in. long attached to stamens projecting downward 1 in. below petals; makes a very striking flower. Up to 40 flowers have been recorded on a single plant. Years before expected bloom: 5 from seed, 2 from scales. Stem branches at tip to form additional flower stalks. Leaves lanceolate alternate or whorled, swordlike with smooth margins. Bulbs, hardy perennial. The bulbs send out horizontal rhizomes and scales produced annually for multiplication of the plant.

Propagation: Seed in a capsule, or best by division of offset scales replanted 1–2 in. deep immediately. Obtain scales after plant dies back in fall. Once established, bulbs can be left undisturbed indefinitely or until new plants are needed. Work organic matter into soil before planting new scales, water deeply, and mulch.

Germination: Stratify 33–38° F for 6 weeks.

Harvest: September–October. Cut capsule from plant. Seeds are in 6 compartment capsules called locules. Let seeds dry in their capsules 6–8 weeks at room temperature. Store with no-pest strip. Individual seed round, tan, 1/4 in., flat. Seeds per oz.: 4,500. Per lb.: 72,000. Lb. per acre: 25. Oz. per 1,000 sq. ft.: 10.

Attracts: Rodents like bulbs. Place 1–2 in. gravel around bulb.

Comments: Tiger lily (*L. tigrinum* or *L. lancifolium*) an alien from Asia, has alternate leaves and dark bulblets in the axils. The day lily (*Hemerocallis fulva*), often found in ditches, is an alien and has unspotted blossoms and swordlike leaves.

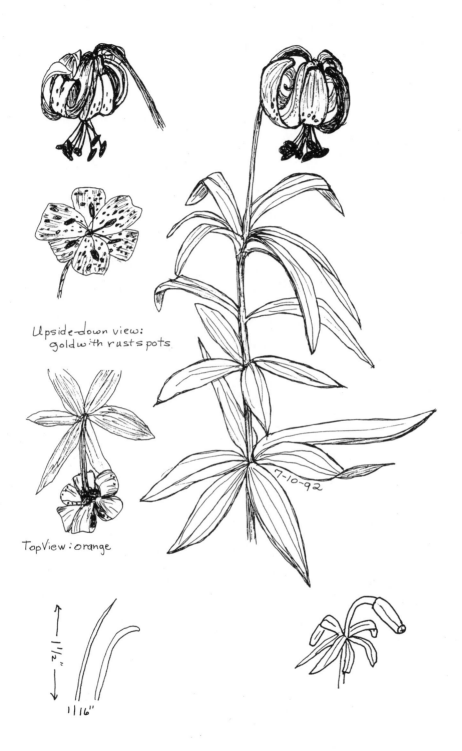

Upside-down view:
gold with rust spots

Top View : orange

7-10-92

1 1/2"

1/16"

Lilium philadelphicum
Wood lily, orange cup lily
Liliaceae (lily family)

Location: Northern grasslands. Infrequent throughout. Well-drained, rich loam. Wet mesic, mesic, dry mesic. Full or partial sun. pH: Acidic 4–6. Border, meadow.

Plant description: Height: 1–3 ft. Blooming time: June. Red-orange, upright, terminal, open bell-shaped flower with 1–5 blooms; 2-in. flower, 6 segments, 3 petals, 3 petallike sepals, each tapering to a stalked base with spaces between stalks that let the rain fall through, 6 stamens with anthers projecting upward. Years before expected bloom: 3–5. Erect stem with whorled leaves, 3–6 per node. Leaves 1–4 in. long, lanceolate. Bulbs about 1 in. in diameter.

Propagation: Difficult to establish and short-lived. Never found long in the same place. Best by division of offset scales planted 1 in. deep. Obtain scales after plant dies back in the fall. Plant several plants together because cross-pollination is necessary for reproduction. Adaptable once established. Adding compost to the soil is beneficial.

Germination: Easy but slow. Early growth is underground, producing only 1 monocotyledon leaf the first year. Plant in fall or store seed at 35° F until spring. Needs stratification 33–38° F for 60 days.

Harvest: September, when foliage has turned yellow. Tie bright yarn on plant so you can find it when seed is ripe. Remove 1–2-in. capsule, 3 sections, densely packed seeds. Individual seed papery winged-flat, rust-colored, tear-shaped, 1/8 in. Seeds per oz.: 4,500. Per lb.: 72,000. Lb. per acre: 25. Oz. per 1,000 sq. ft.: 10.

Attracts: Bees.

Comments: A beautiful flower. Bulbs were eaten by the Dakota and wildlife. A second variety of wood lily is the western form (*L. andinum*), which has scattered leaves. These intergrade west of the Appalachians and have alternate leaves and deep orange or scarlet flowers.

6-17-92

1 1/2"

1/16"

Zigadenus elegans
White camass, death camass, alkali grass
Liliaceae (lily family)

Location: Moist prairies and open rocky areas. Infrequent in north. Calcareous soil. Wet mesic, mesic. Full to partial sun. pH: Neutral-alkaline 6−8. Border, meadow.

Plant description: Height: 1−3 ft. Blooming time: June−July. White flower with yellow center, lilylike raceme 12 in. long with individual blooms 3/4 in. on short stalks. 3 petals and 3 similar sepals; narrow pointed ovals; 6 stamens as long as the petals. At the base of each petal and sepal is a yellow heart-shaped pattern. Good cut flower. Sheath stems with lily-type leaves, mainly basal, 1/2 × 12 in. with protruding midrib under side. Elongated bulbs are onionlike.

Propagation: Best by bulbs. Difficult by seed.

Germination: Needs stratification 33−38° F for 30 days. Best fall-planted outdoors. Monocotyledon seedling.

Harvest: July. Clip stem and store fruit in paper bag. The 3-celled pod, 1/16 × 3/16 in., opens at top, seeds shake out. Individual seed tiny, light gold, tear-shaped. Seeds per oz.: 500,000. Per lb.: 8,000,000. Lb. per acre: 0.5. Oz. per 1,000 sq. ft.: 0.2.

Attracts: Butterflies.

Comments: Bulbs are very poisonous. Do not confuse with edible wild onion or garlic bulbs. If they do not smell like onion, do not eat. White camass (*Z. glaucus*) is also found in thin soil on sandstone or limestone ledges, rare northeast.

253

Grasses

Name and classification: All are native grasses of the Poaceae (Gramineae) family and are monocotyledons. This important grass family has about 525 genera and 5,000 species, providing food for both humans and animals. L. J. Eilers lists 151 native species in Iowa. The most prominent are big bluestem, little bluestem, Indian grass, switchgrass, and prairie dropseed. They are listed in alphabetical order by genus and species, with common names also given.

Location: Native grasses are mostly common to frequent throughout Iowa and the tallgrass prairie as listed with each species. As much as 60 to 90 percent of the vegetation was grass before the prairie was broken. Grasses are the framework of the prairie. Their roots, present for thousands of years, gave the high organic content and black color to the prairie soil. Soil, moisture, and sun requirements are given for each species. The pH range is broad for all the species in this study. Native grass adapts to the variety of soil and hot-dry summers on the prairie.

Plant description: Understanding the characteristics of prairie grass will help you in your prairie seed selection and management. They have several built-in features to ensure their existence. The roots grow very long, spread densely, or do both. Big bluestem roots have been known to be 12 feet long. Leaves will curl in dry, windy weather so that less area is exposed, conserving the moisture in the leaf. Roots store starch as food for the plant. When there has been a dry season, the plant will take time to renourish itself and the roots before it is able to use the energy for making flowers, fruit, and seeds. They withstand drought as well as fires and moderate grazing. This is not only due to the root structure but also because the aboveground growth tissue of grass is located toward the base of the leaf or the shoot, rather than at the tip.

Yes, grasses do bloom, but the bloom is small because it is wind-pollinated and not dependent on insects for pollination. Stems are mainly hollow except at the node, where the leaf attaches. They are also round in comparison to the sedges, which have a triangular stem. Without a showy flower, grass identification becomes more difficult. A useful guide is *Grasses* by Lauren Brown.

Roots are listed as sod-forming or bunch-forming. Sod-forming grasses spread by rhizomes or stolons, growing horizontally to form a dense mat or sod. Once a dense sod is formed, it is hard for other species to penetrate it. Bunch-forming grasses grow vertically in clumps and tend not to crowd out the forbs that are established. Some bunch-forming grasses, as listed, also spread by rhizomes to become sod-forming.

Germination: Special treatments are listed to break dormancy with each species. Dry stratification is sufficient for most prairie grasses. Dry stratification requires the seeds to be exposed to cold, dry conditions for 30 days.

Propagation: Grasses are classified as cool-season and warm-season. Cool-season grasses grow in the cool weather of the spring and fall. They emerge in the spring before the warm-season plants. Cool-season grasses, legumes, and weeds include many aliens that germinate four to six weeks before warm-season prairie grasses. Their competition is a factor that needs to be taken into consideration. They include bluegrass, fescue, bromegrass, timothy, red top, alfalfa, clover, and various trefoils. Cool-season grasses are often sod-forming, but the cool-season native species in this study are all bunch-forming. These include Canada wild rye, June grass, and porcupine grass and have a usefulness in the prairie. Bunch-forming grasses allow forbs room to establish if they mature before the grass roots become dense, and they crowd out weeds. The amount of grass should be kept from 25 to 50 percent of the mix with forbs. Little bluestem and side-oats grama are short enough to emphasize the wildflowers. Big bluestem and Indian grass give more competition. Dropseed is ornamental in small amounts. Switchgrass can become aggressive and should be planted sparingly. June grass is a nice addition for dry soils.

Prairie grasses grow down, not up. The root system establishes itself first, before the grass appears, and continues to be the major part of the plant. The first year the top growth normally amounts to a narrow, straight leaf until late in the summer. These seedlings can be hard to see. Up to 90 percent of a prairie plant's mass may be underground. Inexperienced growers almost always think they have a failure the first year. Most of the time they actually have a good stand, so patience is needed in establishing a prairie. If a cover crop is planted, the areas where it is visible will be a good indication that the native grasses should also be doing well. Number of seeds given by weight is estimated and can vary.

Harvest: Fall is when grass becomes showy. At harvest the grasses have a beautiful array of bronze, orange, and gold colors. Sunlight shining on Indian grass is especially striking. The fruit of the grass family is a grain, an important food source. Grain harvest is described in more detail in chapter 3.

Attracts: Grasses provide cover and seeds for birds. Larger wildflowers and grasses also attract insects, another food source for birds. Many large animals depend on the leafy parts of the grass for forage.

Comments: Grasses were used by the pioneers for fuel, sod houses, thatched roofs, and food. They all have ornamental beauty which extends into fall and winter if they are not harvested. The roots of big bluestem, Indian grass, little bluestem, side-oats grama, and others are good for erosion control and water purification. Grasses also function to support and protect the forbs and to resist weeds. They are drought tolerant and do not require fertilizer.

Andropogon gerardii
Big bluestem, turkeyfoot grass, red hay, beardgrass, turkey claw
Poaceae (Gramineae) (grass family)

Location: Covered thousands of square miles of the tallgrass prairie from the Atlantic Ocean to the Rocky Mountains. Common throughout Iowa. Good loam to clay soil. Tolerates all moisture levels, withstands drought. Full sun or partial shade.

Plant description: Height: 3–8 ft. Blooming time: August–September. Flower has 3 fingerlike branches each 2–4 in. radiating from the top of the stem, shaped like a turkey foot. Coarse, slightly fuzzy flower from bronze to a steely gray-blue color. Leafy stem. Long, white hairs on the upper leaf surface near the base of the leaf. Round hairy stem with reddish tint at its base and blue nodes. Lush, coarse, green leaves. Unlike most grasses, stems are solid or pithy, not hollow. Bunch-forming, 6–12 ft., coarse-branching. Clumps 2–3 ft. will form dense sod.

Germination: No treatment needed. Germinates in April when fall planted.

Propagation: Warm season. Plant late April–June if not fall planted and in a pure stand when used for hay. Growth continues all summer. Debearded seeds produce free-flowing seeds that can usually be seeded with a drill. Should be seeded at a rate of 7–10 lb. of PLS an acre with the Truax drill or double that amount when hand broadcasting. 1 lb. covers about 3,400 sq. ft. In mixed-grass plantings for tallgrass, use 75 percent big bluestem along with Indian grass for your grasses on dry to mesic sites. May also be planted on wet soil for 75 percent of that mix.

Harvest: October–November. Reddish purple to purple-bronze. Fruit arranged in 3 spikes (turkey foot) and has small awns attached to the seed. Some plants will produce seeds the first year. Seeds per oz.: 9,063. Per lb.: 145,000.

Attracts: Delaware skipper, little wood satyr, common checkered skipper butterflies. Forage for deer and livestock, loved by cattle. Do not start grazing until at least 12 in. high or graze below 8–12 in. A rest before freezing is good for root storage but can be grazed after freezing when no longer growing.

Comments: Predominant species of the tallgrass prairie. Ornamental. Prevents soil erosion.

8-31-92

259

Bouteloua curtipendula

Side-oats grama, tall grama grass, mesquite grass

Poaceae (Gramineae) (grass family)

Location: Found in ridges, rocky areas, steep slopes, and well-drained uplands of the tallgrass prairie and Great Plains. Frequent throughout Iowa. Dry, well-drained, moderately calcareous soils. Dry mesic, dry. Full or partial sun.

Plant description: Height: 1–2 ft. Blooming time: July–September. Flower purplish in late summer, inflorescence large with numerous spikelets arranged along 1 side of the stalk, lacking petals, enclosed by scales. 10–50 spikelets droop from 1 or 2 sides of the stalk. Each spikelet is about 1/3 in. long and contains 3–6 individual flowers. Stem rises to form a curly mass of thin leaves 1/8 × 4–12 in. Rough on the upper side and hairy underside. Hairy ligule. Spots often on green leaves. Lower leaves turn whitish and curl when dry. Bunch-forming, interspersed with tall grasses. Dense and only moderately aggressive, spreading by scaly, short, slender rhizomes to form sod.

Germination: No treatment necessary.

Propagation: Warm season, by seed or division. Also grows in cool season; plant in fall. Plant with little bluestem, up to 75 percent combined in mixed grass plantings on dry mesic or dry. 1 lb. covers 2,000 sq. ft., or plant 4 lb. per acre when planting alone.

Seed harvest: September, before fruit starts to drop. Fruit golden-rust in early fall; very delicate oatlike appearance. Seeds strip easily from the stalk when harvesting by hand. Seeds per oz.: 8,000. Per lb.: 128,000 or more.

Attracts: Birds and little wood satyr, common wood nymph, and skipper butterflies. Good forage plant.

Comments: Drought tolerant. Highly ornamental, good with little bluestem and mixed with weaker, smaller flowers. Good on highway slopes and steep areas for erosion control. Also good in between trees in an orchard. Grows vigorously on loamy soils, but will not persist in the face of competition from taller grasses. Blue grama (*B. gracilis*) and hairy grama (*B. hirsuta*) found in west on dry, gravelly hilltops or loess bluffs.

Dichanthelium oligosanthes
Switchgrass, panic grass, wild red top, thatchgrass
Poaceae (Gramineae) (grass family)

Location: Decreases in the bluestem area; found in low moist areas to up-land prairies, streams, and large colonies along roadsides. Prominent in the western edge of the tallgrass prairie and in the eastern Great Plains. Fre-quent to common throughout Iowa. Wide range of soils, even clay, but prefers loamy, sandy soil. Full sun or partial shade. Mesic, dry mesic, dry.

Plant description: Height: 3–7 ft. Blooming time: August–September. Pyramid-shaped flower, up to 20 in. with purplish spikelet. Borne singly at the end of the branch. Strong conical structure. Large, leafy clumps. Stout and erect, green to purple, blades 8–20 in. long. Blade surfaces are smooth but margins are rough. The ligule is a tuft of hairs forming a V-shape where the leaf blade joins the sheath. Sod-forming. Tough, tangled root system with short-scaly rhizomes that send up new shoots.

Germination: Easy and quick, no treatment required. Seeds are viable for 3 years.

Propagation: Warm season. 1 lb. per acre is recommended when planting alone.

Harvest: September–October. Fruit begins dropping in September. 12-in.-long ear, branches hairlike. Feathery open heads are purple, with both the leaves and seed heads turning pale yellow-orange to tan. Individual seed shiny, reddish, hard, and bony. Seeds per oz.: 18,000. Per lb.: 288,000.

Attracts: Delaware skipper, little wood satyr, and common wood nymph butterflies. Important food source for birds and browsing animals. Excel-lent winter and early spring wildlife cover. Often used in Conservation Re-serve Program ground. Wildlife managers use switchgrass solely because it gives a quick stand. Pheasants and quail prefer the mixed stands. Add In-dian grass and big bluestem to give the positive attributes of the original prairie.

Comments: Ornamental for landscaping. Too coarse for the border or small garden; aggressive. Needs strong competition. Good erosion control. Pretty in dried arrangements. Eilers lists 16 native species of this genus.

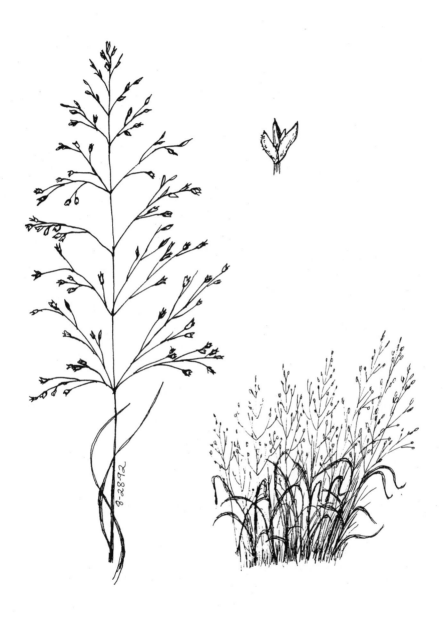

263

Elymus canadensis
Canada wild rye
Poaceae (Gramineae) (grass family)

Location: Upland to lowland prairies, roadsides, open places. Often encircles sloughs along with prairie cordgrass, but also grown on dry soil as well as riverbanks. Common throughout Iowa. Adaptable; from bare sand, dry gravel, and loam to raw clay subsoil. Adapts to all moisture types. Full or partial sun.

Plant description: Height: 3–5 ft. Blooming time: July–August. Densely flowered, bushy inflorescence, with coarse, thick bristles curved outward. Ear 8 in. long, awns 1 1/4 in. long and very rough, single flower. Wide leaf blades and nodding seed heads resemble wheat. Bunch grass. Early vigorous growth and a fibrous, wide-spreading root system make Canada wild rye a valuable ground cover. Forms large colonies.

Germination: No treatment necessary. Germinates best in cool weather.

Propagation: Cool season, comes up fast and holds the soil while not outcompeting the other native grasses or appearing weedy. A short-lived perennial. Plant in fall or early spring. A cover crop of oats may be seeded at a rate of 20–30 lb. per acre, or plant 3 lb. per acre mixed with other grasses. Can be planted up to 5–10 lb. per acre.

Seed harvest: July–October. In summer sends up green seed plumes which turn golden as they ripen and bend when mature. Seed is relatively large and light. Seeds per oz.: 4,782. Per lb.: 76,512.

Attracts: Good forage grass.

Comments: Ornamental plant for landscaping. It was an important part of prairie pastures. Virginia wild rye (*E. virginicus*) has straight bristles and is also frequent to common throughout state. *E. maltei* found rarely northeast and east-central on sandy soil.

8-1-92

Koeleria macrantha
June grass
Poaceae (Gramineae) (grass family)

Location: Prairies, loess bluffs, sandy plains. Infrequent southeast and east, frequent to common elsewhere. Sandy, dry soil to loam. Full sun. Dry mesic, dry.

Plant description: Height: 1–2 ft. Blooming time: June–July. Flattened gray-green spikelets, 1–6 in., dense, unbranched, cylindrical, tapering at the tip. 2 lowest scales of each flower are as long as the others. Years before expected bloom: 1 from division, 2 from seed. Narrow leaves at base and no leaves on stem. Leaf blades 1/8 × 12 in.; dark green, stiff, flat. Inflorescence reaches less than 2 ft. Bunch grass. Grows in scattered clumps and does not form a pure stand of its own.

Germination: No treatment necessary. Seedlings almost invisible when first emerging.

Propagation: Cool season, by division or seed. Grows readily from seeds when planted in early spring or late fall after frost. 1/2 lb. per acre is recommended when planting alone.

Harvest: June–July. Begins dropping in late June. Fruit fluffy, silvery-green, dense, and lustrous. Seeds per oz.: 187,500. Per lb.: 3,000,000.

Attracts: Deer and elk like it while it is green.

Comments: An early invader into disturbed sandy prairies. Good companion for shorter flowers such as the lousewort, puccoon, violet, pasque flower, and prairie smoke. Mature plant mixes well with other prairie species such as butterfly weed, coreopsis, showy goldenrod, and western sunflower. Good for landscaping. The only species of the genus listed by Eilers.

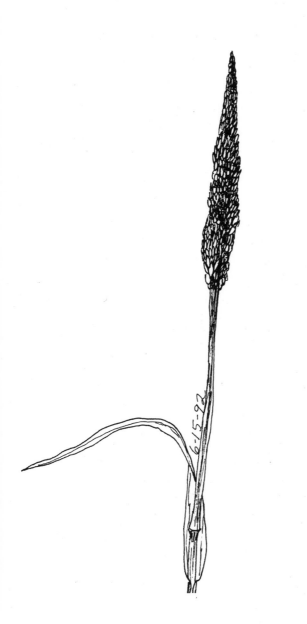

267

Schizachyrium scoparium
Little bluestem, broom beardgrass, wiregrass, broom
Poaceae (Gramineae) (grass family)

Location: At one time grew in 45 states and was the most abundant grass in mid-America. Still common in the Flint Hills of Kansas. Common throughout Iowa. Well-drained lighter soils; medium to sandy-dry. Mesic, dry mesic, dry. Full or partial sun.

Plant description: Height: 2–3 ft. Blooming time: August–September. Fuzzy flower lined along the tan, brown, and wine-red branches. Tiny, lacks petals; enclosed by scales tipped with long, slender bristles. Delicate, erect, single. Years before expected bloom: 1. 1/3-in. spikelets on slender stems that extend beyond the leaves; clusters of spikelets 2 1/2 in. long. Leaf blades to 10 × 1 1/2 in. wide, slightly folded with base sheath stem. Bunch grass. Grows in clumps with space between. Does not usually form sod unless given a lot of moisture. Clumps are 6–8 ft. in diameter, sometimes interspersed with tall grasses. Branching, numerous vertical roots up to 6 ft. deep.

Germination: No treatment. Germinates in April when fall planted. Seedling blue-green.

Propagation: Warm season, best planted in fall, or May–June. 1 lb. covers 3,400 sq. ft. or up to 5 lb. per acre. In mixed-grass plantings, use 75 percent little bluestem on dry, dry mesic, or mesic short grass plantings. Equal amounts of side-oats grama may be used on dry mesic or dry. Should be included in all prairie plantings.

Harvest: Late September–October. Top 1 in. of each branch is a seed-bearing, spikelike raceme. Reddish tan leaves with fluffy seed head; pretty in the fall sunshine, and in the winter the plants turn a colorful orange and purple. Seeds per oz.: 8,800–16,250. Per lb.: 140,800–260,000.

Attracts: Birds and delaware skipper, little wood satyr, common woodland skipper, and nymph butterflies. Hay forage is excellent for cattle, antelope, buffalo, and deer.

Comments: Good support for floppy flowers. Good intermediate grass. It is only moderately aggressive and likes small companions. Will not overshadow prairie flowers, as with dense plantings of the taller grasses. Good in landscapes. Good for erosion control.

Sorghastrum nutans
Indian grass.
Poaceae (Gramineae) (grass family)

Location: Found with the bluestems; upland to moist prairie openings; a dominant species of the tallgrass prairies. Common throughout Iowa. Likes deep, well-drained soil but will tolerate clay soil. Full sun. Mesic, dry mesic, dry.

Plant description: Height: 3–6 ft. Blooming time: August–September. Golden, large inflorescence; single, narrow, 6–10-in. plumelike panicle. Small twisted bristles on the flowers are slightly fuzzy. Closed before and after flowering, but opens away from stem during flowering. Ear 8 in. long. Wide leaf-blades that narrow at the point of attachment. Bunch-grass. Tough, tangled root system. Forms large clumps.

Germination: No treatment necessary.

Propagation: Warm season, plant in the fall or late April–mid June. Plant in a pure stand of 7–10 lb. per acre when used for pasture or hay. Debearding produces a free-flowing seed that can usually be seeded by drill or hand broadcasting. 1 lb. covers 1,400 sq. ft. for a heavy stand or will cover up to a full acre depending on soil, weather, seeding method, and the type of coverage desired. Used in tallgrass mixes; up to 75 percent along with big bluestem on dry and mesic.

Harvest: Late September–early October. Fruit fluffy, appearing as large plumes. Copper color on bronze stems; beautiful on a sunny fall day. Fertile spikelets are 1/4–1/3 in. long and have 2 outer glumes, tipped with awn 3 times as long as the spikelet. Seeds per oz.: 8,300–10,938. Per lb.: 132,800–175,000.

Attracts: Birds and little wood satyr, pepper and salt skipper, and common wood nymph butterflies. Very nutritious, palatable for livestock. Can be baled for hay.

Comments: Can be aggressive. Needs space and competition. Pretty planted behind a wildflower border. Ornamental for landscaping and decorative in dried bouquets. Stands can still be found in Kansas and Oklahoma.

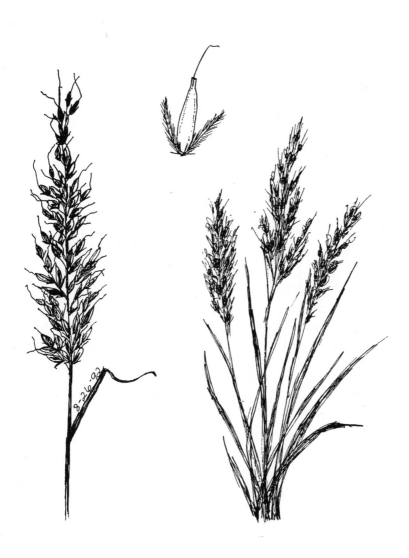

Spartina pectinata
Cord grass, slough grass, ripgut
Poaceae (Gramineae) (grass family)

Location: Wet, marshy areas where water stands in spring (slough), bottoms of ditches, or along shoulders where water collects. Frequent to common throughout Iowa. Heavy, wet, clay soil. Wet, wet mesic, mesic. Full sun.

Plant description: Height: 4–10 ft. Blooming time: July–September. Hundreds of tiny purple blooms. Flattened spikelets are in 2 rows along the rachis; the flower lacking showy petals is very inconspicuous. Branch ears 3 1/2 in. long, numerous, on long stalks. Toothed-edges of the leaf blades are strong, tough, and serrated sharply enough to cut your hand. Leaves up to 30 in. long tapering to a point. Leaves roll up when dry. Stiff branches are widely spaced. Sod-forming grass. Heavy, woody, multibranched roots as deep as 10 ft. with creeping rhizomes. Grows in dense, monotypic patches.

Germination: Double dormancy, takes 2 years to germinate. Few seeds are viable.

Propagation: Warm season, by seed or division of rhizome. Begins growth in April. Often grows in pure stands.

Harvest: October. Bright yellow seeds do not drop until fall, and few are viable.

Attracts: Good protection for wildlife. Attracts birds. Forage grass has been used for hay. Muskrats eat its roots.

Comments: Excellent for stabilizing pond edges, streamsides, and other wet areas. Aggressive. Ornamental plant. Was used for sod houses and thatched roofs, and was twisted into cords and used for fuel by the pioneers. Only species of this genus in Eilers.

273

Sporobolus heterolepis
Prairie dropseed, northern dropseed
Poaceae (Gramineae) (grass family)

Location: Dry to upland prairies, loess bluffs. Common north-central and southwest, infrequent elsewhere. Sandy soil. Full to partial sun. Wet mesic, mesic, dry mesic, dry.

Plant description: Height: 2–3 ft. Blooming time: August–September. Pale pinkish brown to gray head 3 × 12 in., cone-shaped. Bloom insignificant. Years before expected bloom: 2. Stem stout, pithy, and wiry. Throat of sheaths are hairy where blade joins. Many fine-textured, narrow blades of grass 1/8 × 18 in., fragrant. Tip curls inward and margins and midribs are rough. Bunch-forming. Found in open prairies in almost solid stands. Forms hummocks that are round, fountainlike, 3 ft. in circumference.

Germination: No treatment necessary.

Propagation: Warm season, by seed or division of young plants. Plant in May or June when ground is warm or fall plant.

Harvest: September. Seeds drop quickly when maturity is reached. Pinkish brown to grayish black. Seeds can lie dormant for many years. Seeds per oz.: 10,875–14,000. Per lb.: 174,000–224,000.

Comments: Provides a well-defined border when planted 18–24 in. apart. Ornamental.

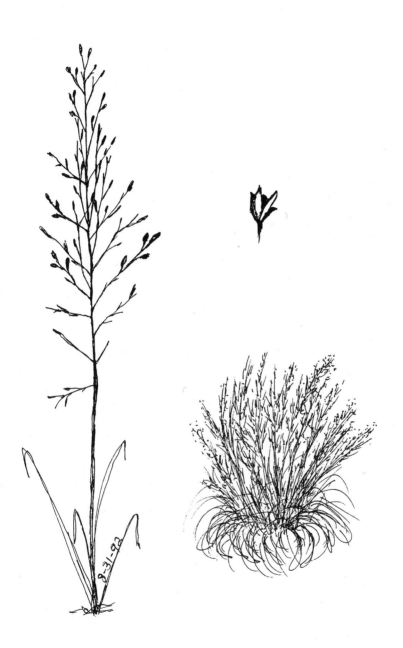

8-31-92

275

Stipa spartea
Porcupine grass, needlegrass
Poaceae (Gramineae) (grass family)

Location: Often found with the bluestems; on dry sites on upland prairies. Frequent to common throughout Iowa. Sandy, well-drained soil. Dry mesic, dry. Full sun.

Plant description: Height: 3–4 ft. Blooming time: June. Rigid and rough awn 4–8 in. on a head 10 in. or more. Glumes 1–1 1/2 in. Unbranched stout, smooth stems. Narrow leaves 1–14 in. with stem leaves 4–16 in. long and basal leaves 1–2 1/2 ft. long. Upper side smooth and underside ribbed. Leaves roll up in the summer as they dry. Bunch-grass. Dormant in the summertime. Grows in small clumps less than 4 in. across with deep roots.

Germination: Stratify for 30 days in cool-damp storage.

Propagation: Cool season, by seed, starts to grow in the fall. Plant sparingly. Up to 2 lb. may be planted on 1 acre if planted alone.

Harvest: Late June as seeds will have dropped by mid-July. Fruit rusty-brown. The seed is very unique with a sharp point and 2-in. wiry awn. Seeds per oz.: 2,132. Per lb.: 34,112.

Comments: Dormant in the summer and may remain green in the winter. Known for the steellike sharp seeds. The awn coils up in response to changes in humidity and screws the seed into the soil to a depth of 1 in. Not recommended where there are children as the "needles" can stick in mouths, bare feet, hands, or skin. Animals have had them driven into their fur, eyes, nose, and mouth. About 6 drove themselves through my shoelaces and into my shoes just walking in the area. Known as "devil's darning needle" by the pioneers. Green needlegrass (*S. viridula*) and needle-and-thread or spear grass (*S. comata*) are native to the Loess Hills.

6-10-92

Glossary

Achene: Fruit or seed that is small and dry, does not open, and contains one seed.

Acre: 43,560 square feet.

Aeration, soil: The exchange of oxygen in the air to the soil. In poorly aerated soil, carbon dioxide becomes higher and oxygen lower.

Afterripening: A period of several months after seed is formed when it will not germinate, characteristic of some seeds.

Alien: Plant from another country; not native to the United States.

Alluvial soil: Soil deposited by flowing water, especially along a riverbed.

Alternate leaves: Single leaves along a stem that are not opposite each other.

Annual: A plant that completes its growth in one growing season.

Anther: The part of the stamen holding the pollen.

Apex: The highest point of anything; tip, peak, top, or vertex.

Awn: A bristlelike appendage fastened to the seed.

Axil: The angle formed by the upper side of a leaf and the stem from which it grows.

Basal: Leaves at the base of the stem.

Biennial: A plant that lasts only two years, producing seeds the second year.

Biome: Large, easily recognizable community units.

Biota: The plant and animal life of a region.

Bipinnate: Multiple leaflets arranged in a featherlike manner on opposite sides of the stalk.

Bog: Depressed land with poor drainage. Wet, spongy ground causes plants to decay from lack of oxygen and contains a thick layer of peat. Characterized by sedges and sphagnum. Acidic in reaction. Precipitation is its only water source, with nutrients coming from rain and snow.

Bracts: Modified leaves, usually at the base of the flower.

Bulb: A short underground stem, swollen, with food-storing scale leaves.

Bunch grasses: Grasses that form clumps or bunches as they grow as opposed to sod-forming.

Burr: A fruit that detaches easily from the plant and sticks to clothing or fur by means of hooks or hairs.

Calcareous fen: A wet, peaty area, often sloped, supplied by internally flowing, spring-fed calcareous water. These fens have many unusual, specially adapted plant species.

Calcareous soil: Soil containing lime, calcium, or calcium carbonate, making it alkaline. Its content of calcium carbonate will effervesce visibly when treated with cold, dilute hydrochloric acid.

Calyx: The sepals of a flower. Outer circle of lower parts, sometimes a papery covering around the capsule, as in the silene family.

Capsule: A dry fruit with one or more compartments, usually having thin walls that split open along one or more lines.

Caudex: The tough, enlarged base of a stem at or below ground level, usually persistent.

Clasping: A leaf whose base wholly or partly surrounds the stem.

Clay: As a soil textural class, soil material that is 40 percent or more clay, less than 45 percent sand, and less than 40 percent silt.

Clone: A group of plants all of whose members are directly descended from a single individual.

Common name: Unscientific name that people have given to identify a plant.

Companion plants: Plants that are found growing together.

Complete flower: Flowers with sepals, petals, stamens, and a pistil all present.

Composite flower: A composite head made up of many flowers (florets) clustered into a head, as in the members of the sunflower family, Asteraceae.

Compost: A mixture of decomposing vegetable refuse, manure, etc., for fertilizing the soil. Causes a slight lowering of the pH, making the soil more acidic.

Compound leaf: A leaf divided into separate smaller leaflets.

Connate perfoliate: Opposite leaves joined at the stem, as in the cup plant.

Corm: The bulblike fleshy part of the underground stem, covered with thin, papery leaves. Not layered or scaly like a bulb.

Corolla: Collective term for the petals of a flower.

Corymb: A flat-topped, indeterminate inflorescence, the outer flowers opening first.

Cotyledon: A leaf of the embryo of a seed.

Cover crop: A close-growing crop grown primarily to improve and protect the soil between periods of regular crop production, or a crop grown between trees and vines in orchards and vineyards.

Cultivar: A plant developed and improved by various horticultural techniques such as selection and hybridization. Such plants carry "cv" with the Latin name and are given a new common name.

Cyme: A broad, determinate inflorescence, the central flowers opening first.

Damping-off: A condition that causes seedlings to deteriorate at the base of the stem and die from too much moisture and fungi.

Deadhead: To remove the flowerhead after blooming so it does not go to seed.

Dehisce: To split apart and discharge seeds.

Dicotyledon: Seeds with two cotyledons in the embryo that have two seed leaves that emerge in the seedling before the true leaves appear.

Disk: The center of flowers in the sunflower family resembling a button and composed of numerous tiny, tubular disk florets, surrounded by a circle of ray florets or petals.

Disk flowers: Tiny, tubular flowers in the buttonlike center of a flower head, such as those found in the sunflower family.

Dormancy: The resting period of plants or seeds which is broken by temperature, moisture, and abrasion of the seed coat.

Downy: Covered with soft, fine hair.

Drupe: A fleshy fruit with a hard stone.

Ecology: Relations between living organisms and their environment.

Ecosystem: A community of plants and living organisms considered together as a unit.

Entire: A leaf margin that is smooth and lacks teeth.

Environment: All the conditions affecting the development of an organism or a group of organisms.

Exotic: An alien plant that has been brought in from another country; not native.

Family: A subdivision of plants with similar characteristics ranking above genus and species; family names of plants having the suffix -aceae.

Fen: Low, flat, marshy land covered wholly or partly with water, characterized by quaking organic soils infiltrated by cold groundwater seepages, making them alkaline, neutral, or only slightly acidic. Sometimes called "hanging bogs" from those created by seepage on a hillside. The soil is muck. The sage willow (*Salix candida*), a showy shrub 1–3 ft. tall, found in eastern Iowa, is an indicator of a fen. Blue lobelia, sneezeweed, flat-topped aster, ladies'-tresses, ladies'-slippers, grass of Parnassus, and fringed gentians are also characteristic.

Fibrous roots: Roots with many thin or branched root elements.

Filament: The anther-bearing stalk of a stamen.

Fine-textured soil: Sandy clay, silty clay, and clay.

Flora: The entire group of plant species growing spontaneously in a particular area.

Floret: A single small flower that may look like a petal. Found in the sunflower family.

Forb: Any herbaceous plant, not a grass or a sedge. Forb is commonly used to describe the broad-leaved plants, known as wildflowers, of the prairie.

Fruit: The ripened ovary or pistil of a seed plant, often with attached parts.

Genus (pl. genera): The main subdivision of a family, includes one or more species. The genus name is capitalized and precedes the species name, which is not capitalized.

Germinate: To sprout, as in the new growth of a seed or the depositing of pollen grains on a stigma.

Glabrous: Without hair, down, or fuzz; smooth.

Glaucous: Having a waxy, whitish coating.

Glochid: A barbed hair or bristle.

Glume: Two empty scales at the base of the spikelet of the grass fruit.

Herb: A plant that lacks woody tissue and dies back to the soil surface at the end of the growing season. Most of the plants in this book are herbs.

Herbage: Stems and leaves considered collectively.

Hip: Fruit of the rose.

Hoary: Having white or grayish hair.

Hummock: A low rounded hill, a hump, a fountainlike formation of grasses.

Humus: Soft brown or black shapeless substance formed through decomposition of plant material forming an upper layer of the soil, more or less the stable part of the organic matter in mineral soils.

Indehiscent: Remaining closed at maturity.

Indigenous or native species: Any species growing on or near a specified site prior to settlement by European immigrants or that has not been introduced to that site by human activity.

Inflorescence: A flower cluster on a plant, or the flowering part of the plant considered as a whole.

Inoculant: A commercially formulated strain of rhizobium added to the soil to aid in the establishment of various members of the bean or pea family.

Introduced: A plant that has been brought into the country; not native.

Involucre: A whorl of leafy bracts surrounding composite flower heads, such as those in the sunflower family.

Irregular flower: Not symmetrical, such as a lipped flower.

Knoll: A mound, hill, or natural elevation of the land.

Lanceolate leaf: Lance-shaped; much longer than wide and tapering to a point.

Leaflet: One of the leaflike parts of a compound leaf.

Legume: Pea family fruit in pods that usually open along two lines, with roots of the plant bearing nodules containing nitrogen-fixing bacteria aided by rhizobia.

Ligule: A strap-shaped corolla in certain composite flowers or a thin membrane attached to a leaf of grass at the point where the blade meets the leafstalk.

Linear: Long, narrow leaf such as a blade of grass.

Loam: A rich soil composed of 7–27 percent clay, less than 52 percent sand, 28–50 percent silt, and 5 percent organic matter.

Lobed: Indented on the edge of the leaf, usually with rounded projections.

Loess: Fine-grained material, dominantly of silt-size particles, deposited by wind.

Marsh: A tract of low, wet, soft land. Characterized by grasses, cattails, or other monocotyledons.

Meadow: A tract of low-lying, moist grassland.

Mesic: The part of the prairie that is neither excessively dry nor moist; moderate moisture.

Midrib: The central vein of a leaf or leaflet.

Moderately coarse-textured soil: Coarse sandy loam, sandy loam, and fine sandy loam.

Moderately fine-textured soil: Clay loam, sandy clay loam, and silty clay loam.

Monocotyledon: Plants with one cotyledon in the embryo of the seed, such as lilies, orchids, spiderworts, and grasses.

Monotypic: Having only one type, as a genus consisting of only one species.

Native: Originated in the area.

Naturalized: A species introduced to a new area which has established itself by successfully reproducing itself for at least one generation, causing it to become established as if native.

Nerve: A leaf vein that is not branched but linear.

Neutral soil: A soil having a pH value between 6.6 and 7.3.

Node: Area where the leaf attaches to the stem, often swollen.

Nodules: Outgrowths of the roots of legume plants that are inhabited by nitrogen-fixing microorganisms known as rhizobia.

Nutrients, plant: Include nitrogen, phosphorus, potassium, calcium, magnesium, sulphur, manganese, copper, boron, and zinc obtained from the soil and carbon, hydrogen, and oxygen obtained from the air and water.

Offset: A short sideshoot arising from the base of a plant; also a small bulb arising from the base of another bulb.

Opposite leaves: Leaves in pairs, one on each side of the stem.

Organic matter: Plant and animal residue in the soil in various stages of decomposition.

Ovary: Reproductive part of the plant, at the swollen part of the pistil.

Ovate leaf: An egg-shaped leaf, broader at the base than at the top.

Palmate: Having three or more divisions or lobes, looking like outspread fingers of a hand.

Panicle: Branching clusters, with compounded inflorescences.

Pappus: A bristle, scale, or crown on seedlike fruits of the sunflower family that aids in dispersing the seeds.

Parasite: A plant deriving its nutrition from another organism.

Peat: The least decomposed of all organic matter found in ancient bogs and swamps, a precursor of coal. Peat contains a large amount of well-preserved fiber that is readily identifiable according to botanical origin. Used as a plant covering, having acidic content, low bulk density, and high water content at saturation.

Pedicel: The stalk of an individual flower.

Peduncle: The main flower stalk or stem holding an inflorescence.

Perennial: A plant that continues to live from year to year from the stem or root stalk.

Perfect flowers: Flowers with both stamens and a pistil but lacking either sepals and/or petals.

Perfoliate: Leaf wraps around stem at attachment.

Petal: A modified leaf attached to the receptacle, one of the segments of the corolla, outside the stamens and inside the calyx. The showiness of petals attracts pollinators to the flower.

Petiole: The stalk to which a leaf is attached.

pH: The H stands for hydrogen, and the p is a mathematical symbol; refers to the acid, neutral, or alkaline soil content. Hydrogen combines with the surface of fine clay particles and decomposing organic matter. Lime replaces hydrogen, neutralizing the soil.

Pinnate leaf: A compound leaf with leaflets along a central stalk.

Pistil: The female organ of a flower, with an ovary, style, and stigma.

Pod: A dry fruit that opens its full length along one or two seams at maturity.

Pollen: The powdery substance produced in anthers containing the male sex cells of flowering plants.

Pollination: The transfer of pollen from an anther to a stigma.

Prairie: A North American grassland dominated by 60–80 percent native grasses and 20–40 percent forbs with less than one mature tree per acre. The term is derived from the French word for meadowland. A sunny grassland with patches of wildflowers.

Preserve: An area of land or water formally dedicated for maintenance as nearly as possible in its natural condition.

Propagation: Increasing the number of plants through seeds, cuttings, or division.

Prostrate: Growing horizontally along the ground.

Pubescent: Covered with fine, soft hairs.

Raceme: A long cluster of flowers on a single stalk, the flowers opening in succession toward the apex.

Rachis: The principal stem of a raceme.

Raptors: Eagles, hawks, falcons, owls, and vultures; birds that feed on smaller animals.

Ray flowers: Flowers that resemble a single petal, arranged around the edge of a circle of disk flowers, in members of the family Asteraceae.

Receptacle: The fleshy tissue at the apex of the floral stalk to which flower parts are attached.

Remnant: A small area that has persisted in a relatively unaltered condition, such as an unplowed prairie.

Rhizobium (pl. rhizobia): Microorganisms that inhabit nodules on the roots of members of the bean family. These organisms have the ability to take nitrogen from the air and create nitrogen compounds, usable by their host plants.

Rhizome: A horizontal underground stem with nodes used for food storage. It usually sends out roots from its lower surface and buds, nodes, and leafy shoots from its upper surface.

Root division: Propagation of plants by cutting vertically between root segments.

Root rot: Degeneration of the roots usually caused by fungi.

Rootstalk: Rhizome.

Rosette: A cluster of basal leaves, appearing to grow directly out of the ground.

Runner: A stem that grows on the surface of the soil, often developing new plants at the tip. Also referred to as a stolon.

Sand: Rock or mineral fragments, mostly quartz, with fragments from 0.05 mm to 2 mm in diameter.

Saprophyte: A plant that obtains all its nourishment from dead organic matter.

Savanna: A grassland covered by more than one mature tree per acre but having less than 50 percent tree canopy cover. Herbaceous prairie vegetation grows in this area of transition between grassland and forest.

Scalping: Removal of the stems and leaves from the seed after threshing.

Scape: The leafless stem of a flower.

Scarification: Breaking the seed hull so moisture can enter to enhance germination.

Seed: A fertilized ovule. The seed contains the embryo, which becomes the new plant.

Seedling: A plant grown from a seed.

Sepal: A small, modified leaf attached to the outer margin of the receptacle and usually green. Some species have more colorful sepals that resemble petals.

Serrate: Having sawlike notches along the edge of the leaf.

Sessile: Without a stalk, as in a leaf when the blade is attached directly to the stem.

Sheath: The part of the leaf that wraps around the grass stem.

Shoot: The aboveground or stem portion of a plant that bears leaves, buds, and flowers.

Silica: A combination of silicon and oxygen; quartz is the mineral form.

Silique: A fruit divided down the middle by a membrane, characteristic of the mustard family.

Silt: Soil with individual mineral particles ranging in diameter from clay to fine sand.

Simple flower: An individual flower on a single stem.

Simple leaf: A leaf with an undivided blade.

Sinuate: Bending or winding in and out or having a wavy margin on a leaf.

Slip: A cutting used in propagation.

Slough: A swamp, bog, marsh, or hollow full of soft deep mud, especially one that is part of an inlet or backwater. Water is found standing in spring but later dries up. Also spelled slew, slue.

Softwood cutting: A propagation by cutting rapidly growing portions of a stem that is green and pliable.

Species: A single, distinct kind of plant with similar distinguishing characteristics within a genus.

Sphagnum: Any of a number of related grayish mosses that excrete antibiotics and raise water acidity; peat moss. Found in bogs, though some species also occur in fens. Used as a soil conditioner because of its water absorbency and as packing material for shipping plants. Historically used as diapers by Native Americans and as surgical dressings in World War I.

Spike: An elongated flower cluster, each flower of which is without a stalk.

Spur: A hollow, tubular extension on a flower, horn shaped.

Stalk: A stemlike structure that supports a single leaf, fruit, or flower.

Stamen: The male flower organ, bearing pollen, consisting of a filament and an anther.

Stem: The main support of the plant, where nutrients and water pass between the leaves and roots.

Stigma: The tip of the pistil which receives pollen grains.

Stipule: One or two leaflike parts at the base of a leafstalk or leaf petioles.

Stolon: A horizontal branch from the base of a plant; a runner aboveground, as in strawberry plants that recline on the surface of the soil and sometimes root. Also called a runner.

Stratification: A moist, chilling treatment to enhance germination of seeds.

Style: The portion of the pistil connecting the stigma and the ovary.

Succession: The way plants naturally increase and decrease in a given area over a period of years.

Synergistic: Working together. The simultaneous action of separate agencies which, together, have a greater total effect than the sum of their individual effects.

Swale: A hollow or depression; especially one in wet, marshy ground.

Swamp: Water-covered land containing trees, not characteristic of prairie wetlands.

Talus: A sloping face of a hill with a wide base.

Taproot: A stout, vertical root, usually thickened, as a carrot.

Tendril: A slender, coiling structure that helps support climbing plants.

Tepal: Used to describe petals and sepals when they are similar, as with lilies.

Texture, soil: The relative proportions of sand, silt, and clay particles in a mass of soil.

Thresh: To beat grain out of its husk.

Thyrse: Flowers clustered around the stem in a compact, cylindrical to tapering panicle, each with its own stalk. Penstemons and mints are examples.

Toothed: Having a sawtooth edge.

Trifoliate: Having three leaves.

True root: Functions to support the plant underground and absorb water and nutrients, the portion lacking buds.

Tuber: A fleshy, enlarged part of an underground rhizome or stolon which stores food.

Umbel: A flower cluster with flower stalks radiating from one point like the ribs of an umbrella.

Undulate: Having a wavy edge.

Venation: The arrangement or system of veins.

Vernal pools: Depressions that collect water over the winter and form temporary pools. As they dry out in the spring, wildflowers bloom at the edge.

Weed: Any undesirable, uncultivated plant that crowds out a desired crop or grows where it is not wanted.

Whorl: A circle of three or more leaves or stalks attached to the same stem node.

Wildflower: An herbaceous plant capable of growing, reproducing, and becoming established without cultivation.

Wing: A thin membranous flap extending along a stem, stalk, or other part of the plant.

Winter annual: A small plant produced from seed in late summer or fall and over-wintering underground to flower and die the next year.

Xeric: The driest part of a site.

Xeriscaping: Landscaping with plants that require little water to match the available soil moisture, so that water is conserved.

Pictorial Glossary

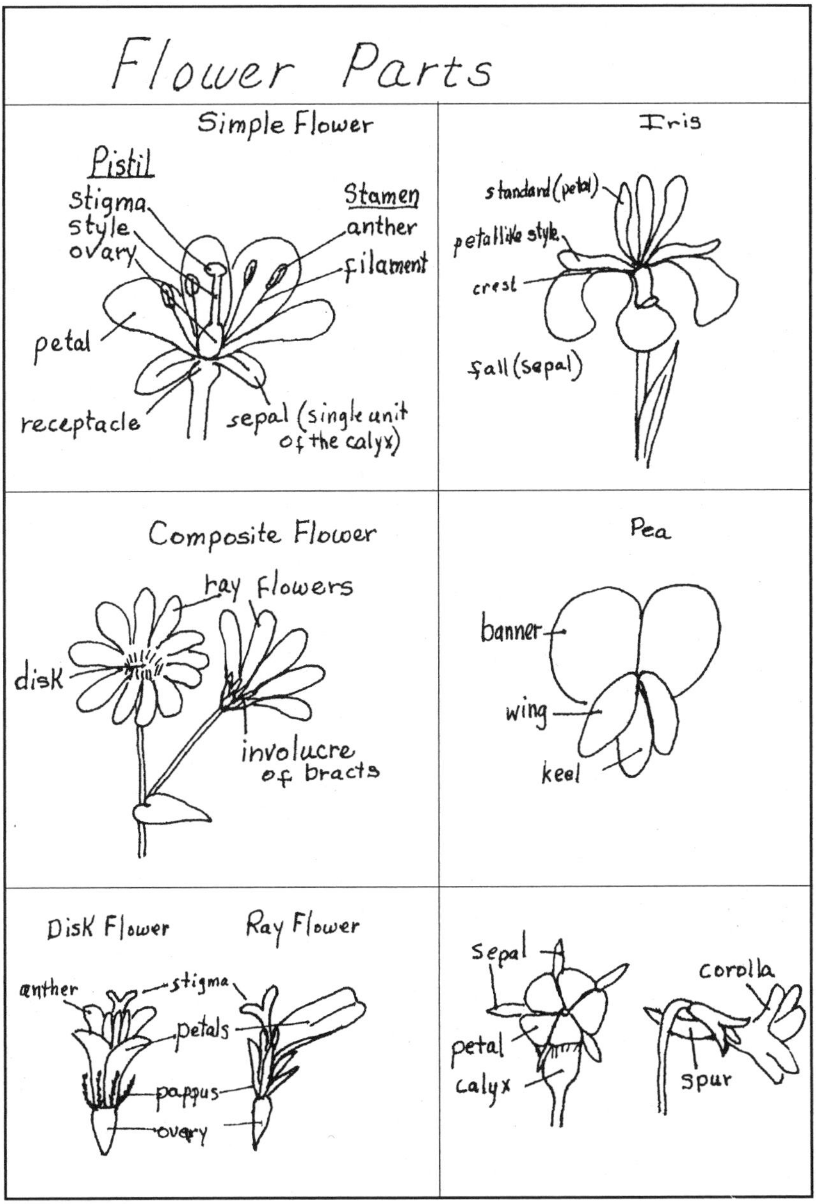

Flower Parts

Simple Flower

Pistil
Stigma
style
ovary

Stamen
anther
filament

petal

receptacle

sepal (single unit of the calyx)

Iris

standard (petal)

petallike style

crest

fall (sepal)

Composite Flower

ray flowers

disk

involucre of bracts

Pea

banner

wing

keel

Disk Flower   Ray Flower

anther

stigma

petals

pappus

ovary

sepal

petal

calyx

corolla

spur

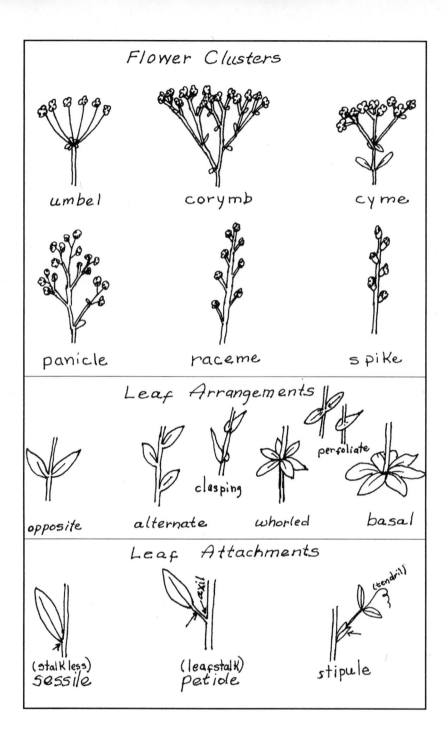

Flower Clusters

umbel   corymb   cyme

panicle   raceme   spike

Leaf Arrangements

opposite   alternate   clasping   whorled   perfoliate   basal

Leaf Attachments

(stalkless) sessile   (leafstalk) petiole   leaf axil   (tendril) stipule

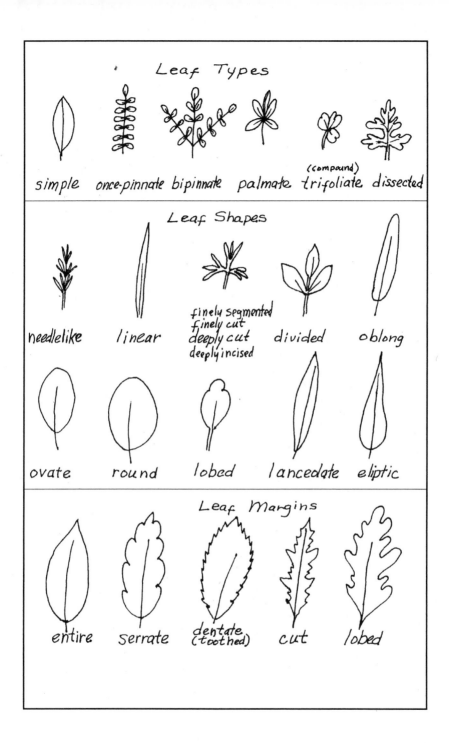

Leaf Types

| simple | once-pinnate | bipinnate | palmate | trifoliate *(compound)* | dissected |

Leaf Shapes

| needlelike | linear | finely segmented finely cut deeply cut deeply incised | divided | oblong |

| ovate | round | lobed | lancedate | eliptic |

Leaf Margins

| entire | serrate | dentate (toothed) | cut | lobed |

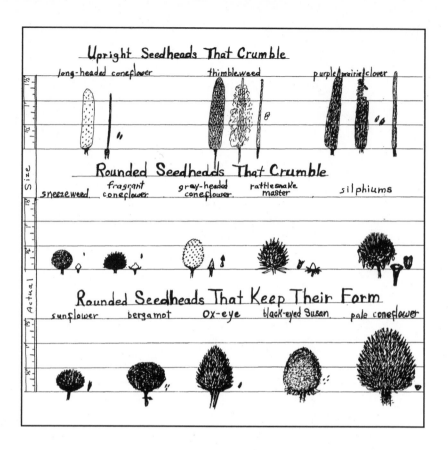

Upright Seedheads That Crumble

long-headed coneflower   thimbleweed   purple prairie clover

Rounded Seedheads That Crumble

sneezeweed   fragrant coneflower   gray-headed coneflower   rattlesnake master   silphiums

Rounded Seedheads That Keep Their Form

sunflower   bergamot   ox-eye   black-eyed Susan   pale coneflower

Size

Actual

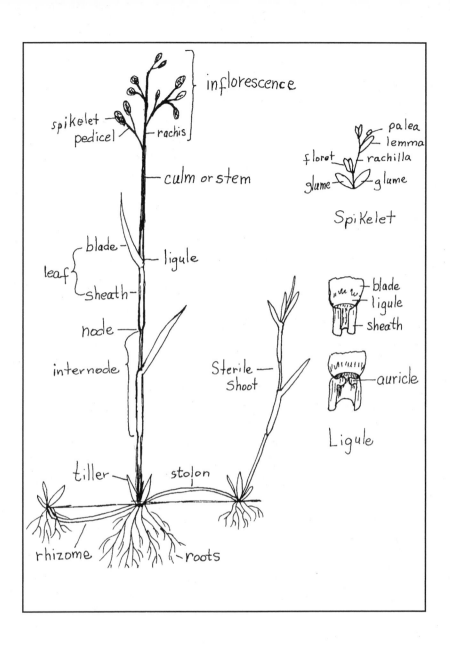

inflorescence

spikelet
pedicel — rachis

culm or stem

palea
lemma
floret — rachilla
glume — glume

Spikelet

blade —
leaf { — ligule
sheath —

node —

internode

Sterile — Shoot

blade
ligule
sheath

auricle

Ligule

tiller — stolon

rhizome — roots

Order of Blooming

Species are listed in the order that they bloom, depending on location and seasonal changes.

APRIL
Pulsatilla patens, pasque flower
Antennaria neglecta, pussytoes

MAY
Astragalus crassicarpus, ground plum
Anemone canadensis, Canada anemone
Viola pedatifida, prairie violet
Pedicularis canadensis, lousewort
Lithospermum canescens, hoary puccoon
Thalictrum dasycarpum, purple meadow-rue
Hypoxis hirsuta, yellow stargrass
Sisyrinchium campestre, blue-eyed grass
Zizia aurea, golden alexanders
Heuchera richardsonii, alumroot
Geum triflorum, prairie smoke
Dodecatheon meadia, shooting star
Phlox pilosa, prairie phlox
Senecio plattensis, prairie ragwort
Vicia americana, vetch
Penstemon grandiflorus, large-flowered beardtongue

JUNE
Iris shrevei, blue flag
Silene antirrhina, sleepy catchfly
Stipa spartea, porcupine grass

Rosa arkansana, sunshine rose
Delphinium virescens, prairie larkspur
Koeleria macrantha, June grass
Tradescantia ohiensis, spiderwort
Echinacea pallida, pale coneflower
Pediomelum argophyllum, silvery scurf-pea
Baptisia bracteata, cream wild indigo
Penstemon pallidus, pale beardtongue
Lilium philadelphicum, wood lily
Heliopsis helianthoides, ox-eye
Zigadenus elegans, white camass
Opuntia humifusa, eastern prickly pear
Ceanothus americanus, New Jersey tea
Anemone cylindrica, windflower
Baptisia lactea, wild indigo
Spiraea alba, meadow sweet
Coreopsis palmata, prairie coreopsis
Mirabilis nyctaginea, wild four-o'clock
Parthenium integrifolium, feverfew
Gaura biennis, gaura
Campanula rotundifolia, harebell
Asclepias tuberosa, butterfly weed
Euphorbia corollata, flowering spurge
Oenothera rhombipetala, sand primrose
Lobelia spicata, spiked lobelia
Amorpha canescens, lead plant

JULY
Verbena stricta, hoary vervain
Desmanthus illinoensis, prairie mimosa
Silphium laciniatum, compass plant
Silphium integrifolium, rosinweed
Silphium perfoliatum, cup plant
Hypericum punctatum, spotted St. John's wort
Potentilla arguta, prairie cinquefoil
Eryngium yuccifolium, rattlesnake master
Oenothera pilosella, prairie sundrops
Asclepias verticillata, whorled milkweed
Allium cernuum, nodding wild onion
Ruellia humilis, wild petunia
Sphaeralcea coccinea, scarlet mallow

Astragalus canadensis, milk vetch
Rudbeckia hirta, black-eyed Susan
Solidago missouriensis, Missouri goldenrod
Verbena hastata, blue vervain
Ratibida columnifera, long-headed coneflower
Ratibida pinnata, gray-headed coneflower
Desmodium canadense, showy tick-trefoil
Spartina pectinata, cord grass
Dalea purpurea, purple prairie clover
Asclepias incarnata, swamp milkweed
Elymus canadensis, Canada wild rye
Lilium michiganense, Michigan lily
Chamaecrista fasciculata, partridge pea
Veronicastrum virginicum, Culver's root
Monarda fistulosa, wild bergamot
Pycnanthemum virginianum, common mountain mint
Bouteloua curtipendula, side-oats grama
Lespedeza capitata, round-headed bush clover
Vernonia fasciculata, ironweed
Eupatorium maculatum, spotted Joe-pye-weed
Eupatorium perfoliatum, boneset
Helianthus occidentalis, western sunflower

AUGUST

Lobelia siphilitica, great lobelia
Liatris pycnostachya, prairie blazing star
Liatris aspera, blazing star
Artemisia ludoviciana, white sage
Hieracium longipilum, hawkweed
Helenium autumnale, sneezeweed
Rudbeckia subtomentosa, fragrant coneflower
Lobelia cardinalis, cardinal flower
Sorghastrum nutans, Indian grass
Prenanthes alba, rattlesnake-root
Dichanthelium oligosanthes, switchgrass
Solidago rigida, stiff goldenrod
Solidago nemoralis, field goldenrod
Andropogon gerardii, big bluestem
Schizachyrium scoparium, little bluestem
Sporobolus heterolepsis, prairie dropseed

SEPTEMBER

Solidago speciosa, showy goldenrod
Gentiana andrewsii, bottle gentian
Aster laevis, smooth aster
Aster novae-angliae, New England aster
Aster azureus, sky-blue aster
Aster ericoides, heath aster

Butterfly Habitats

The following butterflies are classified by family with names of the primary plants and trees that attract them. Emphasis is placed on plants in this book.

Species	Larvae Food Plant	Nectar Plant
Brush-footed (Nymphalidae). Large, most diverse, tiny forelegs.		
American painted lady (*Vanessa virginiensis*)	ironweed	stiff goldenrod, New England aster, milkweed spp., prairie coreopsis, compass plant, dandelion
Buckeye (*Junonia coenia*)	vervain spp.	aster spp., prairie coreopsis, milkweed spp., blue vervain
Great spangled fritillary (*Speyeria cybele*)	violet spp. only	Joe-pye-weed, ironweed, black-eyed Susan, pale coneflower, wild bergamot, cardinal flower, milkweed spp., N.J. tea
Large wood nymph or common wood nymph (*Cercyonis pegala*)	grasses: e.g., Indian grass	wild bergamot, coneflower spp., beardtongue spp.
Meadow fritillary (*Clossiana bellona*)	violet spp.	violet spp.
Milbert's tortoiseshell (*Aglais milberti*)	nettles	ox-eye, goldenrod spp., aster spp.
Mourning cloak (*Nymphalis antiopa*)	willow, elm, aspen, poplar, cottonwood, birch tree foliage	milkweed spp., N.J. tea, sunflower spp.

Species	Larvae Food Plant	Nectar Plant
Painted lady (*Vanessa cardui*)	sunflower spp., pussytoes, pearly everlasting	goldenrod spp., Joe-pye-weed, ironweed, blazing star, wild bergamot, butterfly weed, common mountain mint
Pearly crescentspot (*Phyciodes tharos*)	aster spp.	azure aster, black-eyed Susan, ox-eye, milkweed spp., blazing star, pale coneflower, aster spp., dandelion
Red admiral (*Vanessa atalanta*)	nettles, hops, thistles	blazing star, milkweed spp., pale coneflower, aster spp., dandelion
Regal fritillary (*Speyeria idalia*)	unplowed prairie spp., violet spp.	violet spp.
Viceroy (*Basilarchia archippus*)	fruit trees, aspen, poplar	aster spp., Joe-pye-weed, goldenrod spp., milkweed spp.

Gossamer-wings (Lycaenidae). Small, fast-flying.

Species	Larvae Food Plant	Nectar Plant
American copper (*Lycaena phlaeas*)	docks, sheep sorrel	prairie cinquefoil
Common blue (*Icaricia icarioides*)	lupine	lupine, milkweed spp., sunflower spp., prairie cinquefoil
Eastern tailed blue (*Everes comyntas*)	tick clover, round-headed bush clover	milkweed spp.
Gray hairstreak (*Strymon melinus*)	tick clover, wild bergamot, round-headed bush clover	milkweed spp., goldenrod spp., tick clover, wild bergamot
Marine blue (*Leptotes marina*)	false indigo, lead plant	wild buckwheat
Purplish copper (*Lycaena helloides*)	docks, sheep sorrel	prairie cinquefoil
Silvery blue (*Glaucopsyche lygdamus*)	vetch, lupine	coneflower spp., lupine
Spring azure (*Celastrina ladon*)	N.J. tea	violet spp., milkweed spp.

Milkweed (Danaidae). Tiny forelegs.

Species	Larvae Food Plant	Nectar Plant
Monarch (*Danaus plexippus*)	milkweed spp. only	milkweed spp., goldenrod spp., ox-eye, Joe-pye-weed, ironweed, blazing star, blue vervain, prairie phlox

Species	Larvae Food Plant	Nectar Plant

Satyrs or Browns and Wood Nymphs (Satyridae). Eye spots on wings.

Species	Larvae Food Plant	Nectar Plant
Large wood nymph (*Cercyonis pegala*)	native grasses	pale coneflower, wild bergamot, sunflower spp., ironweed
Little wood satyr (*Megisto cymela*)	Indian grass	various wildflowers

Skippers (Hesperiidae). Quick-flying, dart from perch to flower.

Species	Larvae Food Plant	Nectar Plant
Bunchgrass skipper (*Problema byssus*)	eastern grama grass	various wildflowers
Common checkered skipper (*Pyrgus communis*)	mallow, hollyhocks	aster spp., fleabane, clover spp.
Dakota skipper (*Hesperia dacotae*)	unplowed prairies, native grasses	pale coneflower, long-headed coneflower
Fiery skipper (*Itylephila phyleus*)	native grasses	aster spp., milkweed spp., ox-eye, ironweed
Ottoe skipper (*Hesperia ottoe*)	native grasses, un-disturbed prairie spp.	pale coneflower
Pepper and salt skipper (*Amblyscirtes hegon*)	Indian grass	pale coneflower
Silver-spotted skipper (*Epargyreus clarus*)	tick clover and other legumes, locust, wisteria	Joe-pye-weed, blazing star, milk-weed spp., blue flag, iris, vetch
Tawny-edged skipper (*Polites themistocles*)	native grasses	N.J. tea, purple coneflower

Swallowtails (Papilionidae). Largest, very colorful.

Species	Larvae Food Plant	Nectar Plant
Black swallowtail (*Papilio polyxenes*)	carrot family, parsley	swamp milkweed, prairie phlox, clover spp.
Giant swallowtail (*Heraclides cresphontes*)	prickly ash, hoptree, rue, citrus trees	milkweed spp., goldenrod spp.

Species	Larvae Food Plant	Nectar Plant
Tiger swallowtail (*Pterourus glaucus*)	cherry, birch, aspen, cottonwood, tulip tree, willow, lilac	butterfly weed, prairie phlox, Joe-pye-weed, wild bergamot, monarda, ironweed, sunflower spp.

Whites and Sulphurs (Pieridae). Common, familiar.

Species	Larvae Food Plant	Nectar Plant
Cabbage white (*Artogeia rapae*)	mustard family	aster spp., wild bergamot, milkweed spp., prairie cinquefoil
California dogface (*Zerene eurydice*)	false indigo	thistle, false indigo
Checkered white (*Pontia protodice*)	mustard family	milkweed spp., aster spp.
Clouded or common sulphur (*Colias philodice*)	clover spp., vetch, wild indigo	clover spp., goldenrod spp., aster spp., ox-eye, milkweed spp., prairie phlox
Cloudless giant sulphur (*Phoebis sennae*)	partridge pea, clover spp.	cardinal flower, thistle
Dogface (*Zerene cesonia*)	false indigo, purple prairie clover	prairie coreopsis, vervain spp.
Olympia marblewing (*Euchloe olympi*)	mustard family	
Orange sulphur (*Colias eurytheme*)	wild indigo, vetch, various legumes	clover spp., aster spp., goldenrod spp., prairie coreopsis, ox-eye, milkweed spp.

Family Characteristics

Dicotyledons

Acanthaceae (acanthus family)
Ornamental herbs or shrubs with seeds borne on hooked projections. Flowers often bilaterally symmetrical with showy bracts. Corolla with 4–5 petals, usually 2-lobed upper lip and 3-lobed lower lip. Leaves simple, opposite, smooth with pale streaks or bumps. Fruit is 2-celled capsule.

Apiaceae, Umbelliferae (parsley family)
Flowers grouped into a compound umbel with numerous small petals. Leaves alternate, pinnately compound, finely cut. Fruits split into 2 halves, each 1-seeded.

Asclepiadaceae (milkweed family)
Stems have thick milky juice, opposite or whorled leaves, and flowers in umbellike clusters. Flowers have 5 petals swept back and a 5-parted cup supporting the 2 ovaries. Two pods are formed for the fruits and contain styles with many silky-haired seeds. Pollination by insects is difficult. Attracts many butterflies, including the monarch.

Asteraceae, Compositae (sunflower family)
The largest family of flowering plants. Flower heads are in clusters of many small flowers growing together in a central disk (therefore, composite) and most with a circle of ray flowers supported by small leaflets or bracts. The leaves are simple or compound, opposite, alternate, or whorled. The fruit is 1-seeded with a hard shell. Most seeds have hairs attached to aid in their distribution.

Boraginaceae (forget-me-not family)
Herbs are often covered with hairs. Flowers radially symmetrical, often borne along 1 side of branches or at tip of stem coiled like a fiddleneck. Flower parts mostly in 5's (calyx lobes, stamens). Leaves alternate, undivided, simple. Fruit separates into 4 hard seedlike sections (nutlets).

Cactaceae (cactus family)
Thick, fleshy plants with spines. Leafless. The cuplike flowers have many petals and stamens. Fruit is usually fleshy, often edible, with many seeds.

Campanulaceae (bluebell or harebell family)
Corolla tube opens along upper side; 2 lobes on upper lip and 3 drooping on lower lip. Leaves alternate; plant has milky juice. Fruit is a berry or capsule. Attracts hummingbirds.

Caryophyllaceae (pink family)
Nodes are swollen on the stem, and flowers bloom singly or in a branched or forked cluster. Flower petals and sepals are 5 and stamens 5 or 10, all attached at the base of the ovary. Leaves opposite, simple, notched. Fruit usually a capsule. The hothouse carnation is in this family. Bears a superficial resemblance to phlox.

Euphorbiaceae (spurge family)
Commonly herbs with milky sap. Flowers have 5 petals radially symmetrical; simple or compound leaves with alternate or opposite position. Fruit 3-lobed with 3 1-seeded sections. Among the valuable products of the family are rubber, castor and tung oils, and tapioca.

Fabaceae, Leguminosae (pea family)
Flower has the common sweet pea shape, often clustered. The pea family is related to the rose family. It contains the pea, bean, clover, alfalfa, sweet pea, lupine, wisteria, peanut, and many other species familiar in cultivation. Leaves alternate, pinnately compound, with stipules or tendrils or thorns. Seeds form in a pod that opens along 1 or 2 seams. Inoculants aid in germination.

Gentianaceae (gentian family)
Bottlelike, cylindrical flowers with 4 to 12 petals. Leaves usually stalkless, opposite, simple, and undivided. Fruit usually a capsule.

Hypericaceae (St. John's wort family)
Leafy herbs or shrubs in branched clusters. Flowers radially symmetrical with 5 petals, stamens numerous, all attached to the base of the ovary. Leaves simple, opposite, or whorled with numerous, often black or translucent dots. Fruit usually a capsule.

Lamiaceae, Labiatae (mint family)
Aromatic herbs with square stems and opposite leaves. Flowers small, usually on spikes; 2-lobed upper lip and 3-lobed lower lip. Leaves usually simple, opposite, or whorled. Fruit has 4 lobes, each forming a hard, single-seeded nutlet.

Malvaceae (mallow family)
Herbs that are velvety with starlike or branched hairs. Flowers with 5 separate petals are borne singly or in branched clusters. Many stamens are joined at their

stalks into a tube that joins around the style. Leaves alternate, simple, often palmately veined and lobed or deeply divided. Fruit has 5 or more chambers that separate from one another or form a capsule or berry.

Nyctaginaceae (four o'clock family)
Flowers in small clusters of nodding bells seated in green cuplike circles of joined bracts. Leaves are opposite.

Onagraceae (evening primrose family)
Flowers usually radially symmetrical wtih 4 petals and sepals. Leaves simple, alternate, or opposite. The fruit is commonly a 4-chambered capsule.

Polemoniaceae (phlox family)
Showy flowers in clusters branched in a forked manner. Five flat petals are joined at the narrow corolla tube. Leaves alternate or opposite, simple or pinnately divided. Three-chambered capsule contains the fruit.

Primulaceae (primrose family)
Showy flowers bloom singly or in clusters, radially symmetrical with 5 petals and parts attached at the base of the ovary. Leaves are opposite, whorled, or basal and usually simple. The fruit is in a 1-chambered capsule.

Ranunculaceae (buttercup family)
Numerous stamens and pistils form a button in the middle of the flower. Petals are absent in many species, and the sepals are showy. Leaves are usually alternate, palmately lobed, or divided. The fruit pod or follicle has a seedlike achene or berry.

Rhamnaceae (buckthorn family)
Shrub with small flowers in radially symmetrical clusters with 5 or sometimes 4 petals. Leaves are simple, unlobed, alternate, or opposite. The fruit has a 2- or 3-chambered berry.

Rosaceae (rose family)
Shrub with prickly stems. Flowers radially symmetrical with 5 petals and numerous stamens. Leaves alternate, simple, or compound with stipules at the base of the leaf stalk. The fruit is dry or fleshy. Strawberries, blackberries, and apples are also in this family.

Saxifragaceae (saxifrage family)
Herbs with small flowers borne in racemelike or openly branched clusters, with a flower plan of 4 to 5. Flowers are radially symmetrical with 5 petals. Leaves usually alternate and basal, with a decorative foliage forming a rosette. Fruit is a capsule, small pod, or berry. Closely related to the rose family.

Scrophulariaceae (figwort or snapdragon family)
Showy flowers are bilaterally symmetrical with 4 or 5 petals. They are united forming a corolla with upper and lower lips attached to the ovary (2 lobes above and 3

ing a corolla with upper and lower lips attached to the ovary (2 lobes above and 3 below). The 4 or 5 petals may be more regular. Therefore, not all look like the snapdragons in the garden. Leaves are alternate, opposite, or whorled, simple or pinnately divided. Fruit has 2-chambered capsule or berry.

Verbenaceae (vervain family)
Paired, toothed leaves and small bilaterally symmetrical flowers in slender spikes or flat clusters. Five flat petals are united to a corolla tube. Leaves opposite or whorled, simple. The fruit separates into 4 hard nutlets, each with 1 seed. Teak is in this family.

Violaceae (violet family)
Low plants, flowering with 5 petals. The lower petal is often wider, heavily veined, and extended back into a spur. The lateral petals are usually bearded. The pistil has a thickened head and a short beak. Leaves alternate, simple, but sometimes deeply lobed. The fruit is an explosively opening capsule.

Monocotyledons

Commelinaceae (spiderwort family)
Flowers in a terminal cluster that open 1 or 2 at a time. Bracts are boat-shaped. Leaves linear, parallel-veined, forming a tubular sheath around the stem. Three roundish petals, often blue. Fruit has capsule with 3 chambers.

Iridaceae (iris family)
Flat, swordlike leaves. Showy flowers in 3 parts. Blue-eyed grass has sepals and petals alike, seeming 6-petaled. The iris family differs from the amaryllis family in having 3 stamens instead of 6. It has rhizomes, bulbs, or corms. Fruit is a capsule. The iris family includes several kinds of plants that at first sight do not suggest the iris: gladiolus, freesia, sisyrinchium.

Liliaceae (lily family)
Three- or 6-part flowers, bell-like or triangular. Leaves have parallel veins. Form rhizomes, bulbs, or corms. Three-chambered capsule fruit.

Poaceae, Gramineae (grass family)
Plants with narrow leaves with parallel veins and small, inconspicuous flowers. The stems are mainly hollow except at the node where the leaf is attached. Stems have joints where the leaves attach. Stems are usually round. Flowers are arranged on stalks with two rows.

Sources for Seeds, Plants, and Equipment

ILLINOIS

Bluestem Prairie Nursery, R.R. 2, Box 106A, Hillsboro, IL 62049
Kathy Clinebell, R.R. 2, Box 176, Wyoming, IL 61491
Country Road Greenhouses, R.R. 1, Box 62, Malta, IL 60150
Genesis Nursery, R.R. 1, Box 32, Walnut, IL 61376
Lafayette Home Nursery, 1 Nursery Lane, R.R. 1, Box 1A, Lafayette, IL 61449
Midwest Wildflowers, Box 64, Rockton, IL 61072
Natural Garden, 38W443 Highway 64, St. Charles, IL 60175
Prairie Bluestem Nursery, R.R. 2, Box 92, Hillsboro, IL 62049
Prairie Garden, 705 South Kenilworth, Oak Park, IL 60304
Purple Prairie Farm, R.R. 2, Box 176, Wyoming, IL 61491
Wildflower Source, P.O. Box 312, Fox Lake, IL 60020
Winddrift Prairie Shop, R.R. 2, Oregon, IL 61061

INDIANA

Gardens Alive!, 5100 Schenley Place, Lawrenceburg, IN 47025

IOWA

Allendan Seed, R.R. 2, Box 31, Winterset, IA 50073
Jim Burdette, R.R. 2, Diagonal, IA 50845
Howard Christiansen, R.R. 1, Box 20, Wiota, IA 50274
John Curry, R.R. 2, Box 101, Exira, IA 50076
Farmers Co-op, 300 Osage St., Creston, IA 50801
Lee Farris, R.R. 1, Box 75, Mount Ayr, IA 50854
Heyne Custom Seed Service, R.R. 1, Box 78, Walnut, IA 51577
ION Exchange, Howard Bright, R.R. 1, Box 48, Harpers Ferry, IA 52146
Iowa Prairie Seed Co., Box 228, Sheffield, IA 50475
Keith McGinnis, 309 E. Florence, Glenwood, IA 51534
Nature's Way, R.R. 1, Box 62, Woodburn, IA 50275

Duane Ortgies, 905 Birch St., Atlantic, IA 50022
John Osenbaugh, R.R. 1, Box 106, Lucas, IA 50151
Richard Routh, 406 W. Washington, Mount Ayr, IA 50854
Sexauer Co., 444 S.W. Fifth, Des Moines, IA 50309
Smith Nursery, Box 515, Charles City, IA 50616
Swift Greenhouses, 2724 300th Street, Gilman, IA 50106
Willowglen Nursery & Landscaping, 3512 Lost Mile Road, Decorah, IA 52101

KANSAS
Rolf & Snell Forb Seed, 300 North Adams, Medicine Lodge, KS 67104
Sharp Bros. Seed Co., P.O. Box 140, Hwy. 4, Healy, KS 67850
Wilderness Wildflower Div., P.O. Box 1664, Salina, KS 67402

MICHIGAN
International Bio Enterprises, 14174 Hoffman Rd., Three Rivers, MI 49093
Kalamazoo Wildflower Nursery, 922 Grant, Kalamazoo, MI 49008
Michigan Wildflower Farm, 11771 Cutler Rd., Portland, MI 48875
Wildside, 4815 Valley Ave., Hudsonville, MI 49426

MINNESOTA
Busse Garden, R.R. 2, Box 238, Cakato, MN 55321
Feder's Prairie Seed Co., R.R. 1, Box 41, Blue Earth, MN 56013
Landscape Alternatives, 1465 N. Pascal St., St. Paul, MN 55108
Landscape Alternatives Nursery, 671 Larpenteur Ave., St. Paul, MN 55108
Mohn Frontier Seed & Nursery, R.R. 1, Box 152, Cottonwood, MN 56229
Orchid Gardens, 2232 139th Ave. NW, Andover, MN 55304
Prairie Hill Wildflowers, R.R. 1, Box 191-A, Ellendale, MN 56026
Prairie Moon Nursery, R.R. 3, Box 163, Winona, MN 55987
Prairie Restorations, P.O. Box 327, Princeton, MN 55371
Rice Creek Gardens, 11506 Hwy. 65, Blaine, MN 55434

MISSOURI
Bluestem Seed Co., Box 32, Hwy. 46 E., Grant City, MO 64456
Elixir Farm Botanicals, Brixey, MO 65618
Gilberg Perennial Farms, 2906 Ossenfort Rd., Glencoe, MO 63038
Hamilton Seed Co., HCR 9, Box 138, Elk Creek, MO 65464
J & J Seeds, R.R. 3, Gallatin, MO 64640
E. F. Mangeldorg Seed, 4500 Swan Ave, P.O. Box 327, St. Louis, MO 63166
Missouri Wildflowers Nursery, 9814 Pleasant Hill Rd., Jefferson City, MO 65109
Sharp Bros. Seed Co., R.R. 4, Box 237A, Clinton, MO 64735
Wayne Vassar A-G Grain and Seed, R.R. 4, Clinton, MO 64735

NEBRASKA

P. E. Allen Farm Supply, R.R. 2, Box 8, Bristow, NE 68719

Aurora McTurf Native Grasses, P.O. Box 194, Aurora, NE 68818

Bluebird Nursery, 515 Linden St., Clarkson, NE 68629

DeGiorgi Seed Co., 6011 N St., Omaha, NE 68117

Flowerland, P.O. Box 26, Wynot, NE 68792

Fragrant Path, P.O. Box 328, Fort Calhoun, NE 68023

Horizon Seeds, Inc., P.O. Box 81823, Lincoln, NE 68501

Miller Grass Seed Co., 1600 Corn Husker Hwy., Lincoln, NE 68501

Stock Seed Farms, Inc., R.R. 1, Box 112, Murdock, NE 68407

WISCONSIN

Boehlke's Woodland Gardens, W. 140 N. 10829 Country Aire Rd., Germantown, WI 53022

Country Wetlands Nursery, S75W20755 Field Drive, P.O. Box 126, Muskego, WI 53150

Four Winds Farm Supply, Biological Pest Management, N8806 600th St., River Falls, WI 54022

Kester's Wild Game Food Nurseries, 4488 Hwy. 116 E., P.O. Box V, Omro, WI 54963

Kettle Moraine Natural Landscaping, W996 Birchwood Dr., Campbellsport, WI 53010

Little Valley Farm, R.R. 3, Box 544, Spring Green, WI 53588

Lonergan's, 3048 Paradise Dr., West Bend, WI 53095

Milaeger's Gardens, 4838 Douglas Ave., Racine, WI 53402

Natural Habitat Nursery, 4818 Terminal Road, McFarland, WI 53558

Nature's Nursery, 6125 Mathewson Rd., Mazomanie, WI 53560

Prairie Future Seed Co., P.O. Box 644, Menomonee Falls, WI 53052

Prairie Nursery, P.O. Box 306, Westfield, WI 53964

Prairie Ridge Nursery, R.R. 2, 9738 Overland Rd., Mt. Horeb, WI 53572

Prairie Seed Source, P.O. Box 83, North Lake, WI 53064

Reeseville Ridge Nursery, 309 S. Main St., P.O. Box 171, Reeseville, WI 53579

Retzer Nature Center, W284 S1530 Rd. DT, Waukesha, WI 53188

Wehr Nature Center, 9701 W. College Ave., Franklin, WI 53132

Wildlife Nurseries, P.O. Box 2724, Oshkosh, WI 54901

GARDEN SUPPLIES FOR PEOPLE WITH DISABILITIES

American Horticultural Therapy Association, 9200 Wightman Road, Suite 400, Gaithersburg, MD 20879

Gardener's Eden, P.O. Box 7307, San Francisco, CA 94120

Gardener's Supply Co., Intervale Road, Burlington, VT 05401

Smith and Hawken, 25 Corte Madera, Mill Valley, CA 94941

HARVESTING EQUIPMENT

Grin Reaper (attaches to string trimmer)

Environmental Survey Consulting, 4602 Placid Place, Austin, TX 78731 (512) 458-8531

CLEANING EQUIPMENT

Speed King Hammermill, model 615

Winona Attrition Mill Company, 1009 W. 5th St., Winona, MN 55987 (507) 452-2716

Fanning mill

Clipper Office Tester Seed Cleaner, 805 S. Decker Drive, P.O. Box 256, Bluffton, IN 46714 (800) 248-8318, (219) 824-3400

Seedburo screen shaker and sieves

Seedburo Equipment Company, 1022 W. Jackson Blvd., Chicago, IL 60607 (800) 284-5779, (312) 738-3700

Organizations Promoting Restoration

Butterfly Club of America, 736 Main Ave., Suite 200, Box 2257, Durango, CO 81302

Butterfly Count National Coordinators:
  Paul A. Opler, 5100 Greenview Court, Fort Collins, CO 80525
  Ann B. Swengel, 909 Birch St., Baraboo, WI 53913

Canada Wildflower Society, 1220 Fieldstone Circle, Pickering, Ontario L1X 1B4

Environmental Protection Agency, 401 M Street S.W., Washington, D.C. 20460

Garden Club of America, 598 Madison Ave., New York, NY 10022

Integrated Roadside Vegetation Management, 1268 McCollum Science Hall, UNI Biology Dept., Cedar Falls, IA 50613

Iowa Association of Naturalists, R.R. 1, Box 53, Guthrie Center, IA 50115

Iowa County Extension Offices, Publications Distribution, Printing and Publications Building, Ames, IA 50011

Iowa Department of Natural Resources, Wallace State Office Building, Des Moines, IA 50309

Iowa Department of Transportation, 800 Lincoln Way, Ames, IA 50010

Iowa Natural Heritage Foundation, 444 Insurance Exchange Building, 505 Fifth Ave., Des Moines, IA 50309

Iowa Prairie Network, P.O. Box 516, Mason City, IA 50402

Iowa Prairie Network Newsletter, c/o Dianne Blankenship, Secretary, 2900 Jackson St., Sioux City, IA 51104

Iowa Raptor Foundation, P.O. Box 32, Pella, IA 50219

Kansas Biological Survey, University of Kansas, 2041 Constant Ave., Lawrence, KS 66047

Loess Hills Scenic Byway Brochure, to obtain send SASE to Harrison County Museum/Welcome Center, R.R. 3, Box 130A, Missouri Valley, IA 51555

Michigan Natural Features Inventory, Mason Building, 5th Floor, Box 30028, Lansing, MI 48909

Minnesota Native Plant Society, 1445 Gortner Ave., St. Paul, MN 55108

Minnesota Natural Heritage, Department of Natural Resources, 500 Lafayette Road, St. Paul, MN 55155

Missouri Department of Conservation, P.O. Box 180, Jefferson City, MO 65102

Missouri DNR & Department of Natural History, P.O. Box 176, Jefferson City, MO 65102

Missouri Native Plant Society, P.O. Box 6612, Jefferson City, MO 65102

Missouri Prairie Foundation, P.O. Box 200, Columbia, MO 65201

National Audubon Society, 950 Third Avenue, New York, NY 10022

National Council of State Garden Clubs, 4401 Magnolia Ave., St. Louis, MO 63110

National Parks and Conservation Association, 1015-31st St., NW, Washington, D.C. 20007

National Wildflower Research Center, 2600 FM 973 North, Austin, TX 78725

Native Plant Society of Texas, P.O. Box 891, Georgetown, TX 78627

Nature Conservancy Dakotas Field Office, 1014 E. Central Ave., Bismarck, ND 58501

Nature Conservancy Illinois Field Office, 79 W. Monroe St., Suite 900, Chicago, IL 60603

Nature Conservancy Indiana Field Office, 1330 W. 38th St., Indianapolis, IN 46208

Nature Conservancy Iowa Field Office, 431 E. Locust, Suite 200, Des Moines, IA 50309

Nature Conservancy Kansas Field Office, Southwest Plaza Bldg., 3601 W. 29th St., Suite 112B, Topeka, KS 66614

Nature Conservancy Minnesota Field Office, 1313 Fifth St., SE, Minneapolis, MN 55414

Nature Conservancy Missouri Field Office, 2800 S. Brentwood Blvd., St. Louis, MO 63144

Nature Conservancy National Office, 1815 North Lynn Street, Arlington, VA 22209

Nature Conservancy Nebraska Field Office, 418 S. 10th St., Omaha, NE 68102

Nature Conservancy Texas Field Office, P.O. Box 1440, San Antonio, TX 78295

Nature Conservancy Wisconsin Field Office, 333 W. Mifflin, Suite 107, Madison, WI 53703

Nebraska Natural Heritage Program, Game and Parks Commission, 2200 N. 33rd St., P.O. Box 30370, Lincoln, NE 68503

Prairie Women Adventures and Retreat, Homestead Ranch in the Flint Hills, P.O. Box 2, Matfield Green, KS 66862

Soil Conservation Society of America, 7615 N.E. Ankeny Rd., Ankeny, IA 50021

South Dakota Natural Heritage, 45 E. Capitol Avenue, Pierre, SD 57501

Southern Illinois Native Plant Society, Botany Department, Southern Illinois University, Carbondale, IL 52901

Texas Natural Heritage Program, 4200 Smith School Rd., Austin, TX 78744

University of Missouri, Botany Department, Tucker Hall, Columbia, MO 65201

U.S. Fish and Wildlife Service, Office of Endangered Species, Washington, D.C. 20240

Wisconsin Natural Heritage Program, 101 S. Webster Street, Box 7921, Madison, WI 53707

Xerces Society, 10 Southwest Ash St., Portland, OR 97204

Bibliography

AFIRM (Association for Integrated Roadside Management) Beginning. 1993. *Roader's Digest* 5 (1): 3. Cedar Falls, Iowa: Newsletter of the IRVM County Roadside Assistance Office at the University of Northern Iowa.

Andrews, Ron. 1992. Iowa Wetlands—Wildlife's Field of Dreams. *Nongame News* 8 (3): 7–8. Des Moines: Iowa Department of Natural Resources.

Armitage, Allan M. 1989. *Herbaceous Perennial Plants: Treatise on Their Identification, Culture, and Garden Attributes.* Athens, Ga.: Varsity Press.

Arnold, Dana L. 1992. Weeds and Wildflowers for Wildlife. *Wildflower: Journal of the National Wildflower Research Center* 5 (1): 18–23. Austin, Tex.

Art, Henry. 1988. *Creating a Wildflower Meadow.* Bulletin A-102. Pownal, Vt.: Garden Way Publishing.

———. 1989. *A Garden of Wildflowers: 101 Native Species and How to Grow Them.* Pownal, Vt.: Storey Communications.

———. 1991. *The Wildflower Gardener's Guide: Midwest, Great Plains, Canadian Prairies Edition.* Pownal, Vt.: Garden Way Publishing.

Attracting Backyard Wildlife. 1993. *Iowa Conservationist* 52 (1): 23-page centerfold extra edition.

The Audubon Society Field Guide: North American Butterflies. 1981. New York: Alfred Knopf.

The Audubon Society Field Guide: North American Wildflowers, Eastern Region. 1979. New York: Alfred Knopf.

The Audubon Society Nature Guide: Grasslands. 1985. New York: Alfred Knopf.

The Audubon Society Pocket Guides: Familiar Butterflies. 1990. New York: Alfred Knopf.

Austin, Richard L. 1986. *Wild Gardening.* New York: Simon and Schuster.

Bacon, Kelli K. 1992. Restoring the Link between People and Land. *Iowa Natural Heritage,* winter issue.

Barr, Claude A. 1983. *Jewel of the Plains: Wildflowers of the Great Plains, Grasslands, and Hills.* Minneapolis: University of Minnesota Press.

Bradley, Fern Marshall, and Barbara W. Ellis, eds. 1992. *Rodale's All-New Encyclopedia of Organic Gardening*. Emmaus, Pa.: Rodale Press.

Breining, Greg. 1992. Rising from the Bogs. *Nature Conservancy* 42 (4): 24–29.

Brown, Lauren. 1976. *Weeds in Winter*. New York: W. W. Norton & Company.

———. 1979. *Grasses: An Identification Guide*. Sponsored by the Roger Tory Peterson Institute. Boston: Houghton Mifflin.

Buckley, Tom. 1992. Invasion of the Habitat Snatchers. *River Country Conversations* 6 (1): 10–11. Montrose, Iowa: Lee County Conservation Board.

The Butterfly Garden. 1992. *Country Gardens* 1 (1): 97–105.

Capon, Brian. 1990. *Botany for Gardeners*. Portland: Timber Press.

Carson, Rachel. 1962. *Silent Spring*. Boston: Houghton Mifflin.

Cather, Willa. 1913. *O Pioneers!* Boston: Houghton Mifflin.

———. 1918. *My Ántonia*. Boston: Houghton Mifflin.

Cavagnaro, David. 1993. Bringing Nature's Garden Home. *Iowan* 41 (3): 34–38.

Chamberlain, Izanna. *Prairie Memories*. Iowa City: Rudi Publishing.

Cheater, Mark. 1992. Alien Invasion. *Nature Conservancy* 42 (5): 24–29.

Christiansen, Paul A. 1992. *Distribution Maps of Iowa Prairie Plants*. Ames: Living Roadway Trust Fund, Iowa Department of Transportation.

Coombes, Allen J. 1985. *Dictionary of Plant Names*. Portland, Oreg.: Timber Press.

Cooper, Tom C., and Nyla S. Hunt, eds. 1982. *Iowa's Natural Heritage*. Des Moines: Iowa Natural Heritage Foundation and Iowa Academy of Science.

Costello, David. 1969. *The Prairie World*. Minneapolis: University of Minnesota Press.

The Curious Naturalist. 1991. Washington, D.C.: National Geographic Society.

Damrosch, Barbara. 1992. Let a Thousand Prairies Bloom. *House Beautiful* 134 (11): 32–41.

Dickerson, J. A., W. G. Longren, and E. K. Hadle. Native Forb Seed Production. In *Proceedings of the Sixth North American Prairie Conference*, 218–226. Columbus: Ohio State University Press.

Dickinson, Diana. 1993. Prairie Garden Primer for Midwest Backyards. *Midwest Living* 7 (4): 64–68.

Directory of State Preserves. N.d. Des Moines: Iowa State Preserves Board.

Durrell, Gerald. 1984. *A Practical Guide for the Amateur Naturalist*. New York: Alfred Knopf.

Edsall, Marian S. 1985. *Roadside Plants and Flowers: A Traveler's Guide to the Midwest and Great Lakes Area*. Madison: University of Wisconsin Press.

Ehley, Alan M. 1992. Integrated Roadside Vegetation Management (IRVM): A County Approach to Roadside Management in Iowa. In *Proceedings of the Twelfth North American Prairie Conference*, 159–160. Cedar Falls: University of Northern Iowa Press.

Embertson, Jane. 1979. *Pods: Wildflowers and Weeds in Their Final Beauty*. New York: Scribner's/Macmillan.

Ewald, Paul W. 1982. Hummingbirds: The Nectar Connection. *National Geographic* 161 (2): 223–227.

Fairbanks, Miguel Luis. 1992. Maya Heartland under Siege. *National Geographic* 182 (5): 94–107.

Farney, Dennis. 1980. Can the Tallgrass Prairie Be Saved? *National Geographic* 157 (1): 37–61.

Farrar, Jon. 1990. *Field Guide to Wildflowers of Nebraska and the Great Plains*. Lincoln: NEBRASKAland Magazine, Nebraska Game and Parks Commission.

Fitzgerald, Randy. 1992. Quiet Savers of the Land. *Reader's Digest* (June): 128–133.

Fleckenstein, John. 1993. Iowa's State Preserves System. *Iowa Conservationist* 52 (1): 32–41.

Gardening with Wildflowers and Native Plants. 1989. Gardening Handbook Series 119. Brooklyn: Brooklyn Botanic Garden.

Gibbons, Euell. 1962. *Stalking the Wild Asparagus*. Putney, Vt.: Alan C. Hood, Publisher.

Gore, Al. 1992. *Earth in the Balance: Ecology and the Human Spirit*. Boston: Houghton Mifflin.

Grounds, Roger. 1976. *The Natural World*. New York: Stein and Day.

Hamilton, Geoff. 1987. *The Organic Garden Book*. New York: Crown.

Handbook on Gardening with Wild Flowers 18 (38). 1962. Brooklyn: Brooklyn Botanic Garden.

Harmon, Stanley. 1992. Liatris: A Commercially Successful Wildflower. *Wildflower: Journal of the National Wildflower Research Center* 5 (2): 14–17. Austin.

Harper, Pamela J. 1991. *Designing with Perennials*. New York: Macmillan.

Hemaseth, Lisa. 1993. Wet and Wild. *Iowa Conservationist* 52 (1): 5–9.

Henderson, Carrol L. 1988. *Landscaping for Wildlife*. St. Paul: Minnesota Documents Division.

Henderson, Kirk. 1993. Ecotype plus Cultivar = Ecovar. *Roader's Digest* 5 (1): 1–3. Cedar Falls, Iowa: Newsletter of the IRVM County Roadside Assistance Office at the University of Northern Iowa.

Hensel, Margaret. 1992. Create Your Own Cottage Garden. *Countryside* 3 (4): 62–66.

Hill, Alison. 1991. Resetting the Successional Clock. *Wildflower: Journal of the National Wildflower Research Center* 4 (2): 14–19. Austin, Tex.

———. 1992. Environmental Weeds: The Next Generation. *Wildflower: Journal of the National Wildflower Research Center* 5 (1): 24–29. Austin, Tex.

Howe, Robert W. 1984. Wings over the Prairie. *Iowa Conservationist: A Special Prairie Issue* 43 (9): 5–7.

Iowa Ecotype Project: Germplasm Preservation. 1992. *Roader's Digest* 4 (3): 1–2. Cedar Falls, Iowa: Newsletter of the IRVM County Roadside Assistance Office at the University of Northern Iowa.

Jackson, Jerome A. N.d. Attracting Birds: Take a Walk on the Wild Side. In *Guide to Attracting Birds*, 7–11. Holland, Mich.: Birder's World.

Jacobson, Robert L., Nancy J. Albrecht, and Kathryn E. Bolin. 1992. Wildflower Routes: Benefits of a Management Program for Minnesota Right-of-way Prairies. In *Proceedings of the Twelfth North American Prairie Conference*, 153–158. Cedar Falls: University of Northern Iowa Press.

Jesiolowski, Jill. 1992. America's Ten Least Wanted Weeds. *Organic Gardening* 39 (6): 48–53.

Jimerson, Douglas. 1992. Welcome Wildlife. *Better Homes and Gardens* 70 (5): 69–74.

———. 1993. Butterfly Gardening. *Better Homes and Gardens* 71 (5): 39–45.

Johnson, Cathy. 1991. *The Sierra Club Guide to Sketching in Nature*. San Francisco: Sierra Club Books.

Johnson, Lady Bird. 1988. Texas in Bloom. *National Geographic* 173 (4): 493–499.

Jones, Samuel B., Jr., and Leonard E. Foote. 1990. *Gardening with Native Wild Flowers*. Portland, Oreg.: Timber Press.

Kenfield, Warren G. 1966. *The Wild Gardener in the Wild Landscape: The Art of Naturalistic Landscaping*. New York: Hafner Publishing.

Kilpatrick, James J. 1992. Points to Ponder. *Reader's Digest* (June): 190.

Kindscher, Kelly. 1992. *Medicinal Wild Plants of the Prairie*. Lawrence: University Press of Kansas.

Knobel, Edward. 1977. *Field Guide to the Grasses, Sedges, and Rushes of the United States*. New York: Dover.

Landphair, Harlow C. 1992. Roadside Vegetation: Player or Pest? *Roader's Digest* 4 (2): 1–3. Cedar Falls, Iowa: Newsletter of the IRVM County Roadside Assistance Office at the University of Northern Iowa.

Least-Heat-Moon, William. 1991. *PrairyErth*. Boston: Houghton Mifflin.

Lees-Milne, Avilde, and Rosemary Verey. 1980. *The Englishwoman's Garden*. London: Chatto and Windus.

Leighton, Phebe, and Calvin Simonds. 1987. *The New American Landscape Gardener*. Emmaus, Pa.: Rodale.

Lekwa, Steve. 1984. Prairie Restoration and Management. *Iowa Conservationist: A Special Prairie Issue* 43 (9): 12–14.

Leopold, Aldo. 1966. *A Sand County Almanac, with Essays on Conservation from Round River*. New York: Oxford University Press.

Leoschke, Mark, and John Pearson. 1988. Fen: A Special Kind of Wetland. *Iowa Conservationist* 47 (3): 16–19.

Levathes, Louise E. 1987. Mysteries of the Bog. *National Geographic* 171 (3): 397–420.

Lloyd, Nancy. 1992. A Backyard Wonderland: How to Create Your Own Mini-Wildlife Habitat. *Good Housekeeping* 215 (4): 70–74.

Logan, William Bryant. 1992. To Mow or not to Mow. *House and Garden* 164 (5): 46–48.

Long, Michael E., and a portfolio by Jack Unruh. 1988. Wildflowers across America. *National Geographic* 173 (4): 500–511.

Maclean, Charles. 1992. Butterflies in Flower. *House and Garden* 164 (5): 62–66.

Madson, John. 1982. *Where the Sky Began: Land of the Tallgrass Prairie.* Boston: Houghton Mifflin.

———. 1990. On the Osage: In Oklahoma, the Conservancy Sets the Stage for a Prairie Restoration Effort of Never-before-Attempted Proportions. *Nature Conservancy* 40 (3): 6–15.

Martin, A. C., H. S. Zim, and A. L. Nelson. 1961. *American Wildlife and Plants—A Guide to Wildlife Food Habits.* New York: Dover.

Martin, Laura C. *The Wildflower Meadow Book: A Gardener's Guide.* Charlotte, N.C.: East Woods Press, Fast and Macmillan.

Michael, Pamela. 1980. *A Country Harvest.* New York: Exeter Books.

Mikula, Rick. 1992a. The Good, the Bad, and the Beautiful: A Guide to the Butterflies You're Most Likely to Lure. *Organic Gardening* 39 (6): 28–30.

———. 1992b. Grow Your Own Butterflies! *Organic Gardening* 39 (6): 30–33.

Miles, Bebe. 1976. *Wildflower Perennials for Your Garden: A Detailed Guide to Years of Bloom from America's Long-Neglected Native Heritage.* New York: Hawthorne Books.

Miller, Dorcas S. 1989. *Winter Weed Finder.* Berkeley, Calif.: Nature Study Guild.

Mitchell, John G. 1992. Our Disappearing Wetlands. *National Geographic* 182 (4): 3–45.

The National Wildflower Research Center's Wildflower Handbook. 1989. Austin, Tex.: National Wildflower Research Center.

New Pronouncing Dictionary of Plant Names. 1964. Chicago: Florists' Publishing.

Opler, P. A., and V. Malikul. 1992. *Field Guide to Eastern Butterflies: Peterson Field Guide Series.* Boston: Houghton Mifflin.

Ornamental Grasses. 1988. Plants and Gardens, Handbook 117, 44 (3). Brooklyn: Brooklyn Botanic Garden Record.

Ornamental Grasses for the Midwest. Ames: North Central Regional Extension Publication, Extension Service, Iowa State University.

Orwig, Timothy T. 1992. Loess Hills Prairies as Butterfly Survivia: Opportunities and Challenges. In *Proceedings of the Twelfth North American Prairie Conference,* 131–136. Cedar Falls: University of Northern Iowa Press.

Pearson, John. 1992. Sheeder Prairie: A "People Pasture." *Iowa Conservationist* 51 (7): 55–57.

Peterson, Roger Tory, and Margaret McKenny. 1968. *Peterson Field Guides: Wildflowers, Northeastern and North-central North America.* Boston: Houghton Mifflin.

Phillips, Harry R. 1985. *Growing and Propagating Wild Flowers.* Chapel Hill: University of North Carolina Press.

Pond, Barbara. 1982. *A Sampler of Wayside Herbs*. New York: Greenwich House, Crown Publishers.

Potter-Springer, Wendy. 1990. *Grow a Butterfly Garden*. Bulletin A-114. Pownal, Vt.: Garden Way Publishing.

Prairie Propagation Handbook. 1971. Franklin, Wis.: Wehr Nature Center, Milwaukee County, Department of Parks, Recreation, and Culture, Whitnall Park.

Pyle, Robert Michael. 1992. *Handbook for Butterfly Watchers*. Boston: Houghton Mifflin.

Rappaport, Bret. 1992. Local Weed Laws: Why They Exist and Where They Are Headed. *Wildflower: Journal of the National Wildflower Research Center* 5 (2): 6–13. Austin, Tex.

Ray, Mary Helen, and Robert P. Nichols. 1988. *The Traveler's Guide to American Gardens*. Chapel Hill: University of North Carolina Press.

Reilly, Ann. 1988. *Starting Seeds Indoors*. Bulletin A-104. Pownal, Vt.: Garden Way Publishing.

Roosa, Dean. 1984. Iowa's Prairie Preserves. *Iowa Conservationist: A Special Prairie Issue* 43 (9): 22–26.

Runkel, Sylvan T., and Alvin F. Bull. 1979. *Wildflowers of Iowa Woodlands*. Des Moines: Wallace-Homestead Books.

Runkel, Sylvan T., and Dean M. Roosa. 1989. *Wildflowers of the Tallgrass Prairie: The Upper Midwest*. Ames: Iowa State University Press.

Rushing, Felder. 1992. Wildflowers in Town. *Wildflower: Journal of the National Wildflower Research Center* 5 (1): 6–11. Austin, Tex.

Sandoval, Frances R. 1992. From Vacant Lot to Wildlife Garden. *Wildflower: Journal of the National Wildflower Research Center* 5 (1): 12–17. Austin, Tex.

Schlarbaum, Pat. 1992. Watchable Wildlife—Spring Dancers. *Nongame News* 8 (2): 4–6. Des Moines: Newsletter of the Iowa Department of Natural Resources.

Schramm, Peter. 1992. Prairie Restoration: A Twenty-five-year Perspective on Establishment and Management. In *Proceedings of the Twelfth North American Prairie Conference*, 169–177. Cedar Falls: University of Northern Iowa Press.

Sedenko, Jerry. 1991. *The Butterfly Garden*. New York: Villard Books.

Shreet, Sharon. 1992. Attracting Butterflies to Your Garden. *Flower and Garden* 36 (2): 34–41.

Smith, Daryl D. 1984. Iowa Prairie: A State of Mind. *Iowa Conservationist: A Special Prairie Issue* 43 (9): 3–4.

Smith, Daryl D., and Carol A. Jacobs, eds. 1992. *Proceedings of the Twelfth North American Prairie Conference: Recapturing a Vanishing Heritage*. Cedar Falls: University of Northern Iowa Press.

Smith, J. Robert, and Beatrice S. Smith. 1980. *The Prairie Garden: 70 Native Plants You Can Grow in Town and Country*. Madison: University of Wisconsin Press.

Steffek, Edwin F. 1983. *The New Wild Flowers and How to Grow Them*. Portland, Oreg.: Timber Press.

Stein, Sara B. 1988. *My Weeds: A Gardener's Botany*. New York: Harper and Row.

Stevenson, Violet. 1985. *The Wild Garden*. New York: Penguin Books.

Stokes, Donald, Lillian Williams, and Ernest Williams. 1991. *The Butterfly Book: An Easy Guide to Butterfly Gardening, Identification and Behavior*. New York: Little, Brown.

Stolzenburg, William. 1992. Silent Sirens: Through the Eyes of Butterflies, Scientists Are Finding and Mending Flaws in the Land. *Nature Conservancy* 42 (3): 8–13.

Stuckey, Ronald L., and Karen J. Reese, eds. 1981. The Prairie Peninsula—In the Shadow of Transeau. In *Proceedings of the Sixth North American Prairie Conference*, 278. Columbus: Ohio State University Press.

Sunset-Landscaping Illustrated: Complete Guide to Ideas, Planning, and How-to-do-it. 1984. Menlo Park, Calif.: Lane Publishing.

Szcodronski, Kevin. 1993. All Systems Go. *Iowa Conservationist* 52 (1): 16–23.

Taber, Ruth Ann. 1991. Mycorrhizal Fungi in Wildflowers and Weeds. *Wildflower: Journal of the National Wildflower Research Center* 4 (2): 20–25. Austin, Tex.

Tallon, James. 1992. Along the Way. *Arizona Highways* (March): 2.

Taylor, K. S., and Stephen F. Hamblin. 1963. *Handbook of Wild Flower Cultivation*. New York: Macmillan.

Tekulsky, Mathew. 1985. *The Butterfly Garden: Turning Your Garden, Window Box or Backyard into a Beautiful Home for Butterflies*. Boston: Harvard Common Press.

Thompson, Janette R. 1992. *Prairies, Forests, and Wetlands: The Restoration of Natural Landscape Communities in Iowa*. Iowa City: University of Iowa Press.

Thoreau, Henry David. 1987. *Walden*. Philadelphia: Running Press.

Tufts, Craig. 1988. *The Backyard Naturalist and Backyard Wildlife Habitat*. Washington, D.C.: National Wildlife Federation.

The 25th Environmental Quality Index: 1992, a Year of Crucial Decisions on the Environment. 1993. *National Wildlife* 31 (2): 34–41.

VanBruggen, Theodore. 1983. *Wildflowers, Grasses and Other Plants of the Northern Plains: Black Hills*. Interior, S.D.: Badlands Natural History Association.

Van Gundy, Wendy. 1984. Roadside Prairies. *Iowa Conservationist: A Special Prairie Issue* 43 (9): 9.

Voy, Kermit D. 1985. *Soil Survey of Hardin County, Iowa*. Washington, D.C.: U.S. Department of Agriculture, Soil Conservation Service.

Walcott, Mary Vaux, and ed. H. W. Rickett of the New York Botanical Garden. 1953. *North American Wild Flowers: 400 Flowers in Full Color*. New York: Crown.

Wallace, David Rains. 1987. *Life in the Balance: Companion to the Audubon Television Specials*. San Diego: Harcourt Brace Jovanovich.

Wallace, Mervin, and John Logan. *Methods of Establishing Wildflowers on Missouri Highway Rights-of-Way*. Jefferson City: Missouri Highway and Transportation Department in cooperation with U. S. Department of Transportation; Federal Highway Administration.

Waller, Robert James. 1988. *Just Beyond the Firelight: Going Soft upon the Land and Down along the Rivers*. Ames: Iowa State University Press.

Watts, May Theilgaard. 1955. *Flower Finder*. Berkeley, Calif.: Nature Study Guild.

Weaver, J. E. 1968. *Prairie Plants and Their Environment: A Fifty-year Study in the Midwest*. Lincoln: University of Nebraska Press.

Whye, Mike. 1993. Voices of the Loess Hills. *Iowan* 41 (3): 39–47, 69.

Wildflowers: A Collection of U.S. Commemorative Stamps. 1992. U.S. Postal Service.

Williams, Ted. 1992. No Dogs Allowed. *Audubon* 9 (5): 26–35.

Wilson, Jim. 1992. *Landscaping with Wildflowers: An Environmental Approach to Gardening*. New York: Houghton Mifflin.

Wilson, Kim. 1992. Wildflowers. *Organic Gardening* 39 (9): 43–49.

Wilson, M. 1984. *Landscaping with Wildflowers and Native Plants*. San Francisco: Ortho Books.

Wolf, Robert C. 1991. *Iowa's State Parks: Also Forests, Recreation Areas, and Preserves*. Ames: Iowa State University Press.

Wooley, Jim. 1984. Prairie Chicken Update. *Iowa Conservationist: A Special Prairie Issue* 43 (9): 10–11.

Young, James A., and Cheryl G. Young. 1986. *Collecting, Processing, and Germinating Seeds of Wildland Plants*. Portland, Oreg.: Timber Press.

Zinsser, William. 1992. Roger Tory Peterson: Six Decades of Successful "Guides" Have Not Dimmed This Artist's Vision—or His Vitality. *Audubon* 94 (6): 90–97.

Index

Bur Oak Books